ESCAPE
FROM
BABEL

Toward a Unifying Language
for Psychotherapy Practice

By the same authors

Psychotherapy with "Impossible" Cases:
The Efficient Treatment of Therapy Veterans
Barry L. Duncan, Mark A. Hubble, and Scott D. Miller

Practical Solutions for School Problems:
A Brief Intervention Approach
John J. Murphy and Barry L. Duncan

The Handbook of Solution-Focused Brief Therapy:
Theory, Research, and Practice
Scott D. Miller, Mark A. Hubble, and Barry L. Duncan

The Miracle Method:
A Radically New Approach to Problem Drinking
Scott D. Miller and Insoo Kim Berg

Finding the Adult Within:
A Solution-Focused Self-Help Guide
Barbara McFarland and Scott D. Miller

Changing the Rules:
A Client-Directed Approach to Therapy
Barry L. Duncan, Andrew D. Solovey, and Gregory S. Rusk

Working with the Problem Drinker:
A Solution-Focused Approach
Insoo Kim Berg and Scott D. Miller

Overcoming Relationship Impasses:
Ways to Initiate Change When Your Partner Won't Help
Barry L. Duncan and Joseph J. Rock

A NORTON PROFESSIONAL BOOK

ESCAPE
FROM
BABEL

Toward a Unifying Language
for Psychotherapy Practice

꙰

Scott D. Miller, Ph.D.
Brief Therapy Training Consortium
Chicago, Illinois

Barry L. Duncan, Psy.D.
Private Practice
Port St. Lucie, Florida

Mark A. Hubble, Ph.D.
Private Training and Consulting Practice
Upper Arlington, Ohio

W. W. NORTON & COMPANY
New York   *London*

To John Weakland, whose work and personal
example inspired us to look beyond our traditions
and focus our attention on what works

✣

Portions of chapter 1 first appeared in *The Family Therapy Networker*, 1995,
19(2), 52–58, 62–63.

Quote from David Brandon, *Zen in the Art of Helping*, with permission of Viking
Penguin.

First Edition

For information about permission to reproduce selections
from this book, write to
Permissions, W.W. Norton & Company, Inc., 500 Fifth Avenue,
New York, NY 10110.

Library of Congress Cataloging-in-Publication Data

Miller, Scott D.
    Escape from Babel : toward a unifying language for psychotherapy
practice / Scott D. Miller, Barry L. Duncan, Mark A. Hubble.
    p.   cm.
    Includes bibliographical references and index.
    ISBN 0-393-70219-7
    1. Psychotherapy. 2. Psychotherapy—Philosophy. I. Duncan,
Barry L. II. Hubble, Mark A., 1951– . III. Title.
RC480.M53   1997
616.89′14—dc20   96-38339 CIP

W.W. Norton & Company, Inc., 500 Fifth Avenue, New York, N.Y. 10110
http://www.wwnorton.com
W.W. Norton & Company, Ltd., 10 Coptic Street, London WC1A 1PU

1 2 3 4 5 6 7 8 9 0

Foreword

THE AUTHORS present a lucid, enjoyable, and thought-provoking critique of psychotherapy as it is currently practiced. Consistent with other concerned commentators on the state of psychotherapeutic practice such as Marvin Goldfried, John Norcross, and Paul Wachtel, Miller, Duncan and Hubble ask the reader to focus on certain healing facets of therapy through the use of a unifying language. Unlike those who propose yet another therapeutic system, albeit an eclectic one, these authors have no interest in creating a unique psychotherapy. Instead they draw the reader's attention to a few simple principles that are at the core of therapies. Second only to the enjoyable prose that unfolds throughout the book, their refreshing approach to psychotherapy allows the reader to consider their points of view without feeling persuaded to adapt some new psychotherapeutic system.

Four broad categories of common factors are focused upon and persuasively documented. As the authors point out, these four factors are not particularly exciting from a theoretical point of view. They are, however, empirically and clinically based condensations of the bread and butter of positive patient change. These core elements are addressed in all psychotherapy systems and deserve our utmost attention, regardless of personal preferences for theory-based ways of conceptualizing therapeutic interventions.

The history of psychotherapy is rich with clinical and empirical support for common factors. This text supplies yet another integration of this history while using rich clinical material to illustrate the points of interest. Certainly this text is a stark contrast to many of the current trends in the field, i.e., the current craze for "empirically validated treatments," the development and use of treatment manuals that emphasize techniques with "proven" effectiveness, and the use of the most appropriate treatments for specific disorders. The authors are to be congratulated for standing apart from these trends while still embracing wisdom gleaned from decades of research and the metaphorical world of the wisest therapists and philosophers. The book is a contribution to both novice and professional therapists.

Michael J. Lambert, Ph.D.

Contents

Foreword by Michael J. Lambert   v

Preface   ix

1. TRAPPED IN BABEL   1
   The State of Modern Clinical Theory and Practice

2. ESCAPE FROM BABEL   19
   Building a Unifying Language for Psychotherapy Practice

3. THE UNSUNG HEROES OF PSYCHOTHERAPY   34
   The Contribution of the Client and Chance Events to Treatment Outcome

4. ON THE SHOULDERS OF CARL ROGERS   81
   The Contribution of the Therapeutic Relationship to Treatment Outcome

5. HOPING FOR A CHANGE   122
   The Role of Hope, Expectancy, and Placebo in Psychotherapy Outcome

6. "A GIFT FROM GOD"   161
   A Case Example

7. STRUCTURE AND NOVELTY   182
   The Role of Models and Techniques in Psychotherapy Outcome

8.   GETTING A LIFE   198
        A Case Example

Epilogue   215
Bibliography   217
Index   235

Preface

> Seek facts and classify them and you will be the workmen
> of science. Conceive or accept theories and you will be
> their politicians.
>
> *Nicholas Maurice Arthus (1862–1945)*
> De l'Anaphylaxie a l'immunité

THE IDEA for this book grew out of a conversation that
we had several years ago while sitting drinking beer at
Murphy's Bar in Washington, D.C. The three of us were in
town for the annual Family Therapy Networker conference.
Scott had finished presenting and was wandering the halls of
the Omni Shoreham—the hotel where the conference has
been held for the last nineteen years—bopping in and out of
various workshops, when he happened into Mark and Barry's presentation. Initially intrigued by the rather provocative
title of their workshop—something along the lines of "Reality
versus the Therapy Industry: Myth and Science in Modern
Clinical Practice"—he was persuaded to stay because the content of the workshop closely paralleled an article that he was
writing at the time (see Miller, 1994a).

Following the workshop, the three of us talked for some
time, sharing ideas and swapping stories, before eventually
walking across the street to Murphy's Bar. At first the conversation continued around the content of Mark and Barry's
presentation—in particular, on the problems and challenges

facing the field at the present time. For example, we talked about the many exaggerated claims being made about the effectiveness of particular treatment approaches, about the ever widening number of behaviors and concerns being cast as mental health problems, and about the rapid proliferation of new methods and techniques that seem to come into and go out of fashion with a speed rivaling skirt length and lapel width. We also talked about the division of the helping professions along theoretical, technical, and disciplinary lines and how that division would ultimately affect the survival of the field in this era of increasing public scrutiny and third-party accountability.

In relatively short measure, the discussion began to shift and we started considering potential solutions to the current problems. The discussion was lively and the content diverse. The conversation soon began to coalesce, however, around several common themes. Scott jotted down the ideas on a cocktail napkin and one of us, though we don't remember which, eventually suggested that we work together to turn the ideas into a book. Some three and a half years later, the result of our chance meeting and subsequent collaboration is actually two books: *Escape from Babel* and *Psychotherapy with "Impossible" Cases*.

It is our hope that these companion volumes capture some of the excitement and hope that the three of us experienced that evening at Murphy's Bar. At the same time, however, we want to note that our intention is not to create another model of psychotherapy or add more titles to the already towering heap of basic texts on clinical work. While the books are packed full of practical information for conducting day-to-day therapeutic work, our real aim is to provide a language for clinicians of differing therapeutic orientations to use in speaking with each other about the critical ingredients—about what works, in other words—in helping relationships.

We firmly believe that in this era of increasing scrutiny and accountability clinicians can no longer afford to be divided. As pioneering brief therapist John Weakland wrote shortly before his death in 1995, "The emphasis on having things 'my way' and needing something new each year has distracted us from serious and useful dialogue about what aids people in distress and facilitates change" (p. 16). For the field to survive and clinicians to remain at the helm of the helping professions in the new millennium we must set aside our many apparent differences and find a way to talk, to join together, and to share with each other what we do that works. We must, in other words, find a unifying language of psychotherapy practice.

As the reader will soon gather, the ideas we write about depend heavily on the work of others, in particular, researchers in the fields of psychotherapy outcome and process research and social psychology. We are deeply indebted to the hundreds of researchers whose work we have read as well as cited in this volume—it is from their carefully conducted studies that the unifying language for psychotherapy practice has emerged. In this regard, we want to give special thanks to psychotherapy outcome researcher Michael J. Lambert, whose work, support, and numerous telephone consultations have been critical to our thinking.

Thanks is also owed to several other researchers and clinicians whose pioneering work on the common curative elements in psychotherapy has greatly influenced on our own work. Although the list is not exhaustive, we want to acknowledge Jerome Frank, Lewis Wolberg, Carl Rogers, Sol Garfield, Ken Howard, Alexandra Bachelor, and C. H. Patterson. We also want to thank a number of people whose work, supervision, and support have nurtured and enriched our personal and professional lives. These include Steve de Shazer, Bill O'Hanlon, Lynn Johnson, Hal Miller, Jeffrey Zeig, Larry Hopwood, Karen Donahey, John Weakland,

Scott Fraser, Bob Peach, Aileen Erbacher, Linda Heinz, Mary Talen, Justine Ritter, Doug Buchanan, Ellen Averett, Denny Schemmel, Marita Barkis, and Charlie Gelso. Without these many researchers, mentors, and friends our work would not have been possible. We also want to thank our editor, Susan Munro, for her support and patience throughout these two writing projects.

1

TRAPPED
IN
BABEL

The State of Modern Clinical Theory and Practice

There are many kinds of schools, many kinds of teachings. If you study these teachings you find something excellent being handled down from generation to generation. [However], eventually you will say, "This is best, this is wrong." Under the beautiful flag of religion, philosophy, psychology or whatever, we fight.

Dainin Katagiri
Returning to Silence

Business is devouring science. 'Art does not provide bread' is more true now than ever.

Sigmund Freud
Letters of Sigmund Freud to Edward Silberstein

THERE IS an ancient Zen story about four apprentice monks who approach their Master seeking advice on attaining enlightenment. The Master counsels the young monks to observe strict silence. Upon hearing this, the first young monk responds enthusiastically, "Then I shall not say a word." The second monk then chastises the first, saying, "Ha, you have already spoken." "Both of you are stupid," the third monk remarks. "Why did you talk?" In a proud voice, the fourth monk concludes, "I am the only one who has not talked!"

The behavior of the four apprentice monks is not unlike that of the proponents of various treatment models in the field of therapy. Since the mid-1960s the number of therapy models has grown from 60 to more than 250 (Garfield, 1982; Herink, 1980; Research Task Force of the National

Institute of Mental Health, 1975). This increase constitutes a rise of nearly 400 percent. Worse yet, depending on the way the models are counted, some researchers estimate the actual number to be much higher (Kazdin, 1986).

Like the monks in the story, the proponents of these many treatment models are eager to demonstrate their unique understanding of the therapy process and the superiority of their chosen method. The only problem is that forty years of sophisticated outcome research has not found any one theory, model, method, or package of techniques to be reliably better than any other (Lambert & Bergin, 1994; Lambert, Shapiro, & Bergin, 1986). Indeed, virtually all of the available data indicate that the different therapy models, from psychodynamic and client-centered approaches to marriage and family therapies, work about equally well (Doherty & Simmons, 1995, 1996; Lambert & Bergin, 1994; Shadish, Montgomery, Wilson, Wilson, Bright, & Okwumabua, 1993). *All of the data.* The differences between the various models simply do not make much of a difference in therapy outcome.

While the proponents of a particular model may cite the occasional study demonstrating the superiority of their particular approach, the preponderance of the data indicates that no meaningful difference exists. This is true even of the much ballyhooed cognitive and biological "revolutions" in mental health care. The current popularity of biological psychiatry, for example, could lead a reasonable person to conclude that pharmacological intervention had been proven superior to talk therapy—at least in the treatment of the two most common mental health complaints, depression and anxiety. Recent publicity aside, however, data gathered over the last several decades comparing a variety of psychotropic medications with numerous psychological interventions indicate that they achieve roughly equivalent results (Lambert & Bergin, 1994). More recently, results from one of the most thorough and sophisticated comparative studies ever conducted on the treatment of depression found no significant difference between pharmacologic and psychotherapeutic intervention (Elkin, 1994).

An analogous conclusion holds for the much-touted "cognitive revolution." By now, most clinicians have either read or heard that the cognitive and/or cognitive-behavioral therapies are the "treatment of choice" for generalized anxiety, phobic and panic-related disorders (Barlow, 1988). Results like those reported in a study by Barlow and Wolfe (1981) where 75% of clients were successful in overcoming their phobias are the norm. In the last decade, these and other similar claims made about such common yet difficult-to-treat and relapse-prone clinical problems were influential in both shaping the way clinicians practice and changing the structure of treatment programs across the country. So remarkable were these findings thought to be that a special task force was eventually created within the American Psychological Association to promote and "disseminate important findings about innovations in psychological procedures" (*Task Force Report on Promotion and Dissemination of Psychological Procedures*, 1993, p. 1; Chambless, 1996). Not surprisingly, 80% of the approaches that this committee identified as "empirically validated" belonged to the cognitive or cognitive-behavioral schools of thought.

Unfortunately, the evidence for such claims is far from overwhelming. Though several early large-scale reviews of the literature found a small but consistent advantage for cognitive and behavioral approaches over traditional verbal and relationship-oriented therapies, later studies have showed that this advantage was largely artifactual. Consider, for example, that the 75% success rates cited by Barlow and Wolfe (1981) and others were most often based on the subjects who actually completed the entire treatment protocol—not the number of subjects originally entering the study. When other researchers factored average drop-out rates of 25% into the equation, the success rates of the approaches dropped to modest 50% (Duncan, Solovey, & Rusk, 1992; Prochaska, 1991). Even more troubling were other analyses demonstrating that results favoring the cognitive and behavioral approaches were largely attributable to the highly reactive nature of the outcome measures employed in the research and the allegiance of the experimenters to the methods being investigated. When this latter fact was taken into account in successive analyses of the data, the differences favoring cognitive and behavioral therapies disappeared completely (Lambert & Bergin, 1994)! Given this, the reader will probably not be surprised to learn that the aforementioned task force—the one whose results heavily favored cognitive and behavioral approaches—was created "at the request" of one of the leading figures in the cognitive-behavioral movement.

The latest craze to sweep the clinical world is "brief therapy." Advocates of the various brief therapy approaches are claiming that their chosen methods enable "clinicians to achieve dramatic therapeutic successes more rapidly, more enduringly, more effortlessly, more pleasurably and more reliably than any psychotherapeutic approach" (O'Hanlon & Wilk, 1987, pp. 217–218). Even more radical representations have been made by theoreticians and practitioners on the fringe of the brief therapy movement. For example, in a special issue of the *Family Therapy Networker* devoted to brief therapy, NLP practitioners Andreas and Andreas (1990) claim that their methodology results in "briefer than brief," rapid, one-session, often single-procedure cures.

Such claims could hardly go unnoticed by clinicians struggling to work and survive in the current practice environment. To be sure, the claims have not gone unnoticed by insurance companies, third-party payers, employers, health provider organizations, and government funding agencies, who are always looking for ways to hold down the ever increasing cost of mental health services (Berg & Miller,

1992). Nevertheless, the research shows that the vast majority of claims being made by proponents of brief therapy lack substance (Miller, 1994a).

One of the primary claims made about brief therapy, for example, is that it is, in fact, *briefer*. Of course, the question that immediately comes to mind is how to define the word *brief*. While advocates of the various schools within the brief therapy movement disagree on the specific amount, most agree that brief refers to the time a client spends in treatment and that their approaches help clients spend less time resolving difficulties than other, traditional, "non-brief" approaches (Frances, Clarkin, & Perry, 1984). With regard to the duration of treatment, however, the research literature shows rather convincingly that all therapy is brief. Data collected over the last fifty years consistently show that the average client attends only a handful of sessions *regardless of the treatment model employed* (Garfield, 1971; Koss & Butcher, 1986; Levitt, 1966; Miller, 1994a).[1] In one particularly striking example, Garfield (1989) investigated the length of treatment for clinicians practicing long-term, insight-oriented psychodynamic psychotherapy at the Veterans' Administration in 1949. He found that the average client attended only six sessions! More recently, a national survey of nearly 2,000 randomly selected clinical members of the American Association of Marriage and Family Therapists found that, even though the therapists used a variety of treatment models and worked with a diverse clientele, the number of sessions with families averaged only nine (Doherty & Simmons, 1996).

---

[1]Some find this claim difficult to believe given that their own practices *seem* to be filled with clients who take a long time to reach treatment objectives. Cohen and Cohen (1984) have labeled this the "clinician's illusion," noting that because most case loads are *not* representative of psychotherapy patients in general, therapists tend to overestimate the length of time that the majority of their clients will spend in treatment. Knesper et al. (1985) found, for example, that clinicians tended to overestimate the actual length of treatment by 100 to 170%.

The same conclusions may be drawn about other claims made by the developers of the various brief therapy models. For instance, there is absolutely no evidence that brief therapy results in more effortless, reliable, or even enduring change than "long-term" treatment. Available data suggest that brief therapy achieves roughly the same results as the traditional approaches it is supposed to replace. In short, whatever differences the experts may believe exist between brief and traditional therapy, there is simply no difference in terms of outcome. Additionally, there is zero evidence that any of the brief therapy approaches result in *more* single-session cures for clients' presenting problems. Once again, the research indicates that a single session is the modal number of sessions for all clients in therapy *regardless of the treatment model employed* (Frank, 1990; Talmon, 1990). What's more, this same research has shown that the majority of clients who come for only a single visit benefit enough from that meeting so further treatment is unwarranted—again, *regardless of the treatment model employed* (Talmon, 1990). As senior psychotherapy researcher Jerome Frank (1990) has noted, "*most* patients who quit after a single interview do so because they have accomplished what they intended and . . . on average, such patients report *as much improvement* as those who stay the prescribed course" (p. xi, emphasis added).

When both the average number and the modal number of sessions for clients treated with brief therapy equals the average and modal numbers of sessions of clients treated by other, traditional "non-brief" approaches, claims that brief therapists can "influence . . . client[s] in the direction of completing therapy briefly" (O'Hanlon, 1991, p. 108) begin to ring hollow. Brief therapists do not cause therapy to be brief with their treatment methods any more than Eratosthenes caused the Earth to be round when he measured its circumference (Sagan, 1980). Most of therapy is brief *re-*

gardless of the treatment model employed. Indeed, when brief therapists attempt to set limits on the number of sessions a client may attend in advance, that treatment is typically longer than therapies in which no time limits are set (Orlinsky, Grawe, & Parks, 1994).

After reviewing these and other similar findings for their chapter on therapy outcome in the fourth edition of the *Handbook of Psychotherapy and Behavior Change*, Lambert and Bergin (1994) conclude:

> Research carried out with the intent of contrasting two or more bona fide treatments shows *surprisingly small differences* between the outcomes for patients who undergo a treatment that *is fully intended to be therapeutic*. (p. 158, emphasis added)

Rarely are researchers able to speak with such certainty. In this instance, however, the data are clear: *the model of therapy simply does not make much difference in therapy outcome.*

Because the research has so clearly demonstrated that there is little appreciable difference in outcome between the various therapy models, it is puzzling that so much time and attention continue to be directed toward their discussion in graduate education programs, continuing education seminars, and professional publications. A reasonable person could ask how something that *makes so little difference* could be allowed to continue to dominate professional discussion to the extent that the various theoretical orientations do. Certainly, it is *not* a matter of ignorance. After all, the research showing the relatively homologous outcomes of the various treatment models has been around now for more than a quarter-century (Garfield & Bergin, 1971). So how is it that models continue to dominate professional discussion? The answer is simple: treatment models really *do* make a difference — just not to the client.

CREATING LANGUAGES
THAT DIVIDE:
A TALE OF TWO THERAPIES

The mind is its own opiate. And the ultimate drug is the word.

Thomas Szasz, 1994

As a way of illustrating the point, consider a recent debate between the leading proponents of two popular schools of therapy: de Shazer, of the solution-focused brief therapy school, and White, of the narrative therapy tradition (de Shazer, 1993; White, 1993). The debate between de Shazer and White was sparked when several observers suggested a theoretical and technical similarity between their two methods (see Chang & Phillips, 1993; Johnson & Miller, 1994; Kowalski & Durrant, 1990; Selekman, 1989, 1991; White, 1986).

One particular point of contention centered on the suggestion that the solution-focused concept of "exceptions" and White's notion of "unique outcomes" were similar, if not the same. In the solution-focused literature, exceptions have been defined as "times (rather, depictions of times) when the complaint [for which the client is seeking help] is absent" (de Shazer, 1991, p. 83). On the other hand, the narrative literature has defined unique outcomes as "moments when clients haven't been dominated or discouraged by the problem or their lives have not been disrupted by the problem" (O'Hanlon, 1995, p. 26; see also White & Epston, 1990). In both traditions, the job of the therapist is to "amplify," "reinforce," or simply bring these moments "into the conversation" (Lipchik, 1988; O'Hanlon, 1995; White & Epston, 1990).

As similar as these two definitions sound, both White and de Shazer vigorously opposed any suggestion of similarity between the two concepts. Moreover, they went to extraordinary lengths to draw sharp contrasts between their respective approaches in general. In the end, White (1993) concluded, "the differences in our respective ideas and practices are *far more evident* and significant than the similarities" (p. 123). Not to be outdone, de Shazer (1993) came to an even stronger conclusion, stating "the two approaches are members of *different* families, *different* traditions, and are not 'theoretically compatible' *at all*" (p. 120, emphasis added).

To forestall any potential misunderstanding, it should be noted de Shazer and White are not unique in the field of psychotherapy for stressing their differences rather than highlighting their obvious similarities. As Grosskurth (1991) has documented, this practice dates back to the time of Freud and the earliest days of the psychoanalytic movement. Neither is this practice peculiar to the field of mental health. The question that comes to mind, however, is why model builders in this field would go to such great lengths to highlight the *differences* between their approaches when, as has already been shown, these differences make no difference in outcome. When the very real lack of differential treatment effectiveness is taken into account, debates about difference become little more than arguments over words—fights over how to *talk* about therapy.[2]

Obviously, the emphasis on difference must be about something other than concern for increasing the effectiveness of therapy. What that something might be is, of course, a matter of conjecture. One possibility, however, is that model

---

[2]Neither is the tendency limited to practitioners and model developers. Witness a recent article in the prestigious journal *Psychotherapy Research* in which prominent psychotherapy researcher Donald Kiesler—famous for his 1966 article calling the uniformity of treatment outcomes a myth—continues to asssert that treatment-specific interactions will be found in spite of 30 years of his own and his colleagues' failure to discover any. Here again, one must wonder what motivates the emphasis on difference? What makes it so difficult to admit, as Kazdin (1986) speculates, that "the absence of treatment differences reflects the true state of affairs" (p. 102)?

developers are trying to influence and impress their primary consumers—not clients, but *other therapists*. Therapists are the ones most likely to be interested in one theory or the other, to use the various models to conceptualize and organize their clinical work, and to buy professional books and attend training workshops. Even the research gives some indication that therapists may be the ones most affected by the treatment models they employ. For instance, treatment models have been shown to affect both the way therapists *talk* to their clients and the personal values of the therapist (Kivilighan, 1989; Thompson, 1986). Models of therapy, in other words, may be as useful in influencing the activities of *therapists* as they are in helping clients. From this point of view, proponents of brief therapy should be considered exceptionally skilled salespeople. They have successfully convinced clinicians to buy models that produce the same results as other models presently in use. How could such a large segment of practicing clinicians be sold such a bill of goods?

To succeed in the "therapy model marketplace," the proponents of a particular brand of treatment must somehow manage to make their model stand out from the competition. After all, few therapists would be interested in devoting the considerable amount of time and money it takes to master a particular approach if, as senior psychotherapy researcher Jerome Frank (1976) wisely points out, that "method . . . may be indistinguishable from other methods" (p. 76). Simple economics predicts that developers stand to make the most profit when they have an exclusive product, a product for which there are no competitors, or, at least, for which the differences between it and rival products are considered meaningful *by the consumer*. Should a developer be unable to distinguish his product from others in the marketplace, sales become driven almost exclusively by differences in cost—something that developers of all types of products want to avoid. No one wants a steak with no sizzle!

One way to distinguish a treatment model from others without validating data is to develop a special language or way of talking about the theory and techniques that is exclusive to that model (Coyne, 1982). Possessing a special language imbues the treatment model with an aura of difference that, in turn, justifies the claims of uniqueness made by its developer (Lakoff, 1990). In essence, the models are made to *seem* different because they *sound* different. As in the advertising business, making distinctions with words is tremendously important in the psychotherapy marketplace — worth fighting over, in other words — precisely because words are practically all that separates the models from each other.

As Abraham Lincoln was fond of saying, however, agreeing to call a dog's tail a foot does not mean that the dog really has five feet (Joseph, 1994). Developing special languages may be useful for marketing treatment models to therapists, but it does *not* alter the extant evidence that the various approaches do not differ in effect.[3] Moreover, equating differences in language with differences in effect may ultimately prove very costly to the field in general and the practice of therapy in particular (Garfield, 1987; Hubble, 1993).

Mental health service delivery has been undergoing a period of dramatic change (Berkman, Bassos, & Post, 1988; Cummings, 1986; Zimet, 1989). More than at any previous time in the history of the field, therapists are being held accountable for the services they provide to clients (Clement,

[3]In fairness to de Shazer, it should be noted that he has now made public statements made in private to the first author. Namely, that his intention in developing solution-focused brief therapy had always been to influence the field rather than to have a more effective or efficient treatment approach (de Shazer, 1994). These statements had been published earlier in an article that disguised de Shazer's identity (Miller, 1994a). There is, in fact, evidence that this has always been his position. Over nine years ago, de Shazer traced the development of his solution-focused model stating, "We had no five year plan. *We just wanted to be in the forefront of thinking in the family therapy field*" (Nunnally, de Shazer, Lipchik, & Berg, 1986, p. 77). Judging from the popularity of solution-focused therapy, it would seem that he has been successful.

1994). Third-party payers are stridently insisting that to be paid therapists must "deliver the goods." They want proof of the qualifications of those providing clinical services and documentation about the effectiveness of the services that these professionals provide (Boedecker, 1994). Unlike any previous time in the history of the field, failing to respond to these demands is to court exclusion.

Recently, the field has become the subject of a cascade of mass-market books, articles, and news stories accusing practitioners of greed, fraud, incompetence, failed ethics, and extreme susceptibility to every ephemeral fad that runs through the popular culture. Serious questions have been raised about the right of therapists to practice any form of treatment that has not been empirically tested and had its effectiveness validated. At present, several groups outside the field are promoting legislation, ostensibly for the protection of mental health consumers, that would effectively ban third-party reimbursement for psychotherapy procedures that have not been stringently documented as both safe and effective — and not by therapists, but by the scientific research community, which might or might not include practicing clinicians (*FMS Foundation Newsletter*, March 1, 1995).

Although such proposals evoke outrage in many, we practitioners may have only ourselves to blame. Too many exaggerated claims without experimental backing, fancy and exotic sounding techniques that come and go with the seasons, and loudly publicized internecine quarrels have begun to give therapy a bad name, undercutting its very real and deeply helpful benefits. If the field continues on the same path — that is, churning out and speaking in languages that divide rather than facilitate communication and cooperation among clinicians — efforts to monitor and control the practice of therapy from without will only be hastened.

In this era of increasing scrutiny and demands for accountability, professional dialogue can no longer afford to be the modern equivalent of the Tower of Babel. To adjust to these changes and survive into the new millennium, the field *as a whole* must work together to document that the methods employed by clinicians actually deliver what is promised (Lerner, 1995).

LISTENING TO ~~PROZAC~~
ALKA-SELTZER

In the late 1970s, the makers of Alka-Seltzer surprised the advertising industry by firing the company that created the expression, "I can't believe I ate the whole thing." The announcement came as a shock because the series of clever commercials had so quickly become part of the national vernacular and had garnered such critical acclaim within the industry. Advertising companies all over the world had rushed to produce look-alike commercials. The makers of Alka-Seltzer had one fundamental problem with the commercials—they didn't sell more Alka-Seltzer.

Like the makers of Alka-Seltzer, we may have to "fire" treatment models and their ideological proponents. The reason is simple—they do *not* work. They neither explain nor contribute to effective therapy. Moreover, there is evidence that they may actually prevent practitioners from learning what does. Consider, for instance, a growing body of literature that shows at most only a modest relationship between professional training, education, or experience and therapeutic effectiveness (Berman & Norton, 1985; Christensen & Jacobson, 1994; Clement, 1994; Garb, 1989; Hattie, Sharpley, & Rogers, 1984; Jacobson, 1995; Smith, Glass, & Miller, 1980; Stein & Lambert, 1984)! One large-scale review of the data found that "clients who seek help from *para*professionals are more likely to achieve resolution of their problems than those who consult with professionals" (Lambert, Shapiro, & Bergin, 1986, p. 174; see also Hattie, Sharpley, & Rogers, 1984; Smith, Glass, & Miller, 1980).

Given the average cost of graduate school and continuing education programs, one might expect the relationship between training and effectiveness to be much greater. Unfortunately, existing literature suggests it is not. Then again, as Dawes (1994, pp. 133–177) has pointed out, the ethical codes of most professional organizations do *not* require practitioners to use therapeutic approaches which have been subjected to scientific scrutiny and been proven beneficial — or, at least, not harmful — but only that they use techniques which they have been trained in and can use competently.

Another explanation for these sobering findings is that existing treatment models exert a confirmatory bias on the observations and judgments that clinicians make about clients and the therapeutic process (Dawes, 1994). To illustrate, if a client improves following what, in the current recovery-oriented parlance, is called *abreaction*, then the model that contains the hypothesis about needing to bring denied (or repressed) material into the open is seemingly proven correct. At the same time, the failure of the client to improve following the procedure is *not* taken as evidence that the model is invalid. Rather, this exception to the rule is simply taken as evidence that the denial (or repression) is more severe than originally thought and that more extensive treatment — using the same or even more intensive procedures — will be necessary before the material can be brought into the open (Gilovich, 1991; Jordan, Harvey, & Weary, 1988; Nisbett & Ross, 1980). The model becomes, in essence, "unfalsifiable" since, as Watzlawick (1986) points out, it "is validated by both its success *and* failure" (p. 92, emphasis added).

Rejecting the hegemony of treatment models to escape such problems does *not* mean that therapy in general should be dismissed as ineffective. On the contrary, considerable evidence now exists demonstrating the superiority of therapy to both placebo and no-treatment control groups. Among other findings, this research indicates that the average treated person is better off than 80% of those in a control group who receive no treatment (Lambert & Bergin, 1994; Smith, Glass, & Miller, 1980). Therapists, the research makes clear, are not "witch doctors, snake oil peddlers, or over-achieving do-gooders" (Hubble, 1993, p. 14).

Neither does challenging the central role that treatment models play in the field mean that "anything goes" in treatment or that no guidelines exist for helping therapists navigate the difficult and often ambiguous waters of therapeutic process. In spite of the increasing popularity of postmodern, relativistic thinking in the field of therapy, treatment professionals are not forever doomed, as the theme of the 1992 Family Therapy Networker Conference suggested, to "make it up as we go along" (Miller, 1994a). Indeed, considerable evidence presently exists about the elements and processes of effective therapy. This evidence makes it clear that the *similarities* rather than the *differences* between therapy models account for most of the change that clients experience in treatment. What emerges from examining these similarities is a group of common factors that can be brought together to form a more *unifying language for psychotherapy practice*: a language that contrasts sharply with the current emphasis on difference characterizing most professional discussion and activity; a language that, by focusing on the helpful processes that all treatment models share, has a better chance of uniting clinicians to meet the challenges of the changing health care scene.

The language proposed here is not the same as eclecticism. Despite the increasing number of clinicians who identify themselves as "eclectic," the research makes clear that the eclectic practitioner is a myth (Smith, 1982; Watkins, Lopez, Campbell, & Himmel, 1986). Consider one study, for example, in which researchers found that the modal "eclectic" clinician used only four of the roughly 400 different treatment approaches now available—hardly eclectic. More problematic, however, is that little research exists on the differential or even general efficacy of the integrative/eclectic approaches. This shortage of supportive research is clearly more a function of the relatively recent appearance of these approaches than anything else. Even so, a lack of empirical support means that these approaches—and other methods lacking adequate study and validation—are, by definition, experimental.

The common factors that comprise a unifying language have the advantage of forty years of support in therapy outcome research. They are *not* experimental. Indeed, the greatest support for these factors comes from studies that originally set out to demonstrate the unique effects of one particular approach or another and instead found that all approaches achieve roughly equivalent results. Time and again, research initiated to show—sometimes flaunt—a given therapy's special abilities has, in the end, provided unanticipated and unwanted support for the existence of common factors.

Consider, for example, the work of Sloane, Staples, Cristol, Yorkston, and Whipple (1975) as summarized in "Psychotherapy versus behavior therapy" (Goldfried & Newman, 1992). This study, praised for its procedural sophistication, randomly assigned 90 outpatients to psychoanalytically oriented therapy, behavior therapy, or a minimal-treatment, wait-list control condition. The therapists who participated in the study were all seasoned clinicians and well-regarded supporters of their chosen models (Lambert & Bergin, 1994). As was anticipated, subjects in the two treated groups were better off than those in the wait-list control group when assessed after four months of therapy. Surprisingly, however, subjects in the two treatment conditions fared equally well. Neither approach achieved superior results. In an eight-month follow-up, data acquired on the effectiveness of the therapies continued to demonstrate a finding of no difference. These and other similar findings establish that treatments very different in theory and methods achieve equivalent results.

It should be emphasized that the whole idea of a unifying language based on common factors is not a new one. As early as 1936, Saul Rosenzweig argued that the clinical effectiveness of different therapies depended on their common elements, *not* on their theoretical differences. Later, Jerome Frank (1973), in his ground-breaking book, *Persuasion and Healing*, posited that a core group of factors was responsible for the uniform outcomes of different treatment models. He argued that psychotherapy is best considered a *"single* entity" (italics in original) and offered the following analogy:

> Two apparently very different psychotherapies, such as psychoanalysis and systematic desensitization, might be analogous to penicillin and digitalis—totally different pharmacological agents suitable for completely different conditions. On the other hand, the active ingredient of both may be the same, analgous to two compounds, marketed under different names, both of which contained aspirin. I believe the second alternative is closer to the mark. (pp. 313–314)

Several years later, Strupp, Hadley, and Gomez-Schwartz (1974) added research support to Frank's observations in their classic study, "Specific and nonspecific factors in psychotherapy."

Unfortunately, the language of the common factors does not, in itself, have the same ideological allure that initially draws many practitioners to a given model. It simply does not *sound* unique, special, or intriguingly arcane. Moreover, it lacks the promise of complexity and apparent explanatory power that clinicians have come to expect of psychotherapy theories. Worse yet, it is not spoken by persuasive, charismatic advocates. This, as H. L. Mencken once observed, is often the problem with the truth. He said, "What ails the truth is that it is mainly uncomfortable, and *often dull.* The human mind seeks something more amusing, and often caressing." Despite these disadvantages, the factors that comprise this unifying language do offer something no current model can provide—clear, empirically validated guidelines for clinical practice in this era of accountability (Duncan & Moynihan, 1994).

In the chapters that follow, we spell out the factors comprising this unifying language for psychotherapy practice. In doing so, we recognize that some may argue that paying attention to the factors common to all therapy is itself a type of model or orientation. As one clinician who read an earlier article detailing some of these same ideas put it, "What [will] come next? 'The No-Name, Non-Model'?" (Lisson, 1995, p. 11). As the following chapter will show, however, speaking in a unifying language is not the same as speaking in a uniform voice. The common factors, like notes of written music, may be arranged in different orders and patterns and played in a variety of styles, but they are still based on a common language—a language that allows for maximum flexibility and creativity but that still serves to unify rather than separate the speakers. Therefore, in proposing the specific wording of this language we are far from laying the cornerstone of a new model or concocting a tag-line for selling a "new and improved" brand of therapy. We recognize that nothing would be gained from adding another contender to the already overcrowded field of players vying for the attention of therapist-consumers. The language detailed in the chapters that follow dictates no fixed techniques, no certainties or invariant patterns in therapeutic process, no prescriptions for what should or need be done in order to effect good treatment outcomes. Instead, we will suggest ways for all therapists to recognize and maximize the contribution of common factors already operating in their own clinical work.

2

ESCAPE
FROM
BABEL

Building a Unifying Language for
Psychotherapy Practice

> No psychotherapy is superior to any other, although all
> are superior to no treatment. . . . This is the conclusion
> drawn by authoritative reviews . . . , and well-controlled
> outcome studies. . . . This is really quite remarkable,
> given the claims of unique therapeutic properties made by
> advocates of the various treatments available today.
>
> *Joel Weinberg, 1995, p. 45*

> No theory, just as no profession, can claim preeminence
> for long if it cannot firmly establish that its adherents
> agree on the use of its basic organizing concepts.
>
> *Stuart A. Kirk and Herb Kutchins, 1992, p. 31*

THE PATHOLOGICAL basis of *paralysis agitans*—the shaking palsy—defied medical understanding for more than
a hundred years. With the greying of the population, this
brain-based condition bearing the name of the man who provided the best first description, Parkinson, has become all
too familiar to patients, their families, family physicians, psychiatrists, and neurologists. What is less appreciated are the
singular, almost bizarre, psychological explanations offered
by mental health professionals for the genesis of the disease.

From the earliest accounts, observers noticed that those
afflicted with the disease displayed an "emotional and attitu-
dinal inflexibility, a lack of affect and a predisposition to
depressive illness, which may antedate the development of
motor abnormalities by several decades" (Todes & Lees,

1985, p. 97). In 1875, the famous French neurologist Char-
cot considered that emotions in combination with hereditary
factors were instrumental in bringing on the condition. Over
the years, the notion that a patient's affects were the culprits
in Parkinson's disease has kindled highly speculative but
nonetheless influential explanations.

To illustrate, in the late 1940s Booth hypothesized that
the pre-Parkinson patient lived in a tenuous balance between
striving for independence and freedom from authority while
conforming to social expectations and standards. He further
believed that these patients were inculcated from their childhood with the idea that they should abide by social norms at
the expense of their feelings. According to Booth, this resulted in the development of a social mask to cover or screen
hostile and sadistic impulses. The disease emerged when the
equilibrium of a patient's psychological economy—the social
mask—was upset through frustration, loss of independence,
or eruption of aggression. Although this description fits *most
people* growing up and living in American society, not just
patients with Parkinson's disease, Booth believed that the
factors he had identified were causally linked to the onset of
the disease (Booth, 1948).

Looking back, the purpose of this kind of wild character
analysis was to establish a psychogenic or functional cause
(read: explanation) for Parkinson's disease. Using suppos-
edly "hard" data, such as Rorschach responses, clinical experience, and professional observation, to support their hypotheses, professionals confidently promoted their etiological
hunches—mainly in the vocabulary of psychodynamics.
What is troubling is that this edifice of psychological conjecture stood largely unchallenged until researchers established
that the depletion of the neurotransmitter dopamine in the
substantia nigra (part of the midbrain) accounted for the
debilitating motor disorder (Hubble & Koller, 1995).

Sadly, the story of Parkinson's disease highlights a recurring theme in the mental health professions. Intoxicated by models and a penchant for complex but mostly vacuous psychological theories, clinicians often accord their beliefs the status of clinical reality. Throughout the history of the field, virtually every school of therapy has forcefully championed its own explanation of problem formation, treatment goals, and unique methods for resolving or mitigating clients' complaints. With an immodesty approaching outright hubris, the proponents of each school have insisted that the explanations and outcomes of their paradigm are far superior to other treatment models. As clear as this pattern may be, however, the field seems doomed to repeat it. It is as though there is no end to the impulse to exaggerate the explanatory power and therapeutic effectiveness of psychotherapy models.

Consider, for instance, a recent article in *The Family Therapy Networker* (the magazine with more readers than any other professional publication in the field) on one of the latest trends to sweep the therapy model marketplace: narrative therapy. One writer claimed that the new approach not only has "an immediate impact on troubled people's lives" but, through "its ability to put ideology into action," could also end racism, sexism, and any other political "ism" to which it was applied (O'Hanlon, 1995, p. 24). Or, how about a nationally circulated ad for a therapy called, "NLP Eye Movement Integration." The ad asks the would-be consumer, "Would you like to learn a method that is *faster, simpler, safer, and more effective?*" Well, what provider wouldn't? In this era of managed care, survival increasingly depends on how well and how quickly clinicians can get results—a consideration not lost on advertisers. Lastly, how about the latest book by Albert Ellis (1995), entitled *Better, Deeper, and More Enduring Brief Therapy*, in which readers are promised to learn methods:

> . . . not only useful with less severely disturbed clients, but also with difficult clients such as those afflicted with *personal-*

*ity disorders, psychotic states, organicity, and mental defi-
ciency.* (Brunner/Mazel Bulletin, 1995, p. 6, emphasis
added)

Yet, when Ellis's claims are contrasted with available research on the outcome of brief therapy, the rhetoric simply
does not add up to reality. In reviewing the brief therapy
literature for their chapter in the latest edition of the *Handbook of Psychotherapy and Behavior Change*, Koss and Shiang (1994) found the following:

> [There is] compelling empirical evidence that brief psycho-
> therapy is effective with specific populations. . . . brief ther-
> apy has been found to be *less effective with more severe dis-
> orders, such as those of personality, substance abuse, and
> psychosis.* (p. 681, emphasis added)

What can the practicing clinician conclude regarding most
of the claims made by the developers of treatment models?
Given the very real difference between their rhetoric and empirical reality, it is safe to assume that while creating a great
deal of heat they throw very little light on the subject at hand.

THE VOCABULARY OF
A UNIFYING LANGUAGE

> It is the familiar that usually eludes us in life. What is be-
> fore our nose is what we see last.
>
> *William Barrett*

With almost forty years of research findings in hand, we
can say with confidence that the various manifestations of
therapy are *more alike* than different. Therapies work not
because of their unique explanatory schemes or specialized
language; on the contrary, as was pointed out in the previous
chapter, their success is largely based on what they have

in common. In this regard, veteran psychotherapy outcome researcher Michael Lambert (1994, personal communication) has observed:

> When you watch good therapy being done, you know it and it has a lot of commonalities . . . [G]ood cognitive therapists and good behavior therapists, psychodynamic therapists act an awful lot alike.

It is the very commonalities noted by Lambert that form the basis of a *unifying language* for psychotherapy practice. Fortunately, adopting such a language does *not* mean that therapists must learn an entirely new or even different language of psychotherapy practice. In fact, the words and concepts of the unifying language will already be familiar to most clinicians, based as they are on what all therapists already do that contributes to successful clinical work. For those weary of keeping up with the endless number of new treatment models, the unifying language will certainly be welcomed.

Therapists will also find that their clients are attuned to the commonalities linking all good therapy. Indeed, most speak the language with ease and require no special training. In this regard, when researchers ask clients about the helpful aspects of their experience in therapy, they rarely mention specific, model-driven interventions or techniques. Instead they consistently identify the *same* variables as therapeutic— for example, the importance of "being respected, being understood and being cared for" (Lambert, personal communication, 1992). This same body of research shows that clients also expect their therapists *not* to be bound to any one brand or language of treatment. Consider, for example, a study conducted by Kuehl, Newfield, and Joanning (1990), which found that clients who viewed their therapist as *not* rigidly adhering to a particular point of view were more likely to be satisfied with their experience in treatment.

THE ELEMENTS OF
A UNIFYING LANGUAGE

Four common curative elements, each central to all forms
of therapy despite theoretical orientation, mode (i.e., individual, group, family, etc.), or dosage (frequency and number of sessions), constitute the unifying language. These four
elements, in order of their relative contribution to change in
therapy, are: (1) extratherapeutic factors; (2) therapy relationship factors; (3) model and technique factors; and (4)
expectancy, hope, and placebo factors (Lambert, 1992).

Extratherapeutic factors: Clients and
their environment

> Everything is luck and timing. Ability counts, but ability is
> always third.
>
> *Donald Lamberti, 1995*

In the clinical literature, clients have long been portrayed
as the "unactualized," message bearers of family dysfunction,
manufacturers of resistance, and in most therapeutic traditions, targets for the presumably all-important technical intervention. Indeed, it seems that once people decide to enter
treatment they suddenly become something less than they
were before. They cease knowing their own mind, are dis-
connected from their feelings, certainly have "something"
wrong with them that requires fixing, and, of course, will do
their devilish best to resist the therapist's efforts to help them.
It is curious that the very profession that makes helping a
virtue has also made a cult out of client incompetence. A
testament to the success of this cult of incompetence is the
significant degree to which the pathology- and deficit-based
language of the recovery movement and the *Diagnostic and*

Statistical Manual of Mental Disorders (APA, 1994) have been embraced by American popular culture (Kaminer, 1992).

In the same way that clients are assumed to be fragile or ineffective in some way, therapists are considered the masters and heroes of the therapeutic encounter. There are hundreds of books about great therapists but few, if any, books about great clients.

Nowhere is this tendency more obvious than in professional workshops and conferences where some woebegone individual, couple, or family is recruited for a live demonstration conducted by some recognized expert in the field. Especially desirable for these productions are those clients thought to be at an "impasse" with their current therapist. Before an audience of perhaps hundreds of mental health professionals, clients bare their dilemmas and ill fortune to the "master," who invokes reportedly innovative concepts and techniques to transform the client — at least that is what the audience is paying to see. Underscoring the point, videotapes of these demonstrations can be rented or purchased by practitioners through a proprietary operation called, what else, *The Master Therapists* (trademarked by AAMFT).

As these examples illustrate, much of the writing and thinking about psychotherapy practice places the therapist at center stage in the drama known as *Therapy*. Rarely is the client cast in the role of the chief agent of change. Nevertheless, the research literature makes clear that *the client is actually the single, most potent contributor to outcome in psychotherapy.* The quality of clients' participation, their perception of the therapist and what the therapist is doing, determine whether *any* treatment will work. In fact, the total matrix of who they are — their strengths and resources, the duration of their complaints, their social supports, the circumstances in which they live, and the fortuitous events that weave in and out of their lives—matters more than anything therapists might do. Clients, the research makes abundantly clear, are the true masters of change in psychotherapy; they are always more powerful than their therapists.

In the research literature, the client's contribution to outcome is part of a category of common therapeutic elements called "extratherapeutic factors." These factors are estimated to account for the *major* portion of improvement that occurs in any treatment, a whopping 40%. They refer to any and all aspects of the client *and* his or her environment that facilitate recovery, regardless of formal participation in therapy (Lambert, 1992). As such, extratherapeutic factors are the cornerstone of the unifying language for psychotherapy practice.

All therapies benefit from the operation of extratherapeutic factors, whether or not they are a part of the formal language or technique. By making these factors a part of the everyday lexicon of psychotherapy practice, therapists can enhance their contribution to psychotherapy outcome. In Chapter 3, detailed information and suggestions will be given for both recognizing these factors and including them more deliberately in the treatment process.

The therapy relationship:
Client and therapist together

> I don't believe in just ordering people to do things. You have to sort of grab an oar and row with them.
>
> *Harold Geneen*

The therapeutic relationship is the medium through which the process of therapy is enacted and experienced. While they may use different words and concepts, most therapists and schools of therapy acknowledge the importance of the therapeutic relationship in producing beneficial outcomes.

Over the last forty years, the influence of the therapeutic relationship has been tracked across an array of treatments (e.g., behavioral and cognitive, psychodynamic, experiential, eclectic, group, and pharmacotherapy [Henry et al., 1994]). In all these approaches, a correlation has been found between the therapeutic relationship and psychotherapy outcome. Researchers estimate that as much as 30% of the variance in psychotherapy outcome is due to so-called "relationship factors"—making them second in importance to extratherapeutic factors (Lambert, 1992). In fact, the evidence is so strong that veteran psychotherapy researcher Hans Strupp recently wrote, "*the quality of the interpersonal context* is the sine qua non in all forms of psychotherapy" (1995, p. 70; emphasis in original).

Studies further show that the quality of the client's participation in the therapeutic relationship is the single most important determinant of outcome (Orlinsky, Grawe, & Parks, 1994). Clients who are motivated, engaged, and join in the work with the therapist benefit the most from the experience. Of course, the quality of clients' participation in treatment is greatly affected by the bond or alliance they form with the helping professional. In contrast to what one might expect, the research does not show that the strength of this therapeutic alliance or bond is a function of the length of time a client has been in therapy (Horvath & Luborsky, 1993). Therapists who worry that managed care—with its unrelenting emphasis on cost-effective and time-sensitive therapy— may make having helpful therapeutic relationships impossible can rest a little easier.

Far more important to the formation of a strong therapeutic alliance, the research shows, are what humanistic psychotherapist Carl Rogers considered the "core conditions" of effective psychotherapy—empathy, respect, and genuineness (Horvath & Lurborsky, 1993). The latest research and thinking indicate that strong alliances ʿare formed when *clients* perceive the therapist as warm, trustworthy, nonjudgmental, and empathic. Therapists' evaluations of their success in providing this kind of therapeutic environment for the client are not enough. The core conditions must actually be felt by the client, and each client may experience the core conditions differently (Bachelor, 1988). In this regard, a growing number of studies has found that *clients'* ratings of the therapeutic alliance, rather than therapists' perceptions, are more highly correlated with outcome (Horvath & Luborsky, 1993; Orlinksy et al., 1994). For this reason, the most helpful alliances are likely to develop when the therapist establishes a therapeutic relationship that matches the client's definition of empathy, genuineness, and respect (Duncan, Solovey, & Rusk, 1992).

As was true of extratherapeutic factors, all therapies benefit from the operation of relationship factors, whether or not such factors are an explicit part of a particular model's theory or technique. Adding relationship factors to the unifying language for psychotherapy practice builds on what most treatment professionals already know about successful clinical work and will enable therapists to further enhance the contribution of these important factors to psychotherapy outcome. Recognizing and empowering relationship factors is the topic of Chapter 4.

Therapeutic technique: The doings of therapy

> Techniques are ritualized methods of human relatedness and communication. . . . Techniques and the personal meanings they invoke are always embedded in human relationships.
>
> *Michael Mahoney*

Another element in the unifying language encompasses the category of therapeutic technique. All therapists make use of technical procedures. In any given session, for example, one may see a therapist asking particular questions, listening and reflecting, dispensing reassurance, confronting, providing information, offering special explanations (reframes, interpretations), making suggestions, self-disclosing, or assigning tasks to be done both within and outside the therapy session. There are also technical considerations informing where the therapist and client should sit, when the session should begin and end, who is seen, and even whether or not the client should be offered tissues.

The content of the talk or questions is different depending on the therapist's theoretical orientation and technique. Indeed, as was illustrated in Chapter 1, differences in technique and the language used to describe those techniques are often convenient markers for telling therapists apart and engaging in heated professional debate. Whatever model is employed, however, most therapeutic procedures have the common quality of preparing clients to take some action to help themselves. Across all models, therapists expect their clients to do something different—to develop new understandings, feel different emotions, face fears, take risks, or alter old patterns of behavior.

In spite of the field's interest and investment in technical factors, however, their actual percentage-wise contribution to outcome pales in comparison to extratherapeutic and relationship factors. In his widely cited review of psychotherapy outcome research, Lambert (1992) estimates that the therapist's model and technique contribute only 15% to the overall impact of psychotherapy. Though this finding may be troubling to schools of therapy that have prided themselves on their unique conceptualization of therapeutic process or innovations in intervention methods (e.g., primal screaming, genograms, miracle questions, EMDR, letter writing, etc.), the data are clear: clients are largely unimpressed with their therapists' techniques. As Lambert put it:

[P]atients don't appreciate these techniques and they don't regard these techniques as necessary. They hardly ever mention, ever, a specific technical intervention the therapist made. I'd encourage therapists to realize their phenomenological world about the experience of therapy is quite different than their patients'. The nontechnical aspects are the ones patients mention. Also, when objective judges listen to tapes of therapy, the nontechnical aspects are the ones that correlate with outcome more than any technical intervention. (personal communication, December 9, 1993)

When the practice of psychotherapy is guided by a unifying language, therapeutic technique stops being a reflection of a particular theoretical doctrine or school of therapy and instead becomes the vehicle for enhancing the effects of the other common factors. The immediate result is that therapists spend less time trying to figure out the *right* intervention or practicing the *right* brand of therapy and spend more time doing what they do best: understanding, listening, building relationships, and encouraging clients to find ways to help themselves.

Expectancy, hope, and placebo:
The unsung triad

Contributing the same percentage-wise amount to outcome as therapeutic technique are the final words in the vocabulary of the unifying language — expectancy, hope, and placebo (Lambert, 1992). These factors are responsible for that portion of improvement that clients experience simply by making their way to therapy. Research shows that merely expecting therapy to help goes a long way toward counteracting demoralization, mobilizing hope, and advancing improvement (Frank & Frank, 1991).

As one might expect, the creation of such hope is strongly influenced by the therapist's attitude toward the client during the opening moments of therapy. Pessimistic attitudes conveyed to the client by an emphasis on psychopathology or the difficult, long-term nature of change are likely to minimize or curtail the effect of these factors. At the same time, an emphasis on possibilities and a belief that therapy can work will likely work to instill hope and a positive expectation for improvement. It should be noted, however, that creating this hopeful therapeutic atmosphere is not the same as adopting a pollyannish, "every cloud has a silver lining," attitude toward client difficulties. Rather, hopefulness results from acknowledging both the client's present difficulties *and* the possibilities for a better future.

The research literature shows that hope and expectancy give people a measurable advantage in many areas of life — in academic achievement, managing major illness, and dealing with difficult job situations (Goleman, 1991). In the psychotherapy literature, studies further show that fostering a positive expectation for change may actually be a prerequisite for successful treatment (Snyder et al., 1991; Snyder, Irving, & Anderson, 1991). In Chapter 5, detailed information and suggestions will be given for making these factors an active part of the treatment process.

CONCLUSION

To generations of therapists reared on the proposition that ingenious and intellectually stimulating treatment models and their associated techniques make the real difference in therapy, the four common factors that really count may seem pallid and anticlimactic. Therapists have been subjected to the most intense forms of marketing. Books, continuing education seminars, and graduate school training most often portray the process of producing change as a complicated, technical, and often dramatic business. Faced with the ardors

of day-to-day clinical work, many therapists may feel that
the four factors of the unifying language are simply too inert,
offering little help in addressing the complex problems modern clients bring to the consulting room.

The fact of the matter is, however, that while therapists'
formulation of problems and experience of the therapeutic
process may be complex, the factors that contribute to
successful psychotherapy are not. The data indicate that successful psychotherapy would be best understood as a rather
simple, straightforward, and oftentimes boring business, dis-
tinguishable from other helpful experiences in life only by the
explicit, socially sanctioned contract to be helpful that exists
between a therapist and client. No doubt, the practice of
psychotherapy is not always as easy one. *Easy* and *simple*
are, however, two very different matters. Clinical work may
frequently be trying, but that does not mean that the factors
contributing to successful psychotherapy are necessarily complicated.

The best way for therapists to begin speaking a more unifying language is for them to set aside their chosen model or
theory and look for and identify the four common factors
currently operating in their own clinical work. For instance,
because research has established that the quality of a client's
participation in treatment is the single best predictor of psychotherapy outcome, clinicians might begin by closely examining what they already do in order to engage the client in the
therapeutic process. Given the magnitude of the contribution
made by extratherapeutic factors, therapists would also do
well to look at what they presently do to utilize clients'
strengths and resources in the achievement of treatment objectives. Additionally, therapists can examine what they do
to engender hope and a positive expectation for change in
their clients.

Before reading the suggestions and recommendations contained in the following chapters, therapists might look for

evidence of the operation of the common factors that constitute the unifying language currently operating in their clinical work. Like Dorothy in *The Wizard of Oz*, therapists have always had the means to get back to Kansas. No guru or master therapist, no complex theory of human behavior or "advanced workshop" is necessary. Neither is allegiance to any one model or combination of models, methods, or doctrines. In effective therapy the common factors operate regardless of the model or technique being employed. True, the language may lack the technical precision or theoretical elegance that makes some existing treatment models so compelling. Yet it has the advantage of forty years of empirical support. More important, perhaps, it has the potential to unify clinicians from disparate traditions in their common interest to help those in need of treatment.

3 THE UNSUNG HEROES
OF
PSYCHOTHERAPY

The Contribution of the Client and Chance Events to
Treatment Outcome

> Until lions have their historians, tales of hunting will al-
> ways glorify the hunter.
>
> *African proverb*

> Who should get the credit for this success? Foremost, of
> course, the patient. . . .
>
> *Sandor Ferenczi*

> Although men flatter themselves with their great actions,
> they are not so often the result of great design as of
> chance.
>
> *La Rochefoucauld*

A MAN presented for therapy because he was depressed.
He believed that his depression resulted from longstanding marital problems—problems which started nearly two
years earlier following a terrible fight with his wife. Since
that time, the couple had been sleeping in separate bedrooms
and only speaking to each other when they needed to take
care of business matters.

The therapist worked with the man individually for several
sessions. He continued to be depressed, however, and the
marital problems remained unchanged. Subsequent attempts
to draw his spouse into counseling were not successful. Increasingly, it looked as if the case might end up a failure.
Then something happened that changed everything. Rela-

tives showed up one evening at the couple's home for a visit. Not having seen each other for some time, the two couples talked, laughed, and allowed the hours to slip by unnoticed. When they finally realized the time, it was too late for the visitors to drive home or get a hotel room. The couple invited their relatives to stay over for the night. As there were only two bedrooms in the house, the husband and wife were forced to sleep together in the same room.

For the first time since their argument, the two spoke to one another about matters other than business. Before the night was over they even made love. The talk continued into the next day and they slept together again that night. Much to the therapist's surprise, both showed up for the man's next appointment. They told the therapist what had happened and how their relationship had been improving since that fortuitous evening. The couple continued in therapy for several more sessions, each time reporting improvement in their relationship and the man's depression. Not surprisingly, the couple soon terminated treatment.

In another case, a woman contacted Milton Erickson complaining that she was "very neurotic" (Rosen, 1982). She had heard about Dr. Erickson from some of her friends and desperately wanted him to be her therapist. The only problem was that she could not bring herself to talk about her problem with him or anyone else. Neither would she agree to meet with Erickson personally or continue their conversations on the phone. According to the woman, she just didn't have "the nerve." When she asked if Erickson would still be her therapist, he responded that he would try to help her in any way he could. At that point, the woman indicated that she had an idea.

She told Erickson that she would like to have permission to drive over to his home late in the evening, park in his driveway, and imagine that he was in the car with her talking about the best way to solve her problem. Dr. Erickson agreed. While the exact number of visits is not known for certain, the woman did pay for two such consultations. She solved her problem and even became a subject for some of Erickson's later research on time distortion in hypnosis.

While both of these cases may sound too extraordinary to be useful to practitioners, they do, in fact, illustrate what the research suggests is the single largest contributor to psychotherapy outcome: extratherapeutic factors. These factors refer to events or processes that occur *outside* the context of treatment but which are still instrumental in producing change in clients. Sometimes, as was true in the case of the depressed man, the extratherapeutic factor is a chance event, a freak happening that sets in motion a series of events culminating in the resolution of the problem. At other times, the extratherapeutic factor is a part of the client—her strengths, resources, capacity for growth, and ability to secure support and help from others. It is important to note that these elements exist prior to and are independent of participation in treatment. As may be obvious, these latter factors played an important part in Dr. Erickson's case.

To recap, researchers estimate that as much as 40% of the variance in psychotherapy outcome can be attributed to the operation of extratherapeutic factors (Lambert, 1992; Lambert et al., 1986). As such, they contribute more to outcome in psychotherapy than the therapeutic relationship (30%), the theoretical and/or technical orientation of the therapist (15%), or the operation of placebo factors (15%). More than likely, these factors account for the recent research finding that self-administered treatments work just about as well as those done by a therapist—at least in terms of the most common problems for which people seek treatment, such as depression and anxiety (Bohart & Tallman, 1996; Christensen & Jacobson, 1994; Gould & Clum, 1993).

What is curious about all of these data is that little information exists on how to incorporate extratherapeutic factors into the treatment process. Indeed, the majority of writing and research has been and continues to be on the therapeutic technique, intra-session therapist activity, and the development of treatment models — factors that make a much smaller (15%) contribution to overall psychotherapy outcome. So skewed is the dialogue that a review of the literature uncovered only a single article on the subject (cf. Hunsley & Glueckauf, 1988). This would be of little concern were it not for the fact that these factors make the single largest contribution to outcome in psychotherapy.

Nowhere is the bias toward technique and intra-session therapist activity demonstrated more clearly than among adherents to the strategic school of therapy. Consider, for example, recent articles by one of the leading thinkers of that school, Jay Haley (1993, 1994). In his articles, Haley likens the process of therapy to Zen Buddhism, noting, in particular, that the role of modern-day treatment professionals is similar to that of ancient Zen Masters. Using koan study — those funny and frequently paradoxical Zen stories — and harsh temple rituals as examples, Haley suggests that therapists must use forceful and even devious methods to bring about change in their clients. Insight, advice, instruction, reflection, or simply waiting is not enough to bring about change, according to Haley and the strategic school. *Masters*/therapists must *do something* in order to bring about enlightenment/change in their students/clients. *They* — clients, that is — cannot do it themselves.

The position of Haley and his followers has a certain commonsense appeal. After all, it seems logical to assume that therapists must do something in order to bring about change in their clients. If clients could change by themselves, then they wouldn't have needed to see a therapist in the first place. The problem with this line of reasoning is not so much a matter of truthfulness as it is the degree to which Haley — and the discipline of psychotherapy — apply it in explaining client change.

The references to Zen Buddhism, in particular, reveal the extent of bias toward using technique and intra-session therapist activity to account for change in psychotherapy. Consider, for instance, the koan study and forceful, harsh practices Haley cites as support for his position. Perhaps unknown to Haley, these practices are largely confined to one of the smallest sects of Zen Buddhism — the Rinzai school — which holds that change (or enlightenment in Buddhist terms) does not come about naturally. For this reason, it is believed that adherents must be dealt with forcefully in order to break through the barriers to enlightenment (Kraft, 1988).

While the beliefs and practices of the Rinzai school have become popular in the United States — due largely to the writing of Alan Watts and D. T. Suzuki — the largest and most influential of the schools is actually the Soto Zen sect, which, in contrast to the Rinzai school, does not engage in the activities Haley cites. The reason for the difference is simple. The Soto Zen sect considers apprentice monks, and everyone else for that matter, to be enlightened already. Consequently, no force is needed. There is, after all, no place to go because everyone is already there.

As one might expect, this difference in belief leads to substantial differences in practice. In contrast to Rinzai Masters, the work of Soto Zen Masters is mostly confined to providing the type of environment in which practitioners can "wake up" to their already enlightened status (Uchiyama, 1993). Mostly, this means being supportive and encouraging. Soto Zen Masters know that change is constant and that, sooner or later, their students will "wake up." In the meantime, all they must do is be patient and stay out of the way.

If there is a parallel between the practices of Zen and effective psychotherapy then it certainly lies more with the

Soto than with the Rinzai Zen tradition. *Clients are already enlightened. Change is constant.* Data on extratherapeutic factors make this clear: clients' preexisting strengths, resources, and abilities in combination with fortuitous extratherapeutic events are the largest contributors to psychotherapy outcome. As contrary as it is to the current practice environment, therapists do their best by leaving theories, models, and techniques at the consulting room door and providing the type of environment that validates and nurtures — is mindful of, in Buddhist terms — these factors (Duncan & Moynihan, 1994; Patterson, 1984).

BECOMING MINDFUL OF EXTRATHERAPEUTIC FACTORS

In the material that follows, some descriptions and suggestions are given for becoming more mindful of extratherapeutic factors. Recommendations are also provided for incorporating them into the overall treatment process. This list should by no means be confused with a *prescription* for how one must conduct psychotherapy. In describing therapeutic process, one always risks making complex and dynamic interactions sound like a disembodied set of techniques to be applied in all cases and with all clients. Any instances of this in the material that follows should be attributed to limitations in the authors and their use of language.

Neither should the list be considered comprehensive or exhaustive. Indeed, as these factors contribute to positive outcome regardless of the model being employed, it makes sense to assume that all therapists have developed methods for incorporating them into the treatment process. For this reason, readers may actually benefit most by first taking a few moments to consider how they *already* validate and nurture both client strengths and change-producing chance events in their clinical work. It is not necessary to learn a new method or adopt a different theory of clinical practice in order to empower these important factors in treatment. At present, the Babel of languages spoken by competing treatment approaches has obscured the contribution of these common elements to all successful clinical work. Perhaps by recognizing the unique ways these elements are used, therapists from different theoretical persuasions will be able to cross traditional tribal lines and begin sharing their expertise with one another.

Becoming change-focused

> It is randomness, or chance . . . that seems to be the basic fact, nature's ultimate message.
>
> *Ivar Ekeland*, The Broken Dice

As conscientious professionals, most therapists look forward to the time when their clients begin to improve as a result of being in treatment. However, when that improvement results from factors that bear no relationship to events or processes occurring *within* the therapy—as is always the case with extratherapeutic factors—the changes may be either discounted or overlooked altogether. Therapists avoid this error and ensure the contribution of extratherapeutic factors to psychotherapy outcome by becoming more change-focused in their clinical work. Becoming more "change-focused" literally means that the therapist makes a concerted effort to listen for and validate client change *whenever and for whatever reason it initially occurs during the treatment process*. It means that the therapist trusts in the probability of change and, as a result, creates a therapeutic context in which new perspectives, behaviors, or feelings are welcomed and nurtured.

Having a change focus in clinical work stands in stark contrast to much of the prevailing theory and practice of psychotherapy. If anything, most treatment approaches are *stability-focused* when it comes to understanding and describing clinical work (Miller, 1992). Whether theorizing about systemic homeostasis, the equilibrium maintaining dynamics of ego defenses, or reinforcement contingencies, most models focus on how clients are the same rather than how they are different, better, or improved from week to week. Indeed, identifying stable patterns of thinking, behaving, interacting, or emoting is considered a necessary prerequisite to most therapeutic intervention (see O'Hanlon, 1987; O'Hanlon & Wilk, 1987). The problem is, as was indicated earlier, the degree to which stable patterns of problematic behavior are used to guide most therapeutic intervention. Adopted exclusively, such a focus may cause clinicians inadvertently to overlook changes that are occurring simultaneously with stable patterns of problematic behavior.

The treatment process is replete with opportunities for therapists to be more change-focused, beginning, in most cases, even before formal treatment is initiated.

Pretreatment change

As the name implies, pretreatment change is change that takes place in the client's presenting complaint prior to the formal initiation of therapy. There is perhaps no better example of the operation of extratherapeutic factors in terms of both preexisting client strengths and chance events. Researchers Howard, Kopta, Krause, and Orlinsky (1986), the first to describe such change, estimated that approximately 15% of clients show measurable improvement *prior to* the first session of treatment. Subsequent research has suggested that the incidence of pretreatment change may be much higher. For example, in an exploratory study, Weiner-Davis, de Shazer, and Gingerich (1987) surveyed 30 clients and found that two-thirds (66%) reported positive, pretreatment change related to their reason for seeking treatment — *if* they were asked about it by their therapist at the beginning of the first visit. Lawson (1994) later replicated this research with 82 clients and found that, when asked, 60% reported positive, complaint-related, pretreatment change.

Whatever the exact percentage, the studies conducted to date clearly indicate that beneficial change can and frequently does occur prior to the initiation of formal treatment. For example, change due to the operation of chance events or client strengths may be partly responsible for the approximately 40% of clients who improve enough *not* to need treatment while on a waiting list for services (Lambert, Shapiro, & Bergin, 1986).

Other research even suggests that pretreatment change may play a role in psychotherapy outcome once therapy is underway. Consider, for example, the sizable number of clients who come for only a single session of therapy. Despite the traditional view of such clients as "resistant," "defensive," or even "treatment failures," research indicates that as many as 80% don't return after their first visit because they believe they have received the help they need (Frank, 1990; Frank & Frank, 1991; Talmon, 1990). Surely, therapeutic technique is not the key ingredient in change resulting from a single visit with a clinician. A more parsimonious explanation is that scheduling an appointment with a mental health professional sets in motion a chain of events and client behaviors that ultimately influences the difficulty the client has been experiencing.

Another possible explanation for the phenomenon is what statisticians recognize as regression toward the mean (McCall, 1980). Briefly, the so-called "regression effect" is the observation that the exceptional generally reverts back to the ordinary (Efran & Green, 1994). In a clinical setting where requests for services frequently come at times of great personal distress, there is, in other words, a *natural* tendency for clients to move in the direction of improvement. Back, in other words, toward the center of the continuum and their mean or average daily experience.

Several research projects are currently investigating the degree to which pretreatment change is related to outcome in psychotherapy. One preliminary study conducted by Beyebach, Morejon, Palenzuela, and Rodriguez-Aris (1996) did find that pretreatment change was significantly related to treatment outcome ($r = .261$, $p < .05$). Specifically, those clients in the study who reported that beneficial changes had occurred prior to the initiation of treatment were four times more likely to finish treatment with a successful outcome. Research in other areas also suggests that pretreatment change is a positive predictor of improvement at termination. Consider, for example, data demonstrating the failure of most standardized measures of pathology to differentiate between clients who will and will not ultimately respond to or benefit from psychotherapy. Despite the widespread use of such standardized measures, a growing number of studies suggests that predictions of overall improvement at the conclusion of treatment are more accurate when they are based on the client's report of change or improvement *in the first few sessions of therapy* rather than on therapists' pretreatment assessments of client level of dysfunction. As Garfield (1994) points out in his extensive review of the literature on client variables in psychotherapy, "it does appear as if the patients' (*sic*) subjective feeling of change may really be the *essential* variable. If one can view this as the patient's feeling better or seeing himself or herself as improving early in therapy, then this *early* state of improvement may be indicative of positive outcome at termination" (p. 219).

Treatment professionals can welcome pretreatment changes

in several ways. For instance, during the opening moments
of a first session the therapist may simply inquire about what,
if any, changes clients have noticed since the time they scheduled their appointment for therapy and the first session.

Case Example: Pretreatment
Change All Night Long

As an example of inquiring directly about pretreatment
change, consider the following dialogue taken from the opening moments of a first session with a couple seeking treatment because of longstanding marital problems. The session
started with the therapist asking both partners what brought
them into treatment. The woman spoke first, explaining her
reasons for coming and describing what she hoped would
change about her 35-year marriage. After several minutes,
the conversation then turned naturally to her husband:

Husband: It's so difficult for us to have communication. We
   have very poor communication. It's like a one-way street,
   you know. To me, that is the most . . . That is it as far as
   I am concerned. We cannot communicate about things,
   agree upon things, we are constantly fighting in our marriage. Our relationship, most of the time, I believe I'm
   right, and she believes she's right. One word leads to another and then you got a big old thing that nobody can do
   nothing with. We're yelling at each other and, gawd . . .

Therapist: (*looking back and forth at both partners*) You
   want that to be different.

Wife: Right.

Husband: It's getting worse all the time. Each argument
   pushes you a little further, shifts things, us away from each
   other. I'm getting too old for this, I want some peace.

T: (*to both*) Let me ask you something, since you made the

appointment to come here and tackle this problem have you had any peace? Have you two been communicating?

W: (*ecstatic*) YES! Yes! All night long. We were able to *talk*.

H: (*nodding affirmatively*)

T: (*surprised*) You were able to talk?

W: He talked, then he laid there and let me talk. He let me tell him about some of the things that he would do to flusterate me. The things he would do that would bother me. As well, he would tell me some of the things I did to bother him. And we did communicate since we made the phone call.

T: (*looks questioningly at husband*)

H: (*nodding affirmatively*)

W: (*looks at husband*) How did that happen?

H: (*smiling*) I noticed myself *listening*, really listening. And, glad to hear some of the things that she was saying. (*looks at wife*) That *was* different last night, wasn't it?

Subsequent dialogue continued to amplify the couple's description of the pretreatment change. Specifically, questions were asked to add depth and detail to the episode of pretreatment change that the clients had experienced (Miller & Berg, 1995). In addition, the therapist spent a considerable amount of time during that session exploring what, if anything, each partner had done that might have caused or at least helped the change to occur. For example, the therapist asked both partners how the change had happened, what each of them had done to contribute to this brief, albeit important, change in their usual communication pattern, and what, if anything, either of them might have done to "set the stage" for this instance of success (Miller, 1995). The list of likely antecedent events started small but grew steadily as the session continued. Later sessions were used primarily to build on the pretreatment change identified during that first meeting.

In addition to making such direct inquiries, treatment professionals can simply listen for and then amplify any intra-session reports of pretreatment change. The data appear to indicate that such reports are, in fact, the rule rather than the exception. As evidence of this, recall the studies cited earlier that found that between 60 and 66% of clients report positive pretreatment change. Recall, further, that the 60 and 66% figures were obtained by asking clients about pretreatment change *at the beginning* of the first session of therapy. These same studies found that the total number of clients reporting positive, complaint- or goal-related pretreatment change increased considerably by the end of the therapy hour. Given these findings, the key to successful utilization of extratherapeutic factors would seem to be *listening* for a change.

Case Example: They Say I'm Psycho

As an example of simply listening for reports of pretreatment change, consider the following dialogue taken from the case of a woman referred for psychotherapy by her gynecologist. The client had a longstanding history of dyspareunia accompanied by complaints of severe genital irritation and infection. In spite of years of medical testing, no physical cause had ever been identified for the client's complaints, and the latest in a long list of physicians suspected that the problems were psychogenic. The client began the session by relating some of the history of her problems:

Client: I have seen so many doctors over the last, well, several years. I've had this problem for thirty years. It's serious because, well, you see, I've been married twice and both times this problem . . .

Therapist: Uh huh.

C: It's a little embarrassing. I've, uh, had this redness and
infection — well, the doctors have all said that I don't, have
never had have any infection — but, on my genitals I'm
always swollen and irritated . . .

T: Uh huh.

C: . . . and, well, it has always hurt to have intercourse, you
know, because . . .

T: (*finishing the sentence*) of the redness and irritation.

C: (*with relief*) Yeah. The doctor says I'm psycho . . .

T: Psycho?

C: (*nodding affirmatively*) Psycho . . . psychosomatic.

The client continued for several minutes elaborating her
story and explaining that she had made the appointment for
therapy following a recent visit to a new physician. Unable
to find anything physically wrong with her, this latest doctor
had said that she should consider seeing a mental health professional. The therapist simply listened while the woman related these details. Following a natural break in the process,
the therapist returned to a statement the client had made in
the opening moments of the session:

T: You say that you have *had* this redness and irritation?

C: (*nodding affirmatively*) Mmm.

T: Does that mean to say that there have been some changes
for the better recently?

C: (*surprised*) Well, yes.

T: What's been different?

C: I've tried almost everything. I tried almost every, well, the
doctors have tried all the drugs — creams, steroids, antibi-
otics. Nothing has ever worked, at least not for very long.

T: And lately?

C: Well, I have been applying a mixture of milk of magnesia and Benadryl, just a few drops topically, to the, uh, red, irritated areas.

T: Hmm.

C: And it's much improved over the few weeks that I've been doing it.

T: Is that right?

C: After thirty years, I'd almost given up hope of this ever, well, changing.

T: Of course. And the mixture is helping?

C: Mmm.

Together, the therapist and client explored the differences resulting from the client's discovery. To ensure that the client's solution did not create a real medical problem, the therapist inquired about how the client knew the "appropriate dose" to use on any given occasion, as well as how she would know when the "medicine" was no longer needed. Thereafter, the conversation returned to pretreatment change:

T: Anything else that has been different or helpful lately?

C: (*surprised*) Well, yes. Right now, I find myself in a situation, well, with a man that I've known for most of my life and he's quite a wonderful person . . .

T: (*pleased*) Hmm.

C: . . . and now we, well, have a sexual relationship.

T: (*curious*) That is different?

C: For the first time, last night, it didn't hurt.

T: Is that right?!

C: (*proudly*) Yeah, for the first time.

T: How do you think that happened?

C: Well, for three weeks . . . well, a lot has to do with Steven. We have, well, there hasn't been any pressure. We have gone very slowly and the pain just hasn't been there.

T: The pain isn't there?

C: I guess it helps that I'm in love with Steven and I don't really think that I was in love with my husbands.

T: Sure. What else might be making a difference?

C: Well, I'm not as guarded. He is so careful and, well, thoughtful of me. Early on, we talked and agreed that if there was any hurt then we'd stop and, oh, I think we spend a lot of time just, well, you know, touching and just, laying there, uh, being together.

The therapist and client continued to explore the changes the woman was reporting for the remainder of the meeting. During that time, the client identified several differences in her own and her partner's behavior that were likely responsible for the recent changes. In particular, a considerable amount of time was devoted to the helpful ways the couple had discovered to communicate with each other about their sexual relationship. By the end of the session, the therapist and client agreed that no further sessions were needed.

Whether pretreatment change is reported spontaneously by the client or follows a direct inquiry by the therapist is of little consequence initially. More important in the beginning is simply listening for and validating such reports of change — in other words, welcoming rather than rejecting such reports as evidence of "minimalization," "resistance," "denial," "flights into health," or "escapes from transference."

Between-session change

Extratherapeutic factors contribute not only to change occurring before the formal initiation of treatment, but also to change that takes place once treatment is underway. The research shows, in fact, that *improvement between treatment sessions is the rule rather than the exception*. In one pioneering study, for example, Reuterlov, Lofgren, Nordstrom and Ternstrom (in press) followed 175 cases over the course of treatment and found that at the beginning of any given session 70% of clients reported complaint-related improvement. Even more encouraging, however, was the finding that half of the 30% of clients who initially reported no between-session improvement did identify specific, complaint-related improvement by the conclusion of any given session. On a similar note, a substantial amount of research shows that the majority of client change occurring in therapy happens earlier rather than later in the treatment process. For example, in a meta-analytic study of nearly 2,500 clients seen in a traditional, week-to-week format, 50% were measurably improved by the eighth session and 75% within six months (Howard, Kopte, Krause, & Orlinsky, 1986).

In contrast to these encouraging results, however, the treatment models employed by the majority of therapists most often portray human change as a difficult and long-term process. Indeed, in his massive and systematic review of the current research and thinking on change in psychotherapy, Mahoney (1991) indicates that the view of human change as difficult is "one of the important points of convergence across contemporary schools of thought in psychotherapy" (p. 18). Perhaps reflecting the view of change endemic to these models, surveys of mental health professionals show that a clear majority believe that lasting change takes a long time, perhaps years, to achieve in psychotherapy (Kupst & Shulman, 1979). As may be obvious, the pessimistic or "challenge" view of change shared by most treatment models may inadvertently lead treatment professionals to discount or even overlook between-session changes. This may be especially likely when, as the research indicates is most often the case, change occurs early in treatment or, as is always the case with extratherapeutic factors, is not directly attributable to the therapy or therapist.

Interestingly, treatment professionals might be more mindful and welcoming of between-treatment change if they adopted the beliefs and expectations of their clients. The research shows, for example, that clients' expectations about both the occurrence of change and length of time in therapy correspond more closely with what actually happens in most treatment than do therapists' expectations (Garfield, 1994). For example, the majority of clients expect treatment to be of relatively short duration (e.g., 10 sessions or less) and to experience improvement earlier (e.g., by session 5) rather than later in the treatment process (Garfield & Wolpin, 1963). And, in fact, the research shows that the average client only attends a handful of sessions and that improvement generally corresponds to the median number of sessions attended by most clients (Garfield, 1994; Howard, Kopte, Krause, & Orinsky, 1986).

Therapists can become more receptive to between-session change in several ways. For example, depending on the style of the therapist and presentation of the client, therapists can simply listen for and then amplify any references the client makes during the session to between-session improvement. In addition, during the opening moments of the session therapists can ask clients directly about what, if any, changes have occurred since their last visit.

Case Example: The Blues Ain't Nothin'

Lakisha was a 36-year-old single parent of two children who came to therapy reporting severe depression. Nothing in the first visit with her would have led a therapist to expect early improvement. If anything, her history and present circumstances suggested that her recovery, if it occurred at all, would take a very long time. These initial impressions seemed only to be confirmed when Lakisha returned for her second session and spent the first fifteen minutes recounting the week's difficulties and struggles. Nothing, as she portrayed it, had changed or improved since the last visit. In spite of this apparent lack of progress, the therapist waited for an appropriate opportunity and asked Lakisha directly whether anything had, in fact, improved since the last visit. The result, as the follow dialogue illustrates, was dramatic:

Therapist: Hmm. As you were talking, I was wondering if anything *had* gotten better since our last visit.

Client: Well, basically, I've been OK even though all this, you know, has been going on.

T: Is that right?

C: Yeah, with everything that's happened, you know, I think I done pretty good.

T: Hmm.

C: I'm not crying this time, did you notice that?

T: (*nodding, taken by surprise*) Yeah, I did.

C: I been trying to get out, you know, not stay in the house all the time.

T: That's helped?

C: Yeah, I feel better. It's important for me to, you know, feel better. It's a terrible feeling, feeling down all the time.

T: Right.

C: (*continuing*) And for those people who get down there and don't know, you know, how to come out, I feel sorry for those people.

T: And so, are you saying that you sort of know more about how to come out of this?

C: (*nodding affirmatively*) Yeah, I think that getting myself

outside, walking, or, you know, maybe feeling like, "Today, I don't feel like doing the laundry. I'm not doing the
laundry." (*pounding fist into hand*) You know, not putting that demand on yourself.

T: (*taking notes*) Right, let me get some of this down.

C: (*waiting*)

T: What else?

The client went on to describe other significant changes
that had taken place since the first session, including having
obtained part-time employment. This latter change was particularly important, since much of Lakisha's depression was
related to her current financial situation. As the session pro-
gressed, the therapist continued to listen carefully, inquiring
about other changes and asking questions that added depth
and detail to the client's report (Miller & Berg, 1995). The
therapist also made detailed inquiries about what specifically
the client had done to bring about the changes she was experiencing. Over a handful of sessions, this discussion evolved
into a fairly concrete plan for addressing the difficulties that
brought Lakisha into treatment.

The case example illustrates the potential value of a direct
inquiry about between-session change. More importantly,
however, the case demonstrates the value of *remaining open
to the possibility of between-session change, regardless of the
history or presentation of the client.* Extratherapeutic factors, it will be recalled, can have a beneficial impact on outcome at any time during the treatment process. One can only
speculate about how differently the case might have gone
had the therapist given up on the possibility of change. The
temptation to forgo listening for or asking about such
changes can be especially compelling when, as was true in
the preceding case, clients do not spontaneously report
changes for the better or when an apparent lack of improve-

ment happens to correspond with the therapist's negative expectations for the case. The temptation is only stronger, as the following case will illustrate, when the client not only does not report change but also actively denies it.

Case Example: Nothing Has Changed: Nada, Zip, Zero, Not a Damn Thing!

Regi, a 34-year-old homeless man with a history of chronic mental illness, was referred for treatment by a local outreach program. Workers at the program had grown increasingly concerned about Regi because his personal appearance and level of social interaction had gradually worsened over the last several months. Though occasionally tangential and sometimes difficult to follow in his first visit, Regi managed to identify several specific changes he said he both needed and wanted to make while in therapy. An assignment was given to help Regi initiate a few targeted changes and an appointment was made for the following week.

Regi returned for his second appointment a week later. After spending a few minutes socializing, the therapist asked Regi directly whether any changes for the better had taken place since the last visit. Shaking his head slowly, Regi responded:

Client: Nothing has changed.

Therapist: (*curious*) Nothing?

C: Nada, zip, zero. Not a damn thing has changed.

T: Hmm.

C: The week has just been *terrible*.

Regi spent the next ten minutes detailing the events of the preceding week. Nothing he said gave even the slightest hint of progress. Regi was, for example, still living on the streets and still not receiving the monetary assistance to which he was entitled. As one might expect, remaining open to the possibility of change was a significant challenge for the therapist. The conversation continued:

T: Sounds like this has been another tough week.

C: I did call Habitat for Humanity.

T: (*affirming*) You did?

C: Yeah, but they told me that I need a mailing address.

T: So, you're still working on that.

C: Yeah, but, by the way, I met one of my old girlfriends just this last Saturday.

T: You did?

C: Yeah, it was kinda one of those wonderful things that sometimes happens to a guy.

T: Hmm.

C: (*smiling*)

T: We talked about this last time, getting out and being a bit more social. Tell me, how did this happen?

C: She was coming home from the store, I was going up by Church to work — my boss *finally* gave me some more hours — and . . . (*pausing*)

T: You got more hours in at work?

C: (*nodding but continuing the previous thought*) It just so happened that I was all cleaned up and wearing my favorite shirt (*laughing*)!

T: (*nodding, laughing*)

C: (*laughing*) Maybe I oughta wear that one a little more often.

T: Hmm, maybe I oughta get one and wear it myself!

C: (*laughing*)

T: Gawd, you've said a lot of stuff here, um, can I, can we
go back here for a minute.

In what remained of the hour, the therapist and Regi explored the changes that had been reported. As in the previous
case examples, questions were asked that encouraged Regi to
add depth and detail to his report. In addition, in order to
ensure that the changes Regi was reporting would be repeated in the future, some time was spent clarifying Regi's
role in bringing about these changes. As the next section
demonstrates, such inquiry constitutes a crucial second step
in utilizing change resulting from extratherapeutic factors in
the service of therapeutic outcome.

Potentiating change for the future

Whether change begins prior to or during treatment,
whether it results from the client strengths or a chance event,
a crucial second step in the process of enhancing the effect of
extratherapeutic factors on therapy outcome is helping clients see any such changes—as well as the maintenance of
those changes—as a consequence of their own efforts. Research on self-efficacy leads us to predict that clients who
attribute change to their own efforts rather than to chance
occurrences are more likely to own that change and attempt
to repeat it in the future (Bandura, 1977, 1986). And, indeed, empirical studies have found a strong correlation between the maintenance of change and the degree to which
clients attribute that change to their own efforts (Lambert &
Bergin, 1994). In one telling set of studies, for example,
researchers who gave a placebo to a group of unknowing
clients found that those who attributed the resulting improvement to the inert substance were less likely to maintain gains
than those who viewed the improvement as resulting from
their own efforts (Frank, 1976; Liberman, 1978). Similarly,
by using objective measures, Schuable and Pierce (1974)

demonstrated that those clients who showed an internal sense of responsibility for resolving their problems had significantly better outcomes than those clients who did not.

Obviously, the key here is *perception*—specifically, clients' perception—of the relationship between their own efforts and the occurrence of change. What may have actually— really, truly, or empirically—caused the change is of little importance to the therapeutic process and is, in an ultimate sense, probably unknowable. When the change occurs in the treatment process—before, during, or even after—also matters very little. What is important, however, is that clients come to view the change as resulting at least in part from something they did and can, therefore, do again in the future. Therapists can and do have considerable influence on which view clients ultimately adopt.

Case Example: It Just Happened

Consider the case of Felix, a 41-year-old homeless man who came to treatment because of chronic problems with alcohol and cocaine. Midway into the first interview, Felix spontaneously reported that he had deviated from his usual routine and not used any alcohol or drugs before coming to the scheduled afternoon session. However, when pressed to explain how he had managed to stay away from the drugs and alcohol, the client attributed his success to "luck." Knowing that such a view was unlikely to encourage Felix to do anything other than wait for good fortune to be visited on him again, the therapist persisted:

Therapist: (*curious*) Luck?

Client: Yeah. What can I say? It just happened.

T: (*curious*) It just happened, hmm.

C: Normally I'd've been drinking by now.

T: That's what makes this so . . . interesting. Why you? I mean, why were you the lucky one today?

C: (*thoughtfully*) I don't know.

T: (*nodding*)

C: I've been thinking a lot though.

T: Thinking?

C: Thinking, looking around and at my life. I'm 41 years old and look at me. I don't have a home, my clothes are all free clothes, I have to walk everywhere. I can't even afford to take the bus most of the time.

T: Hmm. Felix, has "thinking," as you say, looking around at your life, and seeing where you're at—is that what helped you make it here sober today?

C: Didn't hurt.

T: That's surprising.

C: What?

T: That it didn't hurt. I mean, if anyone had a good reason to get high . . .

C: (*laughs*) then it is me, yeah, I know.

T: So how come you didn't cave in and go get high today?

As the inquiry continued, Felix gradually assumed more responsibility for the period of success. By the end the hour, he had even identified a couple of actions he had "deliberately" taken to ensure he was sober for the scheduled appointment. This included, for example, skipping breakfast at the food kitchen where he frequently met friends with whom he drank and used drugs. The word "deliberately" appears in quotes here because coming to view the success period as intentional behavior was a process that occurred over the course of the entire session and did not follow from any one event or technique.

One can only imagine how such a small and seemingly

chance occurrence might have been approached from a more traditional alcohol treatment perspective. To begin, coming to the session sober may have been taken for granted and, for that reason, not considered significant by the counselor. More likely, given the near exclusive emphasis on program issues in traditional alcohol treatment programs (i.e., attendance at Alcoholics Anonymous, strict abstinence, etc.), the client may have been confronted (blamed) for what he had *not* yet accomplished rather than given credit for the change that had occurred (Miller & Berg, 1995). Such tactics, though benevolently motivated, serve to punish rather than reinforce the client's sense of self-efficacy with regard to behavior change. They may also create a dependence on external resources (e.g., therapist, programs, substances) rather than internal ones (self, skills, resources, etc.).

Depending on the style of the therapist and the presentation of the client, therapists can help potentiate changes resulting from extratherapeutic factors in any number of ways. For instance, as in the previous case example, the therapist can simply be curious about the client's role in any changes that take place during treatment. Specifically, the therapist can ask questions or make direct statements that presuppose client involvement in the resulting change (Berg & Miller, 1992; Imber, Pilkonis, Harway, Klein, & Rubinsky, 1982; Walter & Peller, 1992). Drawing an analogy to the more common occurrence of assigning blame for negative behaviors, Kral and Kowalski (1989) have called this process "positive blame," noting that, "The act of 'blaming' is meant to assign responsibility of the noted change to the client, which reinforces his/her perceived influence in his/her life" (p. 74; see also, Kral, 1986).

The next section explores additional methods for recognizing and potentiating change in psychotherapy based on becoming more mindful of the client's strengths, resources, and abilities.

Minding the client's contribution to change

> What are therapists good at? They're good at telling peo-
> ple what's wrong with them, that's what they're good at.
>
> — *Dr. Joy Brown*
> *talk radio psychologist,*
> *TalkNet Radio Network, September 19, 1995*

"I have found little that is good about human beings," Sigmund Freud once wrote. "In my experience *most* of them are trash." These are shocking words, especially when one considers that they were penned by the person most practicing therapists would immediately identify as the "father" of the modern helping professions. While few modern mental health professionals openly subscribe to Freud's misanthropic assessment, there is in fact strong evidence that his view has exerted and continues to exert considerable influence — albeit less transparently — on the current theory and practice of psychotherapy.

Consider, for example, the staggering increase in the number of diagnostic categories of mental illness that has taken place over the last forty years. Since the *Diagnostic and Statistical Manual of Mental Disorders* (DSM) was first published in 1952, the number of diagnostic categories included in the volume has increased a whopping 300%. Though there is no evidence that the huge increase in diagnostic categories in any way reflects a similar increase in incidence of mental illness in the general population, the implication is clear: people are sick and getting sicker (Garfield & Bergin, 1994).

Couple the increase in diagnostic categories with pronouncements made by popular mental health experts that upwards of 96% of the American population are either dysfunctional or suffering the effects of growing up in a dysfunctional family, and our current beliefs and practices begin to seem like only a slightly less cynical version of Freud's assessment (Gravitz & Bowden, 1987; Kristol, 1990; Miller & Berg, 1995). While perhaps less explicit than Freud, modern psychotherapy research and practice continue to be based on and guided by the assumption that what is wrong with the people who visit therapists—whether construed in modern clinical parlance as biochemical, intrapsychic, interpersonal, interactional, systemic, cognitive, behavioral, or whatever— is of more importance than what is right—namely, the strengths and resources, experiences and abilities, social supports and world view that they bring to treatment. As Zilbergeld (1983) pointed out in *The Shrinking of America*, "In the [modern] therapeutic view, people [may not be] regarded as vile or as having done anything they should feel guilty about, but *there is certainly something wrong with them*" (p. 195, italics in original).

Perhaps reflecting the wider cultural belief in "original sin," psychotherapy theory and practice continue to stereotype clients as the vessels of pathology, the manufacturers of resistance, and the message bearers of family dysfunction. Rarely are clients given the credit for change occurring in psychotherapy that the research so clearly demonstrates is warranted. The eminent psychotherapist Lewis Wolberg noted this tendency over forty years ago when he observed, "It is unfortunate that so much emphasis has been placed on the evil consequences of emotional and mental disturbance that we are prone to concern ourselves chiefly with destructive pathological effects and forget that constructive regenerative influences may be coincidently present" (1954, p. 14).

If anything, therapists are usually cast in the hero/savior role in the stories of successful psychotherapy that either appear in print or circulate among treatment professionals. Whether the therapist is managing resistance, making interpretations, pointing out dysfunctional thoughts, or asking the "miracle question," stories of successful psychotherapy most often emphasize the therapist's contribution over the client's. These stories not only perpetuate a belief in a magnitude of therapist contribution to change in therapy that is simply not supported by the facts but worse, by continually focusing attention on the therapist's own prowess, may inadvertently lead helping professionals to discount or even ignore the larger contribution to change made by the client.

Client competence

Treatment professionals can begin to cast their clients in their deserved role as the primary agents of change by listening for and being curious about clients' competence and by balancing careful and empathic listening to the difficulties that bring clients into treatment with a mindfulness to whatever strengths, resources, or abilities their lives and circumstances imply. Listening for and being curious about clients' contribution to change in psychotherapy does not mean that the therapist ignores clients' suffering or assumes a blithe, "hear no evil, see no evil" attitude in treatment. Instead, the therapist listens to the whole story: the confusion *and* the clarity, the suffering *and* the endurance, the pain *and* the coping, the desperation *and* the desire.

Case Example: You Can't Help Me

As an example of how the therapist[1] can listen for and highlight client competence in the service of therapeutic change, consider the following dialogue taken from a first session with a blind woman who came to therapy after learning she had lupus — a progressive, degenerative, neurological disease. The woman was very depressed because the disease

---

[1]The therapist in this case was Ron Wilgosh. The dialogue also appears in L. Hopwood and A. Turnell (in press).

was now causing her to lose sensation in her legs, arms, hands, and most tragically, her fingers. The result was that the she could no longer read Braille or engage in most of the activities she had grown accustomed to since losing her sight ten years earlier. The session began with the therapist first familiarizing the client with the consulting room and then asking:

Therapist: What brought you here today?

Client: I just feel really depressed. I can't use my hands, and my legs they're all numb. I'm just like numb all over my body. I don't have any, I can control my left hand, but I don't have the feeling in it . . .

T: (*nodding*) Right.

C: I can't dial a telephone. I have to get the operator to do, to place calls for me. All these things, they're bad because I'm used to doing all these things for myself.

T: Right, right. So you're having to make a lot of adjustments and that's tough, that's hard.

C: (*tearful*) I don't want to live like this, I really don't. I mean, I don't have the thought that I want to kill myself but I don't want to live like this either.

T: There's a lot happening for you at the moment and a lot of it is new to you, how are you coping with this?

C: (*tearful*) I'm not . . . I can't write, I can't read my Braille 'cause I don't have the feeling in my hands, in my fingers. . . . I can't prepare my own meals.

The therapist continued to listen attentively, acknowledge the difficulties the client was experiencing, *and* look for evidence of competence. Maintaining a balance among listening, acknowledging, and looking for competence was a significant challenge for the therapist since, as the dialogue so clearly shows, this client was experiencing and expressing considerable pain and anguish. So much pain and anguish, in fact, that at one point in the session the client flatly told the therapist, "You can't help me because you can't make the feelings [in my hands and legs] come back." Given the amount of suffering this client was experiencing, it would have been very easy and, perhaps, even justifiable on traditional "therapeutic" grounds to forgo looking for competence and simply join the woman in her pain. In this case, however, the therapist managed to maintain a balance that eventually resulted in the following exchange:

C: I don't want to be dependent on people. That was the one hard thing I had to go through when I lost my sight. I lost my sight in September of '80 and that was a real, real, that was a very big adjustment for me . . .

T: I bet it was.

C: I mean, if it hadn't happened to me I wouldn't believe that it was possible that you could actually adjust to it. 'Cause it's very, very hard.

T: Right, so if it hadn't happened to you, you wouldn't believe that you would've been able to adjust to something like that.

C: Right.

T: How did you adjust? How did you do that?

C: For a whole year, I did nothing, didn't eat very much, all I did was sleep. The only time I'd get up and do anything was to go to the bathroom.

T: Mmm hmm.

C: If I had a doctor's appointment I'd get up and go there, come back, and basically all I did was stay in bed.

T: And after that first year what did you start to do that showed you were beginning to adjust?

C: I, uh, went down to the technical college and I was in the program for the visually impaired and learned how to get out and go places by myself, learned how to walk, go to stores, shop . . .

T: (*curious*) You had to learn all of that new? How did . . .

C: Yeah, and every time I managed to accomplish something, I was real pleased with myself . . .

T: Right.

C: I did it until I knew I could do it on my own.

T: Mmm hmm.

C: Once I was able to do it then I didn't have to keep doing it and I went on to something else.

T: So, you sort of practiced it over and over until you felt confident about doing it and then moved on to something else.

For several more minutes, the therapist and client worked together identifying and amplifying the factors that had aided the woman in adjusting to her loss of sight ten years earlier. Not surprisingly, perhaps, this brief interchange became the foundation of competence that this client was able to stand upon, so to speak, in order to confront and eventually adjust to her current problems.

In the second meeting, held a week later, the client reported that she had: (1) resolved to get out of bed; (2) made an appointment for herself at the beauty parlor; (3) dialed the phone by herself and arranged for a taxi ride to the appointment; and (4) decided to attend a support group for people with lupus—all activities which originated *in the client* and which, the reader will recall, had taken her a full year to engage in ten years earlier. At the conclusion of the session, both the therapist and client agreed that no further visits were necessary.

Case Example: Robert's Relapse

As the preceding case demonstrates so well, evidence of client competence can be found in even the most desperate circumstances. It is even possible to notice competence when the client is either not making progress or in the midst of a setback. Consider the following dialogue taken from the fourth session with a forty-something man who has experienced a setback in his attempt to stop using alcohol problematically.

Therapist: How have things been going?

Client: OK, I guess, I've kept exercising. Gettin' up and walking, do some stretches, and such.

T: (*nodding*) Hmm, great.

C: I've been writing too, puttin' stuff on paper, my thoughts and all.

T: (*nodding*) Right.

The client continued for several more minutes describing the events that had gone well since the previous session. The therapist listened attentively, occasionally highlighting evidence of the client's effort and ability. Then the conversation began to shift:

C: (*long pause, breaks eye contact and looks down*) What's gone backwards for me is the drinking thing.

T: (*curious*) It has?

C: I don't know why. Nothing happened, everything was going good. I just started drinking.

At this point, the client elaborated on the drinking episode. According to his report, he had gone to a convenience store one evening following work in order to purchase some cigarettes. While there, he met several old friends who were on their way to a local tavern to have a few drinks and talk. Feeling a bit lonely, the client decided to follow the men to the bar and have a few drinks himself. Before he knew it, however, he had spent the entire evening drinking. The session continued with the therapist gently shifting the focus toward client competence:

T: So, let me ask you then, how did you finally stop?

C: (*laughing*) Well, the bar closed and I went home.

T: (*laughing*) Oh, I see.

C: I just, it was, the next day was BAD. I got up for work and . . .

T: (*interrupting*) You actually got up for work?

C: (*nodding*) I had to, I was sick.

T: I bet, not used to it as much.

C: (*surprised then nodding*) Yeah.

T: So how come you just didn't stay in bed, say, "To hell with it?"

From this point, the conversation began to move in the direction of the client's competence in dealing with the setback he had experienced. In particular, the therapist asked questions that helped the client describe exactly how he had managed to stop the setback and what he was doing to both get back and stay on track. By the conclusion of the session, the client had identified a number of things he had done and had even started viewing the setback as a valuable learning experience rather than a failure.

It should be pointed out that being mindful of client competence does not mean that the therapist must always discover some "real" or "actual" resource or ability within the client—or in his or her history, as in the previous case—that can be utilized to meet therapeutic objectives. Indeed, taking such an active approach can result in failure and, in the process, serve only to heighten clients' (and therapists') existing feelings of hopelessness and incompetence. Rather, the key is the *attitude* the treatment professional assumes with regard to client ability when conducting clinical work. This attitude involves treating clients *as if* they are capable and possess the strengths and resources necessary to solve their problems (Watzlawick, 1986). This attitude was perhaps best summarized by psychoanalyst Alfred Adler when he said he approached all clients, "fully convinced that no matter what I might be able to say . . . the patient can learn nothing from me that he, as the sufferer, does not understand better" (Ansbacher & Ansbacher, 1956, p. 336). Approaching clients in this matter not only helps to combat demoralization and instill hope but, as Adler also noted, "make[s] it clear that the responsibility for . . . cure is the patient's business."

Case Example: Should We Marry or Be Merry?

As a way of illustrating this latter point, consider the following dialogue taken from a first session with a woman who came to therapy because of problems she was experiencing in her relationship. Specifically, the client felt that her three-year relationship had plateaued and was no longer progressing toward marriage. In contrast to the previous case example, the therapist in this case did *not* display an attitude open and friendly to—validating of, in other words—client competence. Notice the attitude the therapist *does* convey and the effect this has on the client:

Client: I don't like the way things are right now but, I don't want to, we have a very nonconflictual relationship, so I don't want to fight with him. We always have a good time. I just want to figure out, you know, should we marry or, uh, (*laughing*) just be merry.

Therapist: Do you think that if people are assertive and let other people know what they want, do you think that makes conflict?

C: (*shifting in chair*) No, I don't, but it's difficult to do.

T: Well, perhaps.

C: I have tried to talk with Michael about this and tell him, you know, but . . .

T: Sometimes people mistake aggressiveness for assertiveness and they say things that thwart the other person, the conversation, and you don't want that to happen?

C: No, but I have tried to talk with him and tell him what I want. Like last week, we were coming home from this party we'd been to and I told him how I was feeling, how I wanted to talk about our, you know, relationship, where we were going.

T: Did he hear you?

C: Yeah, well, at least to start, but then the same old thing, the subject got changed . . .

T: What did you do then?

C: I just laughed to myself.

T: Have you ever heard of a mixed message?

C: Huh?

T: A mixed message, like laughing when you're really angry?

C: (*nodding affirmatively, begins to cry*)

As the dialogue illustrates, the therapist in this case does not approach this client with the attitude that she is capable and has the strengths and resources necessary to resolve the problems that bring her to treatment. In fact, the attitude displayed in the responses—whether technically correct or not—is that this client *lacks* some critical resource(s)—first awareness, then communication skills, and finally information—which, if present, would certainly lead to a resolution of her problem. To be sure, the responses do imply that the client *is* responsible—but for the problem, not the solution. The attitude conveyed through these responses is that the *therapist* is the resourceful and capable participant in this interaction and, therefore, responsible for any solution that develops.

The effect of the interaction on the therapeutic process is immediate and obvious. After some minor protests, the client stops talking and starts to cry. In the time that remained in the session, the client sat quietly while the therapist shared information about different types of communication patterns (e.g., I-messages, assertive versus aggressive communication). A second session was scheduled, but the client did not show up for the appointment.

Working *within* the client's world view

Buried deep in the archives of psychotherapy research is a set of rarely cited but ingenious studies on the nature of language in psychotherapy. In these studies, researchers Patton and Meara (1982) investigated the relationship between client satisfaction with treatment and the similarity and/or difference in the structure and style of language spoken by the client and therapist. In one particularly interesting study, the researchers examined the structure of language of three well-known therapists, Fritz Perls, Carl Rogers, and Albert Ellis, as they worked separately with a client named "Gloria"; the interviews were seen on the now famous teaching film *Three Approaches to Psychotherapy* (Shostrom, 1966). By measuring four different stylistic aspects of spoken language (i.e., the number of sentences, the average sentence length, the average block length, and the average clause depth), the researchers demonstrated what most therapists either know intuitively or learn through hard experience: higher ratings of client satisfaction are significantly and linearly related to similarity in client-therapist linguistic style.

Gloria, the reader will recall from the film, reported the greatest degree of overall satisfaction with the therapeutic work conducted by Fritz Perls and, not surprisingly, the style of language used by Perls and Gloria showed the greatest degree of similarity of all of the interviews on the film.

These and other similar results provide significant clues for successful and efficient clinical work building on and extending the theme of minding the client's contribution to change. The studies suggest, for example, that therapeutic work is likely to be facilitated when the therapist and client speak a language that is similar in word usage, complexity, depth, meaning, and other measures of linguistic style. During their careers, most treatment professionals have the experience of meeting with clients who are able to speak the language of a particular school of psychotherapy with ease but remain mired in their efforts to solve the problems that brought them into treatment in the first place. While the preliminary studies reported by Patton and Meara (1982) were not designed to determine whether the similarity in language between Perls and Gloria was purposeful or the result of chance, they do suggest that an active effort to speak the client's language may lead to higher rates of client satisfaction with the therapeutic process.

Speaking and working within the client's language is one more way for therapists to mind the client's contribution to change. Doing so conveys respect for the client's life experience and world view. It builds on what the client knows about and experiences in his or her daily life *outside* of the therapy office. At a minimum, speaking the client's language will prevent the client from becoming trapped in the particular language that the therapist happens to speak. More importantly, however, conducting treatment in the client's language or world view increases the chances that any resulting change will generalize to the world outside of the therapist's office where, as may be obvious, therapy language is less likely to be spoken.

By now, most clinicians have heard stories about psychiatrist Milton H. Erickson and his uncanny ability to work within the language and world view of his clients. In fact, in the entire treatment literature there is perhaps no greater example of being dedicated to learning and speaking a client's language than published reports of Erickson's work with a schizophrenic man who initially spoke nothing but word salad—schizophrenese (Gordon & Meyers-Anderson, 1981; Haley, 1985, 1986; O'Hanlon & Hexum, 1990; Rossi, 1980). According to the reports, Erickson first hired a stenographer to take down the man's utterances in the hopes of discerning some pattern or meaning in the seemingly random flow of words. When this strategy failed to produce results, Erickson decided to study the transcripts of the man's speech in order to learn to speak "word salad" himself! When he felt he had successfully mastered "a thousand or more" of the client's neologisms, he finally approached the young man and engaged him in conversation (Haley, 1985, p. 224). For three hours, Erickson and the patient carried on a completely nonsensical conversation. As the lunch hour neared, the patient turned to Erickson and spoke his first meaningful words in nine years:

Client: I'm getting tired of this.

MHE: So am I, but I don't mind.

Client: What do you want to know?

MHE: I'd like to take a history of you.

As with most stories about Erickson, this one ends dramatically and successfully. Before the day was over, Erickson had somehow managed to get the history that had eluded scores of previous clinicians. Over time, he and the client become "fast friends." Eventually the client was discharged from the hospital and obtained full-time work.

Fortunately, in most cases, successful utilization of the client's language or world view does not require the stamina or apparent genius of Milton Erickson. Indeed, as the following case illustrates, clinicians can simply listen for and then make a concerted effort to speak in the language the client uses to discuss her life, presenting problem, and goals for treatment.

Case Example: I Don't Have a Problem

Ruth was a 52-year-old client who was ordered into treatment after receiving a citation for driving under the influence of alcohol. Despite previous arrests on similar charges, Ruth maintained that she did not have a problem with alcohol. In the opening moments of the first visit, the therapist listened to the language that Ruth used to describe her reasons for being in treatment and then worked within that language:

Therapist: Ruth, tell me just a little bit about what brings you in today.

Client: I got a, uh, ticket for driving under the influence.

T: (*nodding*)

C: Actually, I only had one or two drinks but I hadn't eaten much and probably some of the medication I take contributed to that.

T: (*sympathetically*) Yeah, and, so, you got a ticket?

C: Yeah, I got my license suspended and I have to come here or someplace for counseling. I've been evaluated, very unfairly I might add, as having a *big* problem.

T: A *big* problem.

C: Yeah, according to these tests, which I don't think are very reliable, uh, that's what they say, and there is no recourse. I have already tried to do something about it but

the State says that if I want my license back I gotta come
here.

T: If you want your license back.

C: Yeah.

T: And, I guess that's what you want?

C: (*emphatically*) Yes, yes.

Up to this point, the language the client uses to describe
her reasons for being ordered into therapy provides many
tempting opportunities for the therapist to begin speaking
the language of a particular school of therapy. For example,
knowing the client's history of problems with alcohol, the
therapist could begin speaking the language of traditional
drug and alcohol treatment. To this end, the therapist might
"confront" Ruth about "denying" or "minimizing" her problems with alcohol. Other languages could also be introduced
into the conversation. For example, aware of familial patterns of alcohol abuse, the therapist might orient the conversation toward Ruth's early life and family history. Given the
vast number of treatment models currently available in the
therapy marketplace, the possibilities for introducing a language that is different from the client's are many.

Please note that "speaking in the client's language" does
not mean that the therapist in this case agrees with the views
expressed by the client. Rather, the client's language and
views are seen as resources for helping the therapist learn
what is important and, therefore, likely to be motivating to
the client. In this excerpt, the therapist is, for the most part,
simply repeating what the client is saying in a similar tone, at
a similar pace, using the same words and sentence structure.
The effect of this on the client appears to be immediate. Ruth
quickly moves beyond her complaints about being forced
into treatment and begins talking about what *she* wants from
coming to therapy. The therapist adopts the frame of refer-

ence inherent in the client's language—"I only want my license back"—and then works within her language to both clarify and add detail to the discussion.

T: They are saying you need to come here for some kind of counseling?

C: Yeah, even though I'm not an alcoholic.

T: Uh huh. Somehow . . . do you just have to come for counseling, is that it?

C: Yeah, just documented that I've been here.

T: (*curious*) So, do just have to show up?

C: Yeah, showing up and you writing a letter to the courts.

T: And, OK, do you have any idea about what they want to see in this letter that will tell them you don't need to come back here anymore?

C: Well, mostly that I've been here, attended.

T: That you attended.

C: That's it, just attended. (*pause*) Well, and that I've read whatever papers you give me, know about what all the laws are, that I'm a safe driver.

T: (*writing*) OK, these are good.

C: I think it's all a money-making proposition. My insurance is going to go up, I have to ask people for rides, I have to pay for this treatment I don't need, it's more than a little upsetting.

T: A pain in the ass.

C: Yeah.

T: Back to this letter, somehow or other they not only have to get this letter that says you've been here, read the papers, know what the laws are, but the other thing you said was that from this they have to get the idea that you'll be safe driver?

C: Yeah, well, I guess they assume that when you've been to counseling that you'll be a safe driver.

T: I'm just wondering if there is anything that we can write in this letter that will convince them that you're a safe driver.

C: Well, most people have to go to A.A. and it's pretty humiliating because you have to go and get signed that you've attended. But they [the State] will say that's good if I've gone.

The dialogue continued with the client and therapist using their common language to jointly identify what else the client needed to do in order to have her license reinstated by the court. By the conclusion of the first visit, the therapist and client had agreed that: (1) the client would attend three A.A. meetings per week and have a note signed at each session verifying her attendance; (2) that she would participate in the A.A. meetings by sharing her own experiences and problems with alcohol; (3) that she would attend group therapy and education classes *and* be an active participant in these classes; and (4) that she would meet once a week with the therapist to monitor her progress in the program and address any personal concerns she had. These agreements, in turn, became the basis for the treatment plan that was developed for the case.

Tapping the client's world outside of therapy

In addition to working within the client's language and world view, mental health professionals can also mind the client's contribution to change by incorporating resources from the client's world outside of therapy into the treatment process. Consider, for example, studies which have shown that nearly half the clients seeking therapy simultaneously look to other sources to obtain help (Bergin, 1971; Veroff, Kulka, & Douvan, 1981). Indeed, in one study, clients in therapy were found to seek outside counsel and advice *more* frequently than members of an untreated control group (Cross, Sheehan, & Kahn, 1980). As researchers Lambert and Bergin (1994) have noted, "Distressed human beings do not sit still like rats in cages waiting for the experiment to end. They act to relieve their stress . . . " (p. 175).

Whether seeking out a trusted friend or family member, purchasing a book or tape from their local bookstore or from late-night television, or attending church or a mutual-help group, clients find support wherever they can outside the formal therapy relationship. In fact, these elements — the clients' strengths and endurance, their tendency to seek and obtain help from others, and their ability to both engage and mobilize whatever social support network they have — are so significant that psychotherapy researchers have the perennial problem of determining whether the results of any particular study should be attributed to the method under investigation or to something clients did to help themselves.

Minding a particular client's world outside of therapy can be accomplished in any number of ways. The therapist can, for example, simply listen for and then be curious about what happens in the client's life outside of therapy that is helpful. Who does the client refer to as being helpful in his day-to-day life? How or what does the client do in order to get these persons to help him? What persons, places, or things does the client seek out between treatment sessions for even a small measure of comfort or aid? How does the client decide to make contact with a particular person or seek out a certain place or activity? What persons, places, or things has the client sought out in the past that were useful? What was different about those times that enabled the client to make use of those resources?

The therapist can also be more directive in the process

by asking, for example, pointed questions about those same elements. Among other things, the therapist may inquire about the helpful aspects of the client's existing social support network, about activities that provide relief, even if temporary, and about the contexts and circumstances outside of therapy in which the client feels most capable, successful, and at ease. In some cases, the therapist may wish to be even more direct, for example, by inviting someone from the client's existing social support network (e.g., parent, partner, employer, friend) to participate in the therapy or by referring the client to resources in the community (e.g., self-help groups, support lines, social clubs).

Whatever stance the therapist takes, it is important to remember that the purpose of this process is to identify not what clients *need* but rather what they *already have* in their world that can be put to use in reaching therapeutic objectives. Given that clients most often present for therapy in times of crisis or desperation, it can be easy to start treatment with the assumption they do *not* have the resources—either personally or in their world outside of therapy—that they need in order to resolve their problems.

Case Example: Recalling Regi

Recall the case of Regi, the 34-year-old homeless man with a history of chronic mental illness. Remember further that, after initially denying any improvement, Regi mentioned meeting an old girlfriend, which led to a process of relating, reviewing, and reinforcing changes that had, in fact, taken place since the first session. As the second session neared completion, Regi brought up a new issue. The problem was that Regi was not receiving the government assistance to which he was entitled. The conversation proceeded:

Client: I sure wish these aid and assistance woes would settle though.

Therapist: Say more about that.

C: Well, you know, start getting my checks and food stamps on a regular basis and not have to worry and wait so doggone long.

At this point, it might be tempting to assume that Regi needs the therapist's help in order to receive the assistance he is due. To this end, the therapist might ask questions in order to assess Regi's knowledge about the social service system, make a referral to an appropriate agency, or even offer to personally help Regi fill out any necessary forms, set up an appointment, or meet with the worker handling his case. In this instance, however, the therapist focuses on Regi's competence in resolving the problem. The result, as the following dialogue illustrates, is that Regi's ability to manage his own affairs is reinforced. In addition, Regi is connected to resources that already exist in his world outside of the therapy office:

T: How would that happen?

C: Well, usually I've got to talk with my accountant.

T: Your accountant?

C: Yeah, my, uh, payee.

T: And?

C: I have to get the monthly report and then take it to my worker.

T: (*nodding*) Your accountant, payee, he's helpful?

C: Oh yeah, sometimes the report is late and that holds things up.

T: I see, what do you do then?

C: I have to contact him more. And also, my worker will want to know what my mailing address is cause I'm no longer at Shelter A. I'm at Shelter B now.

T: So you've got to let her know that you're at Shelter B now.

C: Yeah.

T: How is your worker helpful?

Several more minutes were spent identifying the resources available in Regi's world outside of therapy, as well as reinforcing Regi's ability to mobilize these resources in his behalf. During his third visit, Regi reported that he had contacted his payee and that he would be receiving the monthly report "very soon."

SUMMARY AND CONCLUSION

Extratherapeutic factors make up the single largest contributor to change in psychotherapy. These factors include beneficial chance events as well as the helpful qualities that clients bring with them to the treatment relationship. In this chapter, some recommendations were given for facilitating the contribution of extratherapeutic factors to psychotherapy outcome. One key suggestion was that clinicians become more "change-focused" in their clinical work, listening for and validating client change whenever and for whatever reason it occurs during the treatment process. Other suggestions were given for highlighting the contribution to change made by the client. These included recognizing client competence, working within the client's world view, and utilizing client strengths.

The recommendations and suggestions contained in the chapter should by no means be considered comprehensive or exhaustive. Indeed, there are likely to be an infinite number of methods for conducting and structuring treatment in ways that capitalize on the contribution made by extratherapeutic factors. The particular method employed is much less important than the clinician's mindfulness for change-producing events and processes occurring outside the formal boundaries of treatment.

4

ON THE SHOULDERS
OF
CARL ROGERS

The Contribution of the Therapeutic Relationship to Treatment Outcome

> Some patients, though conscious that their condition is perilous, recover their health simply through their contentment with the goodness of the physician.
>
> *Hippocrates*, Precepts

> Without question, a positive therapeutic relationship is an important requirement for a successful outcome in psychotherapy, *and this applies to all forms of psychotherapy.*
>
> *Sol Garfield, 1989, p. 25, emphasis added*

NOT LONG AGO a client came in for treatment because of a longstanding problem with depression. She talked virtually nonstop for fifty minutes describing the history of her problem and explaining why she believed she had suffered for so long. Near the end of the hour, the client looked at her watch, expressed surprise at how quickly the time had passed, stood, and began exiting the consultation room. On her way out, she turned only briefly to say, "See you next week, same time."

The following week the client returned. Before the therapist had a chance to greet her, she began talking—nonstop again—resuming her story where she had left off the previous week. At various points during the session, the therapist attempted to ask a question or clarify some aspect of the woman's story. Each time, however, the client waved the therapist off and continued talking. After several failed attempts, the therapist gave up trying and simply listened while the woman spoke. As she had the previous week, the client ended the session by looking at her watch, remarking about the time, standing and, while leaving the office, saying "See you next week, same time."

The woman presented herself in a similar manner for the next several visits. Each session, the therapist attempted to ask some questions, make a comment or two about the woman's story, or offer some helpful suggestions. On every occasion, however, the therapist was not able to get in a word edgewise. Frustrated about situation and worried that he was not providing a useful service to the client, the therapist resolved to try harder to interrupt the client in the next — her fifth — session.

Trying a slightly different approach, the therapist met the client in the waiting room instead of having the receptionist direct the client to his office. Sensing an opportunity to have more time with the therapist, however, the client quickly resumed her story where she had left off at the last session. As the hour neared completion, the woman looked at her watch in the same way she had in the preceding sessions. This time, however, she did not end the meeting by commenting on the time and then abruptly leaving the office. Rather, the woman stopped talking momentarily and then announced that this session would be her last. Before the therapist could make his surprise known, the woman added, "I have never been to a therapist like you before. Thank you for listening. You have been tremendously helpful. I feel much better now." The woman stood, shook hands with the therapist, and told him she would be in contact if she ever felt depressed again in the future.

Another client, himself a clinician, had spent years looking for a therapy and therapist that would help him overcome chronic and debilitating feelings of anxiety. He had, for example, sought relief through psychoanalytic psychotherapy, family of origin therapy, and even psychopharmacotherapy, including various antianxiety preparations, antidepressants, and even a course of phenothiazines. All of these attempts had failed, however, compounding his anxiety with feelings of failure. Remembering the patients he had known and worked with over the years, the client-therapist saw himself on the fast track to confinement and eventual disintegration of his personality. He wondered about ending up in a long-term hospital setting similar to the one in which he worked.

In spite of his many disappointing experiences with treatment, however, the client-therapist continued to seek help. Acting on a tip from a friend, he scheduled an appointment with a clinician practicing in a nearby town. He was, needless to say, more than a bit skeptical—not only because of his previous treatment experiences but also because this provider, unlike previous practitioners, was not a doctor, did not work at a prestigious setting, and had not been trained by any recognized experts in the field. Indeed, the provider's pedigree was far from correct in the client-therapist's experience. Desperate for relief, he kept the appointment anyway. Seventeen sessions later, the overwhelming anxiety was gone.

Years later, when asked to clarify why this treatment had succeeded where so many others had failed, the client-therapist indicated that the difference was the *caring* of the provider. "It certainly wasn't her technique, I can say that much," said the client-therapist, "It was her manner, her way of being with me in the room. Everything about her communicated caring. It was almost as though she were saying 'You aren't alone. You will prevail and I will stand by you no matter what happens.'"

While dramatic, there is really nothing new in either of these stories. Indeed, they speak to what all experienced therapists know and have trusted for years: that is, the importance and power of the therapeutic relationship. In the first case, the therapist was denied what he considered his role in the therapy. In other words, to *do* the therapy. For example,

to raise questions, make interpretations, and offer suggestions—in general, to structure the treatment. Simply being
there, however—listening, being present, allowing (in this
circumstance by default) the client to define the therapeutic
enterprise for herself—was actually what ended up making
the difference. In the second case, the client-therapist met a
provider who, in his perception, furnished a relationship
equal in depth to the level of his fomenting anxiety. No doubt
the other clinicians he had known and worked with in the
past had cared, but not in the same way—not in a way that
served to combat the therapist's badly eroded hope that
things could ever improve or be different for him.

The research is clear, however. As much as 30% of the
variance in psychotherapy outcome is attributable to relationship factors (Lambert, 1992; Lambert et al., 1986). Indeed, after analyzing the results of nine major review articles
on the subject, outcome researcher Patterson (1984) concluded:

Although these stories are evocative, recalling perhaps the
reasons many therapists were originally drawn to the field,
they may also seem hopelessly quaint or old-fashioned, ata-
vistic throwbacks to an absurdly naive view of what really
matters in therapy. With the contemporary emphasis on
models and techniques (as detailed in chapters 1 and 2),
attributions of success to something as seemingly vague and
intangible as the "therapeutic relationship" cannot help but
sound misplaced and simpleminded.

> There are few things in the field of psychology for which the
> evidence is so strong as that supporting the necessity, if not
> sufficiency, of the therapist conditions of accurate empathy,
> respect or warmth, and therapeutic genuineness. (p. 437)

Such findings apply to all therapeutic approaches—even
those developed more recently, which tend to downplay the
importance and significance of the therapeutic relationship.

Consider, for instance, a recent qualitative study of solution-focused brief therapy (SFBT)—an approach which has, since its inception, emphasized the contribution of model and technique over relationship factors (Coyne, 1994; Kiser, Piercy, & Lipchik, 1994; Lipchik, 1994; Miller, 1994a; Nylund & Corsiglia, 1994). Indeed, the emphasis on model and technique to the exclusion of other factors has been so marked that Lipchik (1994), one of the developers of the approach, recently observed, "the techniques used in [SFBT] *do* seem so straightforward and unambiguous that it might almost seem as if the client's active participation in the process [isn't] required" (p. 37). When researchers Metcalf, Thomas, Duncan, Miller, and Hubble (1996) interviewed clients and therapists at the center where the approach was developed, however, they found that, while therapists tended to attribute therapeutic success to the use of solution-focused techniques (e.g., specialized interviewing techniques, miracle questions), the clients consistently reported a strong therapeutic relationship as *the* critical factor in treatment outcome (e.g., therapist acceptance, non-possessive warmth, positive regard, affirmation, and self-disclosure).

For clinicians hailing from a variety of therapeutic traditions, research on the importance of the therapeutic relationship is likely to affirm core beliefs—no small feat, as the field has witnessed, in a market that relentlessly exalts the technical aspects of therapeutic commerce. Yet another advertisement boasts, this time for a new approach known as "Thought Energy Synchronization Therapy," that, "its success rate is unbelievable . . . anywhere from 80–97% . . . far superior to traditional techniques." Consistent with other recent trends in the field of therapy, the supposed active ingredient in the approach is a specialized, therapist-delivered technical intervention (e.g., rapid finger tapping on the client's face) that "assists patients in accessing specific thought fields while simultaneously activating the correct combination or sequence of energy meridians." Conspicuously absent from the promotional material mailed to thousands of mental health professionals across the country is any mention of the therapeutic relationship. Of course, this may be due to the fact that the method, as promised by the promoters, provides "amelioration of the problem in a matter of minutes rather than days, weeks, or months."[1]

As far as outcome is concerned, however, relationship factors are second in importance only to extratherapeutic factors. Moreover, in contrast to their somewhat tarnished reputation of being too vague or ephemeral to be of use in this era of increasing scrutiny and accountability, recent research provides some very clear guidelines for ensuring their contribution to psychotherapy outcome.

BUILDING A STRONG
THERAPEUTIC RELATIONSHIP

Carl Rogers' (1951) pioneering view of the therapeutic relationship forever changed the nature of clinical practice and formed the foundation for much of the research on psychotherapy that has conducted over the last forty years. As senior psychotherapy researcher and clinician Hans Strupp once observed, "the impetus given research by [Rogers'] client-centered therapy is at least equal in importance to Rogers' theoretical contributions or the effectiveness of his form of psychotherapy" (1971, p. 44). Early in their training, most therapists spend time learning about and attempting to master what Rogers considered the "core" or "necessary and suf-

---

[1]Not absent from the promotional material is an entire paragraph connecting the new approach to the survival of clinicians in the changing mental health care environment. "The older, more traditional methods . . . will no longer be accepted," a letter from the developers of the approach warns. "It is time to embrace new, rapid and effective modes for helping our clients."

ficient [conditions] to effect change in clients" (i.e., empathy, respect, and genuineness [Meador & Rogers, 1979, p. 151]).

Over the last forty years, researchers and theoreticians have gradually expanded Rogers' pioneering thinking about the necessary and sufficient conditions into a broader concept known as the "therapeutic alliance." Basically, the "therapeutic alliance" emphasizes partnership or collaboration in achieving the goals of therapy by combining Rogers' original thinking about the therapist-provided conditions with the client's contribution to the therapeutic culture (Marmar et al., 1986). In other words, investigators have moved beyond looking only at what the therapist does to promote change (e.g., providing Rogers' "core" conditions) to what happens when the therapist and client work together, side by side, in the service of therapeutic change.

Research on the power of the "therapeutic alliance" now reflects more than 1,000 findings (Orlinsky et al., 1994) and provides several concrete guidelines for enhancing the contribution of relationship factors to treatment outcome, the first being:

> ✂ *Treatment should accommodate the client's motivational level or state of readiness for change.*

For decades, client motivation for therapy has been dichotomized—clients were either motivated or not. The unmotivated client was the bane of everyone's caseload and presumably filled the ranks of so-called dropouts, addicts, and character disorders. Historically, the words "unmotivated" and "resistant" have been used interchangeably and could almost always be counted on to evoke a wave of knowing but anxious nods among case conference participants.

As it turns out, motivation for change is a more complicated affair. First, the idea that there are unmotivated clients is simply not true. All people, all clients, have motivation; only the dead are plausibly unmotivated. It is probably more correct to say the motivation of "unmotivated" clients may not match the therapist's goals and expectations (Duncan, Hubble, & Miller, 1997). For example, the client's intention may be to keep his or her life exactly as it is. This is a valid motivation.

Second, no longer is motivation for change understood strictly as some trait or stable personality characteristic that passively tags along with clients from place to place. Instead, it is a dynamic process — a doing — very much influenced by others' contribution to the interaction. In short, motivation determined as much by context as by personality — or more so.

Motivational readiness and stage of change

With the recognition that motivation for change is partly a product of what people do together, efforts have been made not only to categorize motivational readiness but also to identify the ways clinicians can work in harmony with their clients in order to increase their participation in treatment. Several systems have been proposed and discussed (see Berg & Miller, 1992; Miller & Berg, 1991; Fisch, Weakland, & Segal, 1982; de Shazer, 1988), yet none to date compares to the classification of Prochaska, DiClemente, and their associates. For more than fifteen years, these researchers have been piecing together "the puzzle of how people intentionally change their behavior" (Prochaska, DiClemente, & Norcross, 1992, p. 1102). Their findings are based on thousands of research participants both in and outside of formal therapy, with much attention directed toward those modifying addictions to alcohol, tobacco, and food.

The results indicate that an "underlying structure of change" exists that is "neither technique-oriented nor problem-specific" (Prochaska et al., 1992, p. 1110). That is, the data at hand suggest that no matter what the problem or treatment technique, the actual structure of change remains the same. A central component of this structure is the stage of change.

In their work, six distinct steps or stages of change have been distinguished (Prochaska, 1995). These stages speak to changes in the client's motivation over time and allow an understanding of "*when* particular shifts in attitudes, intentions, and behaviors occur" (Prochaska et al., 1992, p. 1107). Movement through these stages generally happens in two ways. First, change may advance linearly, proceeding gradually and step-wise through the stages from start to finish. The second and by far the most common form of progression is characterized by relapse and a recycling through the stages. This is the process intimated in the popular saying, "Change is three steps forward and two steps back." Sudden transformations in behavior are possible, too, such as the celebrated overnight conversion of Ebenezer Scrooge in Dickens' *A Christmas Carol* (Miller, 1986). For the majority of people pursuing change, however, reaching lasting change takes time and sustained effort. This is the rule rather than the exception.

Support for clinicians' accommodating their clients' motivational level or readiness for change comes from research designed to assess the predictive power of the stages of change. In particular, the stages of change have been found to be better predictors of treatment outcome than more traditional variables such as age, socioeconomic status, problem severity and duration, goals and expectations, self-efficacy, and social supports (Prochaska et al., 1992, p. 1106). As just one example of their predictive power, consider the results of one study reported by Prochaska (1995) on the moderating effect of stages of change in drug treatment for anxiety and panic disorder. Following treatment, stage-of-change measures predicted more of subjects' progress than assignment to either active drug or placebo conditions. In other words, the client's stage of change had more power than the psychoactivity of anxiolytic medication.

Precontemplation

Change begins in the stage called *precontemplation*. Typically, clients in this phase "haven't a clue" that a problem exists. Others may recognize that there is a problem, but the clients have not yet made a connection between a problem in their lives and their contribution to its formation or continuation. In addition, since they do not think they have a problem, these clients are usually not in the mood to either participate in or establish an alliance with a helping professional (Prochaska, 1995). Most often, they have come for therapy at the behest or mandate of someone else. As such, clients in the precontemplative stage of change frequently portray themselves as under duress. Their causative explanation for their predicament is often "bad luck." For instance, one may hear:

> If that cop had been doing his job and catching the real crooks in this town, he wouldn't have been wasting time waiting for me to come out of that restaurant to slap me with this bogus DUI charge. I was in the wrong place at the wrong time. Really, I don't have a problem. *They've* got the problem.

Siding with the referral source against this client will only serve to heighten iatrogenic resistance. In addition, a showdown, without a solid relationship in place, increases the risk of alienating the client and inviting termination or short-lived, hostile compliance.

A different approach is to first accommodate clients' motivation level and then help them take just one step in the change process. Prochaska et al. (1992) found that clients who moved from one stage to the next during their first month of treatment effectively doubled their chances of taking action on their problem in the next six months. For example, in a study that examined outcomes of a smoking cessation program, only 3% of clients who started in the precontemplative stage and were still in the precontemplative stage at one-month follow-up ended up taking action to solve their problem. In contrast, 7% of those clients who moved to the next stage within one month took action to stop smoking within six months (p. 1106). While these percentages may not seem like the greased lightning results suggested by front-runners on the therapy workshop circuit, a 100% increase in the probability of a constructive step is a notable accomplishment.

To help clients in the precontemplative stage take that one step, a light touch is recommended. Having a "light touch" means first and foremost that the therapist is courteous to clients and willing to listen to *their* point of view. The goal is not to *make* clients do something. Rather, in accommodating clients in the precontemplative stage of change, the therapist's job is to create a climate in which clients can consider, explore, and appreciate the pros or benefits of changing. This could include, for example, helping clients become aware of the causes, consequences (positive and negative), and cures of their problems or concerns (Prochaska & DiClemente, 1992, p. 304).

William Miller (1986), who has taken the stages-of-change research to heart in working with clients who have drug and alcohol problems, has developed a model program for accommodating clients in the precontemplative stage of change. The two-session program, known as the Drinker's Check-Up, is advertised in local news media as a public service for drinkers wanting to know whether their alcohol use is harming them. In the first two-hour meeting, objective measures of alcohol-related problems are administered, including alcohol use inventories and a neuropsychological examination incorporating measures sensitive to brain-based deficits secondary to chronic alcohol use. A panel of serum chemistry tests is also given for detecting the effect of alcohol on physical health. A week later, the drinker is provided with the findings. No finger-wagging or coercion is involved. Rather, the results are simply shared with the client and then *he or she* decides what to do with the information. The goal of the program, as may be obvious, is to accommodate the right of clients in the precontemplative stage of change to think and feel as they wish, to studiously avoid any direct pressure to change while simultaneously providing food for thought.

Metaphorically speaking, when clients are in the precontemplative stage of change, the therapist has usually not been invited into their house. While the therapist may have many useful suggestions for arranging clients' furniture or decorating their home, such considerations are secondary to gaining admittance. The challenge is that clients in the precontemplative stage frequently have thick doors with strong locks. To be sure, these doors can be broken down or the locks forced. Once in, however, the therapist will likely have to contend with clients in no mood for interior decorating or even entertaining ideas on how it might be done. Mostly, they will be thinking about how to throw the intruder/therapist out. Should clients be compelled to move things around against their will, they will, once the pressure is removed, put the house back the way they prefer.

No doubt, it is better to be invited. Initially, all clients may be willing to do is open the door a crack and listen. At the entrance, the therapist will want to be friendly, conversational, engaging but not overbearing, concerned, sensitive, and sympathetic. As long as the door remains open the encounter may be considered successful. Later, brief admission to the foyer or hallway may be allowed. Here, the therapist observes all the proprieties of a good guest. That is, he or she stands patiently by the door, follows the lead of the host, compliments the appearance of the house or any objet d'art, and expresses gratitude for having been invited in. With clients in the precontemplative stage, just standing in the hallway should be considered a major success. In time and with enough trust, the client may say, "The more I look at this, the furniture *could* stand to be moved a bit. You seem to know what you are doing. Would you help me with this?"

As an example of accommodating a client in the precontemplative stage of change, consider the following dialogue taken from a first session with a client who was told to come for treatment by his probation officer.

Therapist: So, what brings you here today?

Client: My probation officer told me I had to make an appointment.

T: Really. How come?

C: He says I have a drinking problem.

T: Do you agree with him?

C: No. I'll tell you what I told him. I don't have any problem with alcohol. Period!

T: Geez. So you're confident you don't have a problem and yet you're told you have to be here. That must not feel very fair.

C: That's an understatement. (*Client looks intensely at therapist.*)

T: Well, besides what he wants for you, now that you're here, is there something you might want to talk about?

C: No.

T: That's okay (*said both casually and sincerely*). Well, I appreciate your coming under the circumstances. You didn't want to be here but you made the appointment anyway. You didn't have to do that. I can't help think that, given the pressures you are under and the expectations that the probation officer and perhaps other people have for you, if you don't do something, things are probably going to get worse. (*Client looks surprised and expectant.*) Let me suggest this. I'll set up another time with you to talk about this situation further, but whether you come or not is entirely up to you.

C: I want to think about that.

T: That's fine. Just let me know what you want to do.

In all, as the word *stage* implies, accommodating motivational readiness requires us to be "in phase" with the client. In the earliest stage, if the client communicates an inkling that some action may be necessary, a crucial step forward has been made. And again, moving just one stage in a month doubles — that is, increases 100% — the chances that the client will act in the next six months.

Contemplation

The second stage of change is called *contemplation*. Clients in the contemplative stage of change are renowned for their use of two words, "Yes, but." Frequently, these clients recognize that a change is needed. They may also have a sense of a goal and even know what they need do to in order to reach it. At the same time, however, they are unsure whether the change is worth the cost in time, effort, and energy. In addition, they are frequently unsure or ambivalent about the losses attendant to any change they might make. Miller (1986) describes the client in the contemplative stage as having "an internal balance or seesaw which rocks back and forth between motivations to change on one side and to stay the same on the other" (p. 70).

Accommodating clients in the contemplative stage takes considerable patience, given their tendency to vacillate and be indecisive. Attempts to kick-start change or influence the client with rational argument, guilt, or blame are, in spite of their frequent application and commonsense appeal, usually ineffective and, therefore, best avoided (Prochaska & DiClemente, 1992). A more effective approach entails creating a supportive environment in which the client can carefully consider changing *without* feeling the pressure or need to take action (Duncan, 1989). In certain cases, the therapist might even actively discourage the client from taking action and, instead, simply encourage thinking or observation.

Client: (*with mounting frustration*) . . . I don't know, I don't know, I don't know. . . . Everybody tells me, go ahead and dump him. He's no good for you. You'll meet somebody else. I don't know what to do. (*Client sobs.*) We've been together so long. Five years, almost six years . . . I'm afraid of breaking off the engagement, but lately he's really been treating me badly. Maybe he'll turn around, but my family, my friends say he's no damn good. Why can't I see that? I hate this.

Therapist: How could you not? This situation stinks. (*Client nods.*) From what you said, it seems to me, you *can't* make a decision about this now. You just can't. It's not the right time to make a decision 'cause you *can't* make a decision, no matter what people are telling you to do.

C: That's right. I just *can't*. I can't.

T: Yeah, right.

C: Well, what do I do then?

T: I do have an idea. Would you like to hear it?

C: Of course.

T: You can use it if it feels right to you or discard if it looks like it may make things worse.

C: Okay.

T: I think you may need more information. You can't make a decision because you don't have all the facts you need to make that decision.

C: (*sighs*) Huh, the whole mess seems like I'm trapped in a fog.

T: Yeah, and because you're fogged in right now, things are going to be unclear for a while. Seems to me you're looking for a ray of light, something to illuminate the situation better for you—a light to the way out.

C: You can say that again.

T: So, what I'm suggesting is to just observe for a while. Take your time and look for information, for the facts that will shed more light on this for you. Notice, pay attention, be open to the possibilities that present themselves. Monitor what happens in the relationship, how you feel. But whatever you do, don't try to force yourself to decide when you can't. Does that make sense?

C: Yes, yes it does. I've really been putting a lot of pressure on myself to do something—mostly, I think, to please my parents. They've really been upset with me. I really need to think this one through. (*pause*) It's my life and I'm the one that will have to live with what happens.

T: Would you like to come back?

C: Yes, I think so. I don't know how long this will take. I think I need some time with myself. I love him, but I want to do what's best in the long run. Can I call you?

T: Absolutely.

A classic example of accommodating clients who are contemplating change can be found in the "go slow" injunction from the brief strategic therapy tradition (Duncan, 1989; Fisch et al., 1982).

Therapist: I see what you mean. You have good reason to be careful and cautious. After all, change even for the better requires some getting used to.

Client: You know, I hadn't thought of it that way before.

T: Yes, and because of that, rushing pell-mell or changing precipitously may bring some unanticipated and even unwelcome surprises. I'm thinking that maybe this is a time to go slow, be cautious.

C: Hmm.

T: You know, as your situation becomes more vulnerable to change, we may even want to think about how much change is optimal. Maybe this is not the time to even be thinking about a 100% change.

C: Hmm.

T: Yes, maybe we should be thinking in terms of 80%, or 60%, or 40%, or less than that.

C: (*nodding affirmatively*)

T: Perhaps, maybe no change at all for a while is what's needed here; putting the brakes on completely.

C: I feel like I've got to do *some*thing.

T: Yeah, but take your time with it. I mean, let's face it, this problem didn't develop overnight.

In contrast to what one might think, the advice to "go slow" is not some piece of planned trickery or paradoxical subterfuge.[2] When clients are contemplating change, allying with their ambivalence is perhaps the most empathic stance a therapist can assume. After all, by the time most of these

[2]Until his death, John Weakland, one of the progenitors of the strategic therapy approach, lamented both the reputation and use of the model as a method for tricking clients into changing. In one of the last papers he published, he pointed out the misunderstanding of the approach reflected in "the request 'Give me a paradox for this case' often heard at workshops" (1993, p. 138).

clients have come in contact with a therapist, they have often been exposed to all sorts of exhortations to *do* something— not just from others, but from their own conscience. Expressing the understanding that change requires time, thoughtfulness, and sometimes radical accommodation takes the pressure off and gives the contemplative client the space and support to commit to change.

From the strategic tradition we have also taken a variation of the "go slow" suggestion known as the "dangers of improvement" or "dangers of change" approach (Fisch et al., 1982). This approach is often helpful in accommodating clients who have been in the contemplation stage for a protracted period of time—clients whose lengthy inaction, multiple false starts, or outright treatment failures have led them to be labeled "difficult" or "chronic."

Client: I almost didn't come today.

Therapist: How come?

C: I did it again. I mean, I didn't follow through . . . uh, with what I said I was going to do. Actually, I didn't do much of anything since last time. Things were the same. I guess I talk a good game, but when it comes down to it I'm chicken. (*Client looks down.*)

T: Okay. Let's look at this for a moment. Though I can't stop you, I don't think this is the time to be criticizing yourself. Or, for that matter, for anyone else to criticize you.

C: (*attentive*)

T: So, let's talk about this. Since you were last here, despite your best intentions, you say you sabotaged yourself?

C: Yeah, I've made a career out of that. I could get a degree in that (*laughs*).

T: Hmm (*laughs*). Well, maybe there's another way to look at it. You know, some people might say that not following through is actually a way you have of trying to help yourself.

C: How so?

T: Kind of like protecting yourself, in some unconscious way, from something dangerous that you aren't aware of. Say from a hidden danger.

C: I've heard of that.

T: Yeah, rather than failing, some unconscious part of you may actually be trying to tell you, "Stop, change may bring something, uh, untoward, risky, or unpleasant."

C: Hmm. Sort of like saying, "Don't go one step more."

T: Right, so before you criticize yourself too much for not doing enough, maybe you ought to take some time and really think about what, if any, dangers might lie in store for you if you did change what you say you want to.

C: I mean, I do *want* to change. I don't want to go on like this.

T: Of course, but given how long this has been going on . . .

C: (*finishing the sentence*) Maybe I need to think more about what would happen — if anything bad might happen — if I did change it.

T: I have some ideas, some possibilities, but I don't want to bias your thinking by what I say or turn it in any one direction. I think you need to think about it first.

C: Could you give me a hint how or, uh, what a danger might be?

T: Yeah, some of my clients have talked about the unfamiliarity of change. Change means stepping into the unknown. You never really know what can happen. And sometimes, it becomes easier to live with misery, no matter how painful, because at least it's predictable. There's no guess work. You learn to know it, how it operates, how to limp along with it. While with change, though it looks better, all bets are off. Anything could happen — something better, or something even worse. You just don't know.

C: Well, I don't think I'm afraid of that.

T: Also, I'm not sure, but recalling what you've told me about your family, there may be something else going on. It seems that lately they have been kind of sitting on the sidelines, being quiet and waiting to see what you will do. Once you do begin to change, they may begin to let loose with all the criticisms they've been holding back on. I don't know, but maybe, somehow, at some level, you've picked up on this, that they're going to let you have it big time.

C: (*nodding*) Hmm.

Regardless of the particular therapeutic tradition that is followed or applied in accommodating the client in the contemplative stage, it helps to keep one's finger off the hot button of change. As Prochaska (1993, p. 249) has pointed out, the motto for the contemplative client is, "When in doubt, don't change." Should the therapist attempt to launch such clients into action, they will probably, instead of moving forward, dig in their heels and provide reasons for staying exactly where they are. It is wiser to listen, agree, provide a small friendly nudge when invited, and engage contemplative clients in an exploration of what they stand to both gain *and* lose from changing.

Preparation

The third stage is *preparation*. By the time clients reach this stage they have crossed the Rubicon of change. Since there is little question that change will occur, the main focus becomes identifying the criteria and strategies for success. Preparation is also characterized by clients' experimenting with the desired change—trying it on for size, noticing how it feels, and then experiencing the effects. For example, clients with drug and alcohol problems may delay using temporarily or even modify the conditions under which they typically use (Prochaska & DiClemente, 1992). Obviously, therapists accommodate such clients when they encourage rather than downplay (as has been characteristic of traditional drug and alcohol treatment approaches) the significance of such early problem-solving efforts.

In comparison with the two previous stages—where clients' relationship with change is tenuous and delicate—forming a therapeutic alliance with clients in the preparation phase proceeds more smoothly. Indeed, in most treatment approaches, these clients are often considered the ideal—their customership is on a sure footing and their intention is to take action on their problem in the next month (Prochaska et al., 1992).

Clinicians accommodate clients in the preparation phase when they help them sort through and select their treatment goals, as well as explore and map out potential paths that might be taken to reach those goals. While it is always advisable for the client to be the instigator of change, the therapist can take a more active role in raising possibilities, presenting treatment options or change strategies, and constructively challenging the client's problem-solving abilities. As during all the stages, however, choice is important. Clients in preparation need to be active in choosing and designing their own strategy for change. The reason for this is simply human nature. As Miller (1986) observes, people will "persist in an action when they perceive that they have personally chosen to do so" (p. 71). Therapists are most likely to be helpful when they present a variety of alternatives or methods that clients can use to achieve their goals. In contrast, implying that there is only one way leads to resistance and increases the risk of premature termination. Hardly anyone, even when strongly motivated to make a change, likes to be told what to do (Fisch et al., 1982).

Action

Following preparation, the *action* stage commences. Clients in the action phase present with both firm commitment and a plan for the future. Because of a tendency to conflate the action stage with change in psychotherapy, many traditional treatment models erroneously identify this stage as the one in which *the* treatment takes place (Miller, 1986; Prochaska et al., 1992). By overlooking (or downplaying) the work that takes place in the earlier stages, however, programs are developed with a bias toward clients in preparation or action but ultimately little utility for clients in either contemplation or precontemplation.

Treatment programs sow the seeds of their own failure when, by design, they do not accommodate clients' readiness for change or motivational level. As an example, consider the history of poor outcomes associated with drug and alcohol treatment approaches. For the last forty years, the field has been dominated by what can only be viewed as action-oriented treatment approaches, in spite of overwhelming evidence that "the vast majority of addicted people are *not* in the action stage" (Prochaska et al., 1992, p. 1105). To illustrate, among smokers only 10–15% are prepared for action, while 30–40% are in contemplation, and 50–60% in precontemplation. While well-intentioned, such mismatching leads to overserving of a few, misserving of others, and exclusion of the vast majority of individuals who might benefit from professional assistance.

Maintenance

In the *maintenance* stage change continues. Now, however, stress is placed on what clients need to do in order to maintain or consolidate their gains. The mantra for those in the maintenance stage comes from Karl Menninger, the dean of American psychiatry, who once said, "Anticipation is the best defense." Providers can accommodate clients in the maintenance stage by helping them anticipate the challenges that might provoke regression or relapse. As they are identified, prevention plans are developed. For instance, if, in the past, driving down a certain street increased the risk of a stop at a certain bar, a prevention plan might specify a new route for the recovering drinker to take until the street no longer served as a cue for alcohol consumption.

Therapists also accommodate clients in the maintenance stage by helping them design retention plans for the inevitable lapses that accompany any change. Should clients find themselves sliding down the slippery slope of relapse, the retention plan provides handholds to grab so the slide to the bottom need not continue. For example, if the drinker drives down the street, goes into that bar, and has the first drink or two, a prearranged retention plan might kick in that defines the specific actions for the client to take to stop further drinking. The plan might identify a person for the drinker to call or some other predetermined concrete step. As was the case with clients in the action phase, the therapist can suggest options other clients have found helpful or help clients draw up unique and personal approaches.

Termination

According to Prochaska (1993, p. 253), in the final stage of *termination*, "there is zero temptation to engage in the problem behavior, and there is a 100 percent confidence (self-efficacy) that one will not engage in the old behavior regardless of the situation." So defined, the stage of termination may actually be an ideal rather than a realistic or achievable state of change. More than likely, most people stay in the maintenance phase. That is, they continue to be mindful of possible threats to their desired change and monitor what they need to do to keep the change in place.

In all, the stages-of-change model offers one way for therapists to think about the design and implementation of treatment that has been found to increase the client's participation in therapeutic relationship. As the extensive work and research in this area demonstrate, clients will more likely engage in change projects when their therapists and other interested parties "assess the stage of a client's readiness for change and tailor their interventions accordingly" (Prochaska et al., 1992, p. 1110). At the same time, the research shows that failure to accommodate the client's state of readiness can spell the failure of the most expensive, thoughtful, extensive treatment programs.

The second guideline follows from the first:

✂ Treatment should accommodate the client's goals for therapy.

Closely related to accommodating motivational readiness is the process of tailoring treatment to fit with clients' goals for therapy. Accommodating treatment interventions to clients' goals literally means taking the time to explore *clients'* thoughts, feelings, and attitudes about the nature of their problems as well as their ideas about how therapy might best address those problems. In spite of the current and historical practice of basing treatment intervention on psychiatric diagnosis, theory-specific problem etiology, or therapist-generated treatment plans, research on the therapeutic alliance makes clear that treatment is both more effective and more efficient when client goals are accepted at face value *without* reformulation along doctrinal lines and when those goals, in turn, determine the focus and structure of the intervention process. Indeed, the more conscious, deliberate, and focused the attempt to draw the client into goal and intervention construction, the less significant explanatory models and techniques come to seem.

As evidence of the importance of tailoring treatment interventions to clients' goals, consider research on the treatment of clients with drug and alcohol problems. Until recently, the routine practice of most drug and alcohol treatment has been to assign clients to standardized programs with little or no regard to their own goals or individual characteristics (Miller & Hester, 1989). The result, as noted earlier in this chapter, is a history of poor treatment outcomes. More recently, studies examining the effects of accommodating treatment to clients' goals have found that clients are more likely both to enter treatment earlier in the development of a drug or alcohol problem and, once in treatment, to follow through with whatever suggestions and recommendations are offered (Miller, 1987; Miller & Hester, 1989; Sanchez-Craig, 1980).

Such research indicates that treatment intervention is best understood as a collaborative process—something that client and therapist do together rather than something that is done to the client to produce a therapeutic effect (e.g., follow this directive, take this medication, go into trance). The therapist and client work together, in other words, on the construction of interventions, so that they fit with the client's experience and interpretation of his or her problems. In this way, interventions become an expression or instance of the therapeutic alliance in action. As such, they cannot be separated from the relationship in which they occur and have no meaning or power on their own. As researchers Butler and Strupp point out, treatment interventions "gain their meaning and, in turn, their effectiveness from the particular interaction of the individuals involved" (Butler & Strupp, 1986, p. 33).

Therapists can accommodate intervention to clients' goals in several ways. They can, for example, simply listen and then amplify the stories, experiences, and interpretations that clients offer about their problems, as well as their thoughts, feelings, and ideas about how those problems might best be addressed. Therapists can also make direct inquiries about clients' goals for treatment and ideas about intervention.

One useful way to inquire directly about clients' goals for treatment is to ask outcome questions. Basically, any question that helps clients begin to describe how they would like their life to be different as a result of coming for therapy can be considered an outcome question (Johnson & Miller, 1994; Miller, 1994a). In this regard, the therapist might ask:

- How did you hope that I might be of help?
- What is your goal for treatment?
- What did you (hope/wish/think) would be different as a result of coming for treatment?
- What did you want to change about your (life/problem, etc.)?
- What would have to be minimally different in your life to consider our work together a success?

Research from several fields indicates that treatment goals that have been specified in small, concrete, specific, and behavioral terms and that clients perceive as both desirable and attainable are more likely to influence their behavior in the desired direction (Bandura & Schunk, 1981; Berg & Miller, 1992; Locke, Shaw, Saari, & Latham, 1981; Miller, 1987). Indeed, in one study, researchers Beyebach, Morejon, Palenzuela, and Roriguez-Arias (1996) found that the presence of treatment goals with such qualities increased the likelihood of a successful therapeutic outcome by a factor of two. For this reason, therapists should help their clients describe their goals for treatment in the smallest, most specific, concrete, and behavioral terms possible.

Negotiating concrete, specific, and meaningful treatment goals can be a challenge since, as Beyebach et al. (1996) also found in their research, some clients experience considerable difficulty articulating their goals in precise terms. With such clients, it can be helpful to slow down the process of defining treatment goals and spend more time developing a broad, yet rich and compelling, overview of the outcome the client desires. Thereafter, the client and therapist can slowly work backwards from the broad and general to the detailed and specific.

As one example of working backwards from the broad to the specific, consider dialogue taken from the middle of a first session with a client who presented for treatment for what she could only describe as an "existential crisis."

Client: Everything, everything . . . it's just, nothing *means* anything to me anymore.

Therapist: Your artwork, your acting.

C: Yeah, I mean, there was a time when I was pumped just to be working.

T: Uh huh.

C: Now, I don't even care. If I'm working, if I'm painting, huh.

T: Right now it's like you don't even care.

C: (*nodding*)

T: (*continuing*) But you'd like to care . . . About something.

C: Yeah. Normally, I'm a really passionate person. I have

feelings about everything (*laughs*). I'm into experiencing life, you know, I know this sounds clichéd, but being in the moment, moving . . .

T: You *are* a passionate person.

C: Yeah.

T: You're into experiencing life, being in the moment, moving . . . ?

C: (*nodding affirmatively and continuing*) Moving from thing to thing, being alive!

T: Right.

C: But now, its like (*shaking head*), it's like the faucet has been turned off.

T: Hmm, that's an interesting way of putting it.

C: (*quiet*)

T: (*thoughtfully*) So, it's not that the well has gone dry, I mean, there's water in the pipes, it's just that the faucet has been shut off tight.

C: Yeah, in a way (*laughs*). It's like I can't access this part of me that's, you know, usually, that's always there.

T: Right. Let me ask you something about that, sort of sticking with this very, um, nice picture you've created here. I'm thinking about how we could tell that our work had turned the faucet back on, not a gush now, but a dribble.

In the conversation that followed the client was able to describe the outcome she desired from therapy in specific and concrete terms.

With regard to eliciting clients' ideas about potential treatment interventions or homework tasks, one helpful approach is to provide some time at the conclusion of each session for the client to reflect on both what has transpired during the interview and what steps need to be taken prior to the next session. This process is illustrated in the next case example.

Case Example: Testing the Theory

Steve was an unemployed father of three who presented for therapy with complaints of depression and suicidal ideation. In spite of much effort on the part of the therapist, little progress seemed to be made during the first interview. For example, Steve experienced considerable difficulty specifying, with any degree of clarity, what he wanted from coming to treatment. Worse yet, any conversation about goals only seemed to exacerbate his feelings of hopelessness and pessimism about the future.

At the conclusion of the interview, the therapist instructed Steve to take a few minutes to himself to think about what had transpired during the session — in particular, any thoughts or ideas he had about what he could think more about or do prior to the next visit that might be helpful in resolving the difficulties that brought him to treatment. When the session resumed after several minutes, the following conversation took place:

Therapist: OK, so before I share some of my thoughts, any ideas you've had about the session or about things you need to think more about or do in the coming week?

Client: Well, when I thought about you asking me, you know, during the session, what do I *want* from coming here and some small signs that I was making progress, (*with emphasis*) that was hard.

T: (*nodding*) Uh huh.

C: I could feel myself getting really frustrated.

T: Mmm huh, yeah.

C: And I worry, you know, so what if I do do some small things? Will that really make a difference?

T: Right.

C: So I do set the alarm or get up in the morning, so I do take a shower and stuff, will that really help me? I mean,

will that make it easier for me to deal with the fact that I
don't have a job?

T: Right.

C: And I guess that's the part of me that has given up.

T: And the other part?

C: I know I have to do something. I mean, I know that I
can't just sit around anymore. I have to do something.

T: Any thoughts about what?

C: Well, as much as I don't like it, I think I have to test the
theory that one small change can make a difference.

T: Okay.

In his feedback to Steve, the therapist essentially reinforced
the idea of thinking about and then taking some small steps
in the direction of change. In the next visit, Steve reported
some small changes he had made in what had been his daily
depression routine. The same process of taking a few minutes
to reflect on the session and make plans for the coming week
was then repeated until the presenting problems were resolved.

The next guideline concerns the nature of the developing
relationship:

> ⚭ *Treatment should accommodate the client's*
> *view of the therapeutic relationship.*

For years it was believed that therapist behaviors associated with helpful therapeutic relationships could be standardized and then taught to therapists-in-training (cf. Hammond,
Hepworth, & Smith, 1977; Jensen, 1977; Truax & Carkhuff, 1967). As noted earlier, thousands of therapists spent
time in graduate school learning and attempting to model

standardized versions of behaviors that the research was demonstrating to be effective in establishing a positive therapeutic relationship. At the same time, research showed that providing the "core" or "necessary and sufficient conditions" of effective psychotherapy was more complicated than the standardized therapeutic skills training packages seemed to imply (Frank, 1964; Garduk & Haggard, 1972; Speisman, 1959). For example, studies found that identical therapist behaviors generated positive responses in some clients while generating negative ones in others (Murray & Jacobsen, 1971).

The problems with these early studies on standardized therapeutic skills have largely been explained by subsequent research. Basically, this later research has showed that the therapist's provision of the "core" or "necessary and sufficient" conditions is not enough. This is because clients have been found to vary widely in their experience of the conditions that make up helpful therapeutic relationships. For example, in a study of therapist-provided empathy, Bachelor (1988) found that 44% of clients experienced their therapist's empathy as cognitive, 30% as affective, 18% as sharing, and 7% as nurturant. Successful therapeutic relationships, the data indicate, are those in which the definition of the therapist-provided variables are extended to accommodate the client's own unique experience of those variables — in other words, the *client's* definition of therapist-provided warmth, empathy, respect, genuineness. In fact, the data indicate that clients' ratings of these conditions yield stronger predictions of outcome than therapists' ratings (Bachelor, 1991).

As far as practice is concerned then, the alliance literature indicates that clinicians stand the greatest chance of facilitating the contribution of relationship factors to psychotherapy outcome when they actively tailor their provision of the core conditions to the client's definition of those variables. Some suggestions for accomplishing this challenging task follow.

Empathy

> If only
> I could throw away
> the urge
> to trace my patterns
> in your heart
> I could really see you.
>
> *David Brandon*
> Zen in the Art of Helping

Empathy emerges as a discerning and thoughtful appreciation of the situation that brings the client into contact with
the clinician. Therapeutic empathy is not, therefore, an un-
changing, reflexive, or even specific therapist behavior (i.e.,
the reflection of feelings). Rather, it is better understood as
an attitude that places the client first, before prior training or
theory-specific definitions of what empathy should be.

Being empathic begins by giving undivided attention to
what the client is saying, attempting to understand the client's experience, and then sharing that understanding with
the client. Of course, this does not mean that the therapist
must understand everything the client says. Clients frequently
report that they experience an empathic connection even
when they know the therapist doesn't exactly understand
what they are feeling or experiencing. What seems to matter
most is that clients perceive the therapist as trying, even
struggling, to understand what they deem important and
meaningful.

Unfortunately, much of what has been written about and
considered empathic has focused almost exclusively on the
therapist's identifying and connecting with the client's negative feelings and personal experiences (e.g., clients' pain or
suffering, their despair or feelings of hopelessness, their present difficulties and the history of their complaint). However,
since client strengths and resources contribute greatly to psy-

chotherapy outcome, we would do well to adopt a broader view of empathy, a view that encompasses the light as well as the dark, the hope as well as the despair, the possibility as well as the pain.

Case Example: It Would Be
Better If I Weren't Around

As just one example of adopting this broader conceptualization of empathy, consider the following dialogue taken from the first session with a client who came for treatment of depression. Within the opening moments of the meeting, the client began describing her near-overwhelming feelings of hopelessness and recent thoughts of suicide. As the excerpt illustrates, the therapist listens attentively to the client, acknowledging her present difficulties while simultaneously connecting with her hope for improvement in the future.

Client: I've just been feeling as if nothing is going to change.

Therapist: Mmm.

C: I'll tell you what, it's so bad, that, well, I almost canceled today. I thought that no one could help me.

T: Even though you weren't sure this could help, you decided to come anyway? To do something for yourself?

C: (*nodding*) You know, I've been so desperate. Sometimes I even think that, well, it would be better if I weren't around.

T: You desperately want things to change, to get better, so much so that you've even thought it would be better if you weren't around.

C: Yeah. I'm not sure though that you, anyone, will be able to help me.

T: Uh huh, you're not sure.

C: And I'm a really hard worker. Lately, it doesn't seem like it matters.

T: With all of the hard work you do you deserve something better.

C: Yes.

T: I'm curious—even though you weren't sure that this could help you came anyway?

C: (*nodding*) I have to do something and this was the one thing that I thought I could do.

T: That really strikes me. Given the way you've been feeling, it would be easy to understand if you'd given up, canceled today.

C: That's not me.

The dialogue that followed was increasingly oriented around the client's strengths and hope for change in the future. As the session evolved, the client and therapist began working together to identify some small steps the woman could take to turn that hope into reality.

Respect

> If you have respect for people as they are, you can be more effective in helping them to become better than they are.
>
> *John W. Gardner*
> No Easy Victories

The core condition of respect is the assumption that all clients can make more satisfying lives for themselves. Respect is reflected in the attitudes and behaviors that value the client as a person of worth above theoretical perspectives, treatment techniques, and diagnostic considerations. It is manifested, too, by sensitivity to the acceptability of the therapist's conduct to the client.

The key, as with empathy, is perception. *Perceived* respect is strengthened when therapists modify their approach when clients regard it as unhelpful. In this regard, respect is cultivated and maintained when the therapist avoids engaging in any behavior that might insult the client (e.g., criticism, rejection, speaking down to the client or using professional jargon or language that the client does not understand). Clients are not blamed when the therapy is not progressing well. Argument, unnecessary reassurance (a subtle way of deskilling the client), or pressure is not used to get the client to fall in line and accept the therapist's will or opinion. Rather, time is spent clarifying the purpose of any question or procedure, listening attentively to the client's ideas and attitudes, and affording the client the opportunity to voice different values and preferences (Wolberg, 1977).

A metaphor for respect may be found in the example of good ambassadorship. Clients may be regarded as representatives of foreign countries or cultures. The therapist, as a good ambassador, relies on protocol and tact, learns and follows as much as possible the norms and mores of the culture, and frames comments and proposals diplomatically. The goals of ambassadorship remain: to exert beneficial influence, define common ground and interests, secure cooperation, and cement alliances. The overall lessons of ambassadorship apply as much to therapy as they do to the management of international relations (Hubble & Solovey, 1994).

Genuineness

> Be as you would seem to be.
>
> *Thomas Fuller, M.D.*, Gnomologia, *1732*

> Know what you see, don't see what you know.
>
> *Addie Fuhriman, personal communication, 1984*

The client's experience of the therapist's genuineness emerges in unexpected ways and unexpected places. David Viscott described just such an instance in his well-known and entertaining work, *The Making of a Psychiatrist* (1972). According to Viscott, a client named Ernie was waiting for his appointment at an outpatient mental health service when he happened to overhear his doctor, Bert, urinating in the toilet of the adjoining bathroom. According to Ernie, this chance occurrence led him to conclude that any psychiatrist feeling secure enough to relieve himself straight into the middle of the commode, without worrying who heard the sound, must be sure of himself and able to help him. In his commentary, Viscott observed:

> I don't think circulating tape recordings of psychotherapists in the bathroom is going to stamp out mental disease, but this humanizing detail of Bert's life did make Bert more real for Ernie. . . . (p. 128)[3]

As the story implies, clients want their therapists to be authentic, the "Real McCoy," a "class act" without a hint of self-indulgence at their expense. In other words, they want their therapist to be admirable, honorable, and humane, and to possess a strong sense of personal integrity.

In contrast to what might be assumed, therapists stand the greatest chance of being perceived in this fashion when they conceptualize, intervene, and approach clients *tentatively*. Tentativeness conveys that the therapist is willing to be wrong and is open to change. Until the desired effect is achieved, the clinician adjusts the work through experimentation. In being tentative, the therapist avoids making special

---

[3]As unique as this example sounds it is not the first. In 1932, psychoanalytic pioneer and member of Freud's inner circle, Sandor Ferenczi, noted how a client improved after hearing him use the toilet in her home (Ferenczi, 1985).

claims to a corner of reality. Indeed, instead of wearing the inscrutable mantle of the expert, the therapist presents as a partner or collaborator who, by virtue of training and experience, may be able to offer productive input, suggestion, and guidance.

As such, being genuine requires a measure of humility — regarding both the limits of psychotherapy and the inherent diversity and complexity of human beings. Shows of certainty yield to representing accurately what is known and not known about therapy and human behavior. Humility, moreover, is found in the ability of the therapist to take criticism from the client, admit mistakes, and to say, "I am sorry."

Validation

The effectiveness of the relationship is reinforced through the client's experience of validation. Validation accomplishes several important aims. First, it legitimizes or justifies the client's concerns. Many times clients have been told to "buck up," "stop making mountains out of molehills," "get your head on straight," "there's nothing the matter with you," "every cloud has a silver lining," "where did you get that idea," "oh, that's silly," and myriad other forms of advice that devalue the problem and the client for having it. For clients to be affirmed by the therapist, to know that the therapist wants to hear their side of the story, combats the minimization and disparagement they often bring with them to the session. It is as though the therapist is saying, "I want to listen and understand. You're not stupid or a pariah for thinking and feeling the way you do."

Second, the therapist not only acknowledges that a problem exists for the client but also accepts its significance. That is, if the problem was important enough to bring to therapist, then that importance is accepted and validated. Relatedly, the therapist recognizes the ways in which the problem has troubled or brought pain to the client. Here the client's struggle and attempts to master the dilemma are recognized. During sessions, as clients describe their situation, acknowledgment may take the simple form of "Yes," "I see," "Oh my," even "Ummm." Or the therapist might say, "In the past, this problem has made your life feel unbearable. Others have not seemed to understand the suffering it has caused you. You have struggled with it mightily, but lately it seems to have grabbed hold of the best of you. It is no wonder you feel discouraged and beaten down."

Finally, through validation the therapist expresses a belief in the client and his or her strength to withstand and eventually overcome the problem:

> Despite all that the problem has done to you, here you are ready to stand against it again. I don't know whether you are ready to hear this or not, but I can't help but believe this is a statement of courage, inner strength, resiliency, and a decision to prevail. I'm not sure if other people in your circumstance could have endured as much as you have and yet kept their determination to make a better life.

Validation speaks to the aspect of the therapeutic bond that has been most studied, namely therapist affirmation. Affirmation is defined as acceptance, nonpossessive warmth, or positive regard. Orlinsky et al. (1994) reviewed nearly 90 findings suggesting that the client's perception of therapist affirmation is a significant factor in promoting a positive outcome. Clients want their therapists to like them; they do not want to be condemned for their problems.

Validation is involved in all aspects of the therapeutic process, from interviewing to intervening. Intervention at its best demonstrates the therapist's validation of the client's world (i.e., the legitimacy of the client's concerns, their perceived importance, and the therapist's belief in the client's ability to resolve the concerns).

Case Example: Shooting the Breeze

Fred had been in therapy for twenty years, struggling with agoraphobia. He had become very skeptical about psychotherapy and seemed quite pessimistic about the success of a new attempt at therapy. His future was also looking fairly dim. The therapist validated Fred's cynicism as appropriate considering all his previous efforts to change and complimented him for his courage and tenacity in trying again. In spite of the long history, the therapist believed in Fred's ability to overcome the problem. Fred's struggle with agoraphobia was viewed as both important and legitimate, given his troubled past both in and out of treatment.

By chance, Fred entered therapy during the NCAA basketball finals. He was an avid fan and enjoyed discussing the various teams, coaches, and players. Over time, more of each session was spent discussing basketball and, after basketball season was over, biking. Fred became very animated during these discussions, and the therapist enjoyed his company.

During one session, almost incidentally, the therapist and Fred constructed a list of the most difficult to the least difficult activities or tasks for Fred to perform. By the next appointment the client had accomplished the three most difficult items on his list. After this, Fred and the therapist continued their friendly discussions and the client made significant changes, progressing from leaving the house only to attend therapy to starting a painting business and biking regularly. At termination, he credited the "shooting the breeze" sessions, not the desensitization hierarchy, saying that he felt the therapist really understood him. He reported that in previous therapies casual conversation was discouraged in favor of discussing his problems. Apparently, the problem focus did not coincide with his view of what a therapy relationship should be. For Fred, empathy and respect entailed an appreciation of more informal conversation and attention to life outside the agoraphobia. He wanted a person he could talk to, a person who would stand down from a professional role and relate more as an equal.

Other aspects of this case might be highlighted, but it was the validation and acceptance of the client's initial pessimism and, later, his way of relating or doing therapy that became primary in promoting his change. The empirical literature supports this conclusion. Fred's story suggests less time might be spent worrying about which intervention to use and more in monitoring the client's response to what is helpful in the relationship.

SUMMARY AND CONCLUSIONS

Relationship factors make up the second largest contributor to change in psychotherapy. Clients who rate the relationship highly are very likely to be successful in achieving their goals. Regardless of how chronic, intractable, or "impossible" a case may appear, if the client's view of the relationship is favorable, change is more likely to occur (Duncan et al., 1997). In this chapter, several suggestions were given for ensuring a positive view of the therapeutic relationship. These included: (1) accommodating treatment to the client's motivational level or readiness for change; (2) accommodating treatment to the client's goals and ideas about intervention; and finally, (3) accommodating the core conditions to fit the client's definition of those variables.

It has long been debated whether or not the relationship factors are necessary *and* sufficient to promote change. Many question the degree to which they are sufficient, preferring to believe in the power of a particular method or theory. The research indicates that it is the client's perception of the relationship that determines sufficiency. Therapists' own evaluations of their success in creating the alliance are not enough. The most helpful alliance will develop when the therapist works to establish a therapeutic environment that fits with the client's sensibilities and individual frame of reference.

5 HOPING FOR A CHANGE

The Role of Hope, Expectancy, and Placebo in Psychotherapy Outcome

> I cannot forget what one of my patients once answered when I asked him, "What do you believe was the reason that I could succeed to cure you after all these years of misery?" He answered, "I became sick because I had lost all hope. And you gave me hope."
>
> *Alfred Adler*
> *quoted in Hoffman, 1994, p. 311*

> Belief sickens, belief kills, belief heals.
>
> *Robert Hahn*
> *quoted in O'Regan, 1985*

THERE SEEMED to be little hope for saving the couple's marriage when they first presented for treatment. After twenty years of marriage, the man had moved out of the house several months earlier. Recently he had started dating. The woman, on the advice of her attorney, had quickly filed for divorce and obtained a court order barring her husband from coming within 500 feet of her, the house, and their belongings. Even though a professional mediator had been appointed by the court to negotiate the terms of their divorce, the process had quickly become bogged down in a morass of bitter and angry feelings. Frustrated with the couple's lack of progress, the mediator recommended psychotherapy.

The couple spent the majority of the first session alternately making cutting remarks and arguing with each other. The only point of agreement seemed to be that they would not have come unless "ordered" by the court-appointed mediator. During the first hour little, if any, progress had been made; moreover, the therapist felt fairly discouraged about the prospects of helping the couple and even feared that more failure would only add to their escalating anger and resentment. In concluding the meeting, the therapist simply thanked the couple for coming in, apologized for not having been very helpful, and expressed hope that the next session might be more helpful. The man and woman then stood, shook hands with the therapist, and left the office.

Given the events of the first session, the therapist was a bit surprised when the couple showed up for their appointment the following week. Even more suprising, however, was that they were sitting together, talking, when the therapist came into the waiting room. Once in the therapist's office, they both said that their relationship had begun to improve following the last session—so much that now they were reconsidering their decision to divorce. When the therapist asked the couple to explain the change, the man and woman agreed that it was due to the comments the therapist had made at the end of the first visit—namely, the offer to see them again and the statement about *hoping* the next visit would be more helpful. Somewhat bewildered, the therapist asked for clarification. "You're a marriage counselor," the man said, looking at the therapist. "Why would you want to see us again unless there was some hope of saving our marriage?"

Years earlier and on a different continent, a man lay dying in a small provincial hospital (Allport, 1964). The medical staff had all but given up hope of curing him. The problem was simple: the staff could not figure out what was making the man ill. Fortunately, a famous diagnostician was scheduled to visit the hospital in a few days. The local doctors told the man that they could probably cure him if the mystery illness were accurately diagnosed by the famous doctor.

When the doctor finally arrived at the hospital the man

was very close to death. Making his way to the patient's bedside, the doctor took one look at the man and then muttered, "Moribundus"—the Latin word meaning "being in the state of dying"—and moved on to the next patient. Several years later, the man, who did not speak or understand a word of Latin, managed to track down the famous diagnostician. "I've been wanting to thank you for your diagnosis," the man said, "The doctors told me that if you could diagnose me, I'd get well, and so the minute you said, 'Moribundus,' I knew I'd recover" (p. 7).

While the particulars of these stories differ, the curative factors involved in both are the same: hope and expectation. In the first example, the therapist's inadvertent comment about hoping to be helpful, combined with a fairly routine suggestion for rescheduling, imbued the clients with a renewed sense of hope, which in turn led them to redouble their efforts to save their troubled marriage. In the latter case, the dying man's expectations about the famous doctor facilitated his recovery in spite of—or perhaps because of— his misunderstanding of the doctor's true assessment.

Research confirms the importance of hope and expectation in psychotherapy. As has been reported in earlier chapters, as much as 15% of the variance in treatment outcome may be attributable to what are typically referred to as "placebo factors" in the literature (Lambert, 1992; Lambert et al., 1986). While this may not sound like much, one need only consider that *placebo factors make the same percentage-wise contribution to change as technique and model factors* in order to appreciate their significance in psychotherapy. Research further shows that clients give high marks to the role of hope and expectation in treatment. For example, Murphy, Cramer, and Lillie (1984) found that 58% of clients identified the instillation of hope as a curative factor in psychotherapy. Other studies have found significant correlations between clients' expectations for change and subsequent improvement in therapy, especially during the initial stages of treatment (Garfield, 1994).

Expectations can help; however, they can also forestall or even work against healing. Consider a case reported by Cannon in 1942. A doctor was called to treat a native of North Queensland, Australia, who lay dying for no apparent medical reason. Physical examination and routine hospital tests could not uncover any cause for the native's illness, and he subsequently died. An autopsy was conducted on the body, but still no medical reason for the man's illness and death was found. Even though no physical cause was identified, however, the physician knew why the man had died. On the death certificate he listed the cause of death as "bone pointing." Bone pointing is part of a death spell used by some Australian natives on their enemies. Researchers have documented the powerful and devastating effect of such spells, which often, as the story by Cannon illustrates, result in the death of the intended victim. Given that all physical causes were ruled out, the only remaining explanation for the death was the native's *expectations* regarding the power of the spell.

BONE POINTING IN PSYCHOTHERAPY

> The assumption that behavior we dislike or condemn is due to internal problems is religious, however, not established by empirical science.
>
> *Robyn Dawes, 1994, p. 282*

From the time of Freud, most modern psychotherapy theory has focused on identifying the underlying causes of mental suffering. Indeed, as distinguished psychologist and philosopher Paul Watzlawick has noted, the assumption has been "that the discovery of the *real* causes of the [client's] problem is a *conditio sine qua non* for change" (1986, p.

92). The idea, of course, is that knowing the underlying cause of a particular problem would lead, as has so often been the case in physical medicine, to the identification and/ or development of effective treatments (de Shazer, 1991).

Over time, various causes have been advanced by various psychotherapy theories. For example, owing to their emphasis on early life experiences, psychodynamic theorists have traditionally located the cause of mental health problems in childhood. Cognitive therapists, on the other hand, with their emphasis on thought processes, identify the cause of suffering as problematic or dysfunctional patterns of thinking. Psychiatrists, with their training in physical medicine, are increasingly convinced that biology is the key to mental illness, while family therapists have, not surprisingly, located the cause of personal, familial, and to some extent societal dysfunction in the family system.

The list of supposed causes goes on and on, extending very quickly beyond these more popular schools of thought to include causes such as past-life traumas, abduction into UFOs, and forced participation in highly secretive but well-organized satanic cults (cf. Carlinsky, 1994; Morrock, 1994; Putnam, Guroff, Silberman, Barban, & Post, 1986; Roper Organization, 1992; Weiss, 1988). Unfortunately, however, in spite of nearly one hundred years of hypothesizing, no consensus exists among clinicians, theoreticians, or researchers regarding the root (and presumed real) causes of most problems treated in psychotherapy. Rather, it seems that the etiology of a particular client's problem depends, for the most part, on the particular therapist that the client happens to see. Clients seeing recovery-oriented therapists, for example, soon discover that they were raised in dysfunctional families, while those seeing treatment professionals trained in Rational-Emotive Therapy quickly learn that irrational thinking habits are at the root of their current problems (Cummings, 1986; Frank & Frank, 1993; O'Hanlon, 1990).

Given the very real lack of scientific or professional consensus, the routine practice of indoctrinating psychotherapy clients into a particular clinical belief system is, at best, ethically questionable. More troubling, however, is that research on how change occurs both in and outside of psychotherapy seriously challenges the long-held assumption that understanding the cause of a problem is necessary for changing or resolving it (Beutler, 1989; de Shazer, 1988, 1991; Held, 1991, 1995; Prochaska & DiClemente, 1982, 1984). Indeed, this research is finding that the factors that contribute to the eventual change in and/or resolution of a mental health problem frequently bear *no relationship* to the factors that caused the problem in the first place. As two of the most prominent researchers in this area, Prochaska and DiClemente, summarize, the "acquisition of problems is often unrelated to [their] modification or change" (1984, p. 2).

According to this growing body of literature, therapeutic time is spent more productively when the therapist and client focus on and enhance the factors responsible for change-in-general rather than on identifying and then changing the factors a theory suggests are responsible for causing problems-in-particular. Along these lines, researchers de Shazer, Berg, Lipchik, Nunnally, Molnar, Gingerich, and Weiner-Davis (1986) note, "[The] aim [of therapy] is to start the solution process rather than to stop the complaint," and to do so, they go on to say, "It is not . . . necessary to construct a rigorous explanation of how the trouble is maintained" (pp. 210, 212). On the contrary, *a strong argument can be made that indoctrinating clients into a particular model of problem causation might actually function as a kind of psychotherapy-style bone pointing*, undermining the very factors responsible for the occurrence of change by drawing clients' attention to whatever a particular theory suggests is causing their suffering. This is especially likely to be the case with placebo factors, where the search for larger, deeper, and, in most psychotherapy theories, pessimistic and pathology-oriented causes may actively work against the creation of hope and a positive expectation for change.

One can only speculate what the outcome might have been for the man awaiting the famous diagnostician had he been able to understand Latin. There are enough stories about the effects of negative expectations, however, to lead a reasonable person to conclude that the doctor's true assessment might have become a self-fulfilling prophecy (O'Regan, 1985). As author and Nobel laureate Isaac Bashevis Singer once observed, "If you keep saying things are bad, you have a good chance of being a prophet." As contrary as it may seem to traditional training, therapists are more likely to facilitate hope and expectation in their clients when they stop trying to figure out what is wrong with them and how to fix it and focus instead on what is possible and how their clients can obtain it.

FACILITATING HOPE AND A POSITIVE EXPECTATION FOR CHANGE

In the material that follows, some suggestions are given for facilitating hope and a positive expectation for change in clients. The recommendations should not be considered comprehensive or exhaustive. Indeed, some of the most potent ways for therapists to facilitate hope and positive expectations for change have already been presented in the previous chapters—in particular, forming strong therapeutic alliances with clients and incorporating clients' strengths into treatment. Neither should our suggestions be considered prescriptive. As pointed out in previous chapters, descriptions of therapeutic process always run the risk of making complex and dynamic interactions sound like disembodied sets of techniques that can be applied across cases and clients. For this reason, as you read, recall that it is not the particular suggestions or techniques themselves, but, rather, the degree to which those techniques or suggestions facilitate hope and a positive expectation for change, that is critical to the change process.

Having a healing ritual

> Every system of change makes use of rituals that are designed to attract and maintain the client's attention as well as make the healing magic appear more powerful and impressive.
>
> *Jeffrey A. Kottler, 1991, p. 58*

In the late 1980s, a new approach for the treatment of clients with histories of severe traumatic experiences burst onto the American therapy scene. The approach, known as Eye Movement Desensitization and Reprocessing (EMDR), seemed able to achieve results with the most intractable cases and to do so in significantly less time than existing treatments (Shapiro, 1989). The procedure was simple enough—clients recalled traumatic experiences while watching their therapist's fingers move back and forth every half second or so for a period of 5 to 15 seconds. According to proponents, the eye movements helped traumatized individuals "rebalance brain processes" in much the same way that rapid eye movements (REM) in normal sleep helped nontraumatized individuals process daily experience. This physiological explanation, in combination with the apparent success of the simple procedure, catapulted EMDR to the center of professional and public attention and has made it the standard of care for an increasing number of mental health problems in clinics around the country (Bower, 1995).

There is only one problem—there is little scientific evidence that EMDR has any therapeutic effect beyond placebo and/or other factors known to be effective with traumatized clients (e.g., exposure; Acierno & Hersen, 1994). Indeed, one of the only studies (Lytle, 1993) that has been conducted comparing EMDR to an active placebo condition found that subjects treated with the procedure fared no better than those treated with the active placebo treatment, although both groups achieved immediate results that were significantly better than those obtained by subjects in a nondirective control condition.[1] That same study suggests that something more commonplace than the induction of eye movements might be responsible for the results associated with the procedure.

In Lytle's (1993) study, the treatment administered to subjects in the active placebo control group was very similar to EMDR—with one important exception. Rather than *moving* their eyes, subjects in the active placebo control group were instructed to *fix their gaze* on a spot on the wall while recalling traumatic memories. That subjects engaging in eye *fixation* achieved results equivalent to those engaging in the technically opposite eye *movement* procedure suggests that something other than the supposed physiology-altering technique might be responsible for the improvement of subjects in both groups—namely, the client and therapist's involvement in an active, structured, specialized, and technical healing ritual that both believed would be therapeutic.

Rituals are a shared characteristic of healing procedures in most cultures and date back to the earliest origins of human society (Frank & Frank, 1993; Frazer, 1922; Van Gennep, 1960). Their use inspires hope and a positive expectation for change by conveying that the user—be it medicine man, shaman, astrologer, or therapist—has a special set of skills

---

[1] One other well executed study has appeared in the literature. In this study, Wilson, Becker, and Tinker (1995) found that participants undergoing EMDR experienced decreases in presenting complaints and increases in positive cognition. However, since the researchers employed a delayed-treatment rather than active-placebo control group, it is not possible to say that the EMDR—as opposed to other factors operating in the therapy (e.g., exposure)—was responsible for the observed effects.

for potentiating healing. That the procedures are not in and of themselves *the* causal agents of change matters little (Kottler, 1991). Rather, what matters is that the participants have a structured and concrete method for mobilizing the placebo factors in the recovery process.

When viewed as a healing ritual, EMDR is nothing new to the practice of psychotherapy. Healing rituals have been a part of the practice of psychotherapy dating back to the modern origins of the field (Wolberg, 1954, 1977). Whether instructing clients to lie on a couch, talk to an empty chair, chart their negative self-talk, give themselves positive affirmations, or—as is currently in vogue—listen to feedback from an anonymous team sequestered behind a one-way mirror, mental health professionals are basically engaging in healing rituals. Indeed, given that comparisons of psychotherapeutic techniques have found little differential effectiveness, they may all be conceived of as healing rituals—technically inert but nonetheless powerful and systematic methods for enhancing the effects of placebo factors.

The perennial question facing therapists is what particular ritual to use when working with an individual client. Given the large number of choices available to clinicians, answering this question may seem, at first glance, to be overwhelming. Some guidelines are possible, however, chief among them being the therapist's belief in and commitment to whatever therapeutic ritual is employed in treatment.

✕ *The therapist should believe in the procedure or therapeutic orientation.*

Research confirms that therapists enhance the placebo component of the procedures they employ when they truly believe in and are confident that the procedures will be therapeutic. As researchers Benson and Epstein have noted, treatment professionals "who have faith in the efficacy of their treatments . . . are the *most* successful in producing positive placebo effects" (O'Regan, 1985, p. 17). Having faith in a particular procedure or therapeutic orientation does not mean that the therapist adopts a "damn the torpedoes, full speed ahead" attitude. Neither does it mean that the therapist must actively court clients' favor or preach the "power of positive thinking." Rather, faith in a given therapeutic procedure or orientation is best conveyed through the beliefs therapists hold regarding the probability of change in general. In this regard, therapists who believe that probability favors client change are more likely to enhance the placebo component of the procedures they use.

✣ The therapist should show interest in the results of the procedure or orientation.

Placebo effects are further enhanced when therapists show an interest in the results of whatever technique or orientation they employ. Psychologists have long known that people in research studies are more likely to respond in the predicted direction when they know the purpose of the experiment in which they are participating (Matheson, Bruce, & Beauchamp, 1979; Smith & Glass, 1987). Clinicians can put this same phenomenon to work in the service of therapeutic change by engaging in treatment activities that convey a positive expectation of and hope for client change. For example, as was pointed out in Chapter 3, therapists can make a practice of inquiring about the beneficial effects of treatment at some point during each session. Even more proactively, therapists can ask their clients to notice and record any changes for the better that occur between sessions (Kral & Kowalski, 1989). As may be obvious, such a homework assignment conveys the therapist's hope for and expectation of improvement, which may in turn create an observational bias on the part of the client favoring therapeutic change.

Case Example: Sharon and
Her "Scum Ex-Husband"

As an example of showing an active interest in the results of therapy, consider the following dialogue, which occurred at the conclusion of a first session with a female client whose husband had recently abandoned her and their five minor children. In the session, the woman was alternately tearful and angry as she recounted the events of the preceding three months, during which her husband had completely depleted their savings accounts, racked up large credit card debts, and begun cohabitating with another woman. For most of the session, the therapist simply listened attentively as the client related her story. As the end of the session neared, an appointment was set for the next week and the following exchange took place:

Therapist: Okay, so this same time is good?

Client: (*nodding*) Mmm huh.

T: (*writing in the appointment book*) Four o'clock on Thursday then. Would you like me to write that down here on a card?

C: You probably better, I'm not, I can't, I haven't been keeping very good track of things.

T: (*writes on card and hands to client*) All right.

C: (*takes card, begins to put on coat*)

T: Sharon, before you go, I just want to ask you how—or if, I guess I should say—coming in today was helpful?

C: (*positively*) I think so.

T: How so?

C: Well, I think just being able to come here and . . . *talk*.
Let it out. You know I don't really have anyone that I can
talk to like this. My mother (*shakes head negatively*), you
know, like I said, she just . . . she just doesn't understand.

T: Uh huh.

C: And my scum husband, soon to be ex-husband, he won't,
I don't, I can't talk to him.

T: So how was talking to me helpful?

C: I could just let it out. I've been holding it in and together
. . . for my kids, you know.

T: You were able to "let it out."

C: Yeah.

T: And, help me understand, how was "letting it out"
helpful?

C: (*pause*) I feel . . . better. Everything's not penned up inside (*pause*). I feel . . . calmer.

T: And how do you see that calmness making a difference
this next week?

C: (*thoughtful*) Hmm. I hadn't really thought about it like
that.

The client and therapist talked for a few more minutes
about how the effects of the first session of therapy might be
seen in the coming week. The therapist then concluded the
meeting by asking the client to observe and notice, "any of
these or any other changes that occur for the better between
now and the next time we meet." The interest in results inherent in this assignment, as well as the conversation that pre-
ceded it, both conveyed and constructed an expectation of
improvement in the client's presenting problem. In the handful of sessions that followed, the therapist continued to create
an expectation of change by making similar inquiries about

the results of the treatment and by linking those results to the client's life outside of therapy.

> ✨ *The procedure or orientation must be credible and persuasive from the client's frame of reference.*

The placebo effects of a given therapeutic procedure are likely to be enhanced when that procedure coincides with and is complementary to clients' preexisting, pretreatment beliefs about their problem(s) and the change process. As the French philosopher and mathematician Pascal once noted, "People are generally better persuaded by the reasons which they have themselves discovered than by those which have come into the minds of others." The research also indicates that "acceptability" to the client of a particular procedure or orientation is a major determinant of its implementation and ultimate success (Beutler, 1971; Beutler et al., 1978; Kazdin, 1980; Murphy, 1996; Reimers, Wacker, Cooper, & De Raad, 1992; Witt, Elliot, & Martens, 1984).

Consider a study conducted by Hester, Miller, Delaney, and Meyers (1990) comparing the efficacy of traditional alcohol treatment, which views problem drinking as a disease, with a learning-based counseling approach, which views problem drinking as a bad habit. Given the volume of studies showing that existing treatment approaches achieve roughly equivalent results, the researchers were not surprised when, at the conclusion of the study, both approaches were found to be equally effective. What was surprising was the difference that emerged between the two groups when the clients were contacted six months later. Basically, the researchers found a difference in outcome between the two groups that stemmed from the beliefs the *clients* held about the nature of alcohol problems *prior to* the initiation of treatment. Specifically, clients who believed that alcohol problems were caused by a disease were much more likely to be sober at six-month follow-up if they had received the traditional alcoholic treatment, while clients who believed that alcohol problems were a bad habit were more likely to be successful if they had participated in a therapy that had treated them as such.

Traditionally, the personal characteristics of *therapists* were thought to determine the credibility and persuasiveness of the treatment they administered. Research conducted over the over the last forty years, however, has proven otherwise (Orlinsky et al., 1994). Hundreds of studies, conducted by different investigators, employing a variety of research methods, have examined characteristics such as therapists' age, gender, shared lifestyle, personal therapy experience, socioeconomic status, race, cultural background, level of education, and even manner and style of dress—all with very disappointing results (Beutler, Machado, & Neufeldt, 1994). The lack of significant findings in this area, in combination with the results of studies similar to those of Hester et al. (1990), illustrates that credibility and persuasiveness are not characteristics of the therapist but, rather, the result of a complementary and dynamic interaction between the client's frame of reference and the therapist's theoretical orientation and treatment techniques.

Case Example: I Have to
Learn from My Mistakes

A therapist can foster a more credible and persuasive therapeutic interactions by deliberately utilizing treatment procedures that fit the client's frame of reference. As an example of this, consider the case of a man who came to therapy because of difficulties he was experiencing at work. Briefly, the man was a newly promoted, mid-level supervisor who was in considerable personal distress because he was constantly being criticized by those he was supposed to supervise. In the opening moments of his first session of therapy, the man described the situation at work and his feelings.

Client: I have a problem that I need to talk about.

Therapist: Okay.

C: I am a welfare worker, working with the disabled, and, uh, I have a lot of difficulties with my colleagues, especially the workers that are under me, the ones that are supposed to be my assistants.

T: Uh huh.

C: They always pick on me, pinpoint my mistakes; they talk about me behind my back.

T: (*sympathetically*) They do?

C: They don't like me. They call me at home, always tell me that I forgot to do something. They leave me notes on my desk pinpointing my mistakes.

T: Mmm.

C: I always follow up because I know I make mistakes. I call them back or go to see them, I always ask them for more specific information so that I can correct my mistake. But when I do that they accuse me of trying to push my responsibility off on them.

T: Right.

C: But that is me, I always want to know what is my mistake. Yeah, I always want to be open and even ask them for feedback so that I can learn. Learn from my mistakes.

T: (*laughing*) Sounds like you've been successful.

C: Yeah, but now I don't know what to do, they're telling me all the time, picking at me, making my life miserable. I want to learn, I want to improve and be a good supervisor. Now, I feel like I don't want to ask for their feedback at all.

Following this last statement, the man went on to relate how the difficulties at work were affecting him personally. He was having difficulty sleeping and had isolated himself from his family and friends. Prior to noting these difficulties, however, the client had given enough information for the therapist to begin entertaining ideas about treatment procedures that would be both complementary to the man's frame of reference and, at the same time, helpful in resolving the difficulties he was having at work. For example, given the client's statements about valuing learning, the therapist might consider using some type of behaviorally-oriented, skills-based learning approach. This is, in fact, the approach the therapist eventually adopted. Near the end of the first session, the therapist used the client's frame of reference (i.e., wanting to learn from his mistakes) as the rationale for teaching him some new skills for dealing with problems at work.

T: You know what I just realized?

C: What?

T: You're making another mistake.

C: What do you mean?

T: I think you're making a mistake.

C: You do?

T: Yep, and I know you're the kind of person that wants to learn from his mistakes so I've got to point this out to you.

C: (*leans forward*) Good, this is what I need.

T: This is going to sound a little crazy but I think your mistake is that you let those under you know that you don't know you've made a mistake when they call to let you know that you have.

C: (*interested*) Say that again.

T: I think the mistake you have been making is that you let those under you know that you didn't know you'd made a mistake when they've called to let you know that you had.

C: Ah hah (*pause*). *I let them know that I don't know I've made a mistake.*

T: That's right.

C: (*pause*) But I still need to learn from my mistakes.

T: Right, you still need to learn from them. That's good.

C: Uh huh.

T: But your mistake is that you keep letting them know that you have to learn from them, and then you can't be the boss.

C: Right! Never let them see me sweat.

T: (*nodding affirmatively*) So you have to learn a new way of talking with them.

C: Uh huh.

T: A way that ensures that you get the information you need, about any mistakes that have been made, but also lets them know that you're the boss.

C: (*nodding*)

The session concluded with the therapist introducing the client to some concepts from assertiveness training. In particular, the difference between assertive communication—the kind that would help him establish and maintain more appropriate relationships with his assistants—and aggressive communication—the kind that would jeopardize those relationships and likely prevent him from receiving the feedback he desired. A handful of later sessions built on this foundation by providing more detailed information and an opportunity to practice the skills with the therapist.

> ✼ *The procedure or technique should be based on, connected with, or elicit a previously successful experience of the client.*

In 1968, researchers Batterman and Lower administered placebos to people suffering from rheumatoid and osteoarthritis. Like many others conducting studies in this area, the researchers found that the people receiving placebos experienced significant relief from the pain often associated with these two debilitating conditions (O'Regan, 1985). More interesting, however, was their finding that people who had previously been treated successfully for pain with an active analgesic agent experienced *more* relief when given a placebo than those people who had not been treated successfully for their pain prior to receiving the placebo. Combined with similar reports from the literature, these findings strongly suggest that the placebo effects of any given procedure or orientation are likely to be enhanced when they are based on, paired with, or elicit a previously successful experience of the client.

Therapists can pair therapeutic procedures with their clients' previous experiences of success in any number of ways. First and foremost, however, is simply listening for or inquiring about the client's usual method of or experience with change. For example, paying particular attention to:

- How does change usually happen in the client's life?
- What causes change to occur?
- What does the client do to initiate/facilitate change?
- What do others do to initiate/facilitate change?
- What is the usual order of the change process (i.e., first/second/third) with regard to these concerns and problems?
- What events usually precede/occur during/follow the change?

As just one example of pairing treatment procedures with clients' prior experiences of success, consider the case of an eight-year-old child who was brought to therapy because of a persistent problem with bed-wetting (Miller, 1992). During the first visit, it was learned that bed-wetting was a problem *except* when the child slept on the hardwood floor. According to the child, she was more inclined to get up and use the bathroom when sleeping on the floor because it was less comfortable than her bed. At the end of the first session, the therapist incorporated the success experience into the treatment by assigning the child the task of "continuing to have dry beds while sleeping on the hardwood floor." Later sessions used the child's success experience in combination with the behavioral modification technique of fading (see Martin & Pear, 1983). Basically, over the course of treatment, the therapist helped the child transfer her initial success of sleeping on a sheet on the hardwood floor, to sleeping on a sleeping bag on the hardwood floor, then to a mattress, and finally to sleeping on the mattress on the bed.

Having a possibility-focus

> The essence of genius is taking things that other people think are ridiculous and seeing them as possibilities. These people are visionaries.
>
> *Charles Martin, 1989, p. 2*

"Patients are deceptive in the therapeutic encounter," say therapists Gediman and Lieberman (1995) in their book *The Many Faces of Deceit: Omissions, Lies, and Disguise in Psychotherapy*. Why? According to the authors, "The patient fools himself or herself in an effort to protect self esteem" and gain the "sadomasochistic gratification" associated with "putting one over on the therapist." The cure? If therapy is to have any chance of being successful, therapists must learn to detect the many signs of deception, since, the authors forcefully argue, "The patient . . . cannot be helped until the lies come out into the open and are dealt with" (p. 7).

As pessimistic as the statements by Gediman and Lieberman (1995) sound, there is a significant body of data indicat-
ing that they are right about one thing: people do "lie," in a
manner of speaking, to both themselves and others in a way
that protects their self-esteem (Taylor, Wayment, & Collins,
1993). The research shows, for example, that people inflate
their own personal strengths and attributes, overestimate
their degree of personal control, and have a strong tendency
to view the future more optimistically than is warranted by
objective facts (Taylor & Brown, 1988). On this point, at
least, there is little disagreement. What is less certain, however, is whether the lying and self-deception identified by
Gediman and Leiberman are the *causa finalis* of mental and
emotional maladjustment they seem to think. On this point,
the data strongly suggest the opposite.

Over the last ten years, research has been conducted showing that positive illusions — the things that Gediman and Leiberman identify as lies — are characteristic of normal, healthy,
well-functioning individuals, *not* abnormal, unhealthy, or
dysfunctional ones. As Taylor (1989), one of the primary
researchers in this area, puts it, "in many ways, the *healthy
mind* is a self-deceptive one" (p. 227; emphasis added). In
fact, the data indicate that the people who are most likely to
suffer from problems such as anxiety, depression, negative
mood, or chronically low self-esteem — the problems that
bring the majority of clients into treatment — are those who
are for whatever reason incapable of sustaining such illusions
(Taylor & Brown, 1988). Contrary, then, to what Gediman
and Leiberman (1995) recommend in their book, the research on positive illusions suggests that helping clients has
less to do with forcing them to see the truth than it does with
helping them believe there are possibilities — the possibility of
change, of accomplishing or getting what they want, of starting over, of succeeding or controlling their life. Basically, the
possibility of whatever.

There are a variety of ways for therapists to be more "possibility-focused" in their clinical work. One of the first is to orient clinical work toward the future.

⚭ *Treatment should be oriented toward the future.*

One of the most robust findings from the literature on positive illusions is that healthy, well-adjusted people tend to view the future with more optimism than is warranted by objective facts. Indeed, the research shows that people who are optimistic experience more positive life events and are better at coping with and avoiding negative ones than people who are pessimistic (see Markus & Nurius, 1986; Perloff, 1983; Weinstein, 1980, 1982, 1984). While common sense might suggest that being psychologically well-adjusted *causes* or, rather, *enables* people to be optimistic about the future, the research indicates that quite the opposite is true; that is, being optimistic actually enables people to be better adjusted psychologically (Taylor et al., 1993).

Clearly, there are benefits to helping clients develop more optimistic expectations for the future. One way for therapists to do this is to orient their clinical work more toward the future. Traditionally, psychotherapy has focused more on the past than the future. The idea has been that, for clients to have better tomorrows, therapists must first help them create better yesterdays. As Frank and Frank (1993) suggest, however, it is not revisiting or, in psychodynamic parlance, "working through" the past but, rather, challenging the pessimistic assumptions clients have about the future *as a result of their past* that facilitates hope and positive expectations for change in treatment. Clients, research convincingly shows, come to therapy not because they have problems but because they have become demoralized about their chances of resolving them (Frank, 1973; Garfield, 1994; Rabkin, 1983). As a result of a remote event or more recent history, they have given up hope of changing and, instead, act as if their problems are going to be permanent (Seligman, 1975, 1990).

The first therapist to recognize the possibilities inherent in future-oriented clinical work was the Austrian-born psychiatrist Alfred Adler. Departing sharply from his Freudian colleagues and their tradition of focusing on the past and identifying pathology, Adler (1964a) advocated focusing on the future and treating clients "as if" they possessed all the skills, resources, and insight necessary to resolve their problems. The future-oriented "as if" quality of his work can be seen in a number of treatment procedures he pioneered. Perhaps the most notable of these was a technique he called simply, "The Question." Still in use by Adlerian therapists today, the method involves first asking clients to imagine that the therapist has a magic wand or magic pill that eliminates their symptoms and then encouraging them to think about the resulting differences in their life (Mosak, 1978). Yet another example of a future-oriented Adlerian technique is giving clients a homework assignment to act "as if" they *already have* the kind of life, skills, or outcome from treatment they desire (Adler, 1963).

Future-oriented clinical work has become increasingly popular over the last ten years (Kessler & Miller, 1995). While known by different names (e.g., age progression, time projection, pseudo-orientation in time, end result and goal imagery approaches, interventive interviewing, solution-oriented/focused treatment, the NLP outcome template, and externalizing), all of the existing future-oriented models share the common characteristic of helping clients create a vision of the future when the problems they are struggling with have either been resolved or are no longer a problem (see Berg & Miller, 1992; de Shazer, 1985, 1988; Frederick & Phillips, 1992; Hollon & Beck, 1994; Johnson & Miller, 1994; Phillips & Frederick, 1992; Miller, 1992; Miller &

Berg, 1995; Penn, 1985; Torem, 1992; White & Epston, 1990). As two practitioners of future-oriented treatment, Butler and Powers, point out, "the simple act of imagining a different future can free clients from a hopeless perspective . . . and enable clients to construct their own solutions" (1996, p. 231).

Case Example: The Black Cloud

A woman who came to therapy because she was feeling "severely depressed" described her lifelong battle with depression as the "black cloud that hangs over every aspect of my life." For several minutes, the therapist simply listened attentively while the client described her struggle with the "black cloud." When a natural break occurred in the flow of the conversation, the therapist introduced a future orientation with a question similar in nature to the one originally proposed by Adler (Mosak, 1978).

Therapist: Suppose, Michelle, somehow or other, through our work here together, we are able to move this "black cloud," so that it's no longer hanging over you, affecting you?

Client: (*shaking head negatively*) That would be . . .

T: That would be?

C: I just can't imagine, I've felt this way for so long, the cloud has been there for so long.

It is not uncommon, as this dialogue illustrates, for clients to experience some difficulty when first attempting to shift their orientation from the past to the future. Indeed, some difficulty should be expected. Given some time and an appropriate amount of support and encouragement from the therapist, most clients are able to respond (Miller, 1995).

T: Right, the cloud *has* been there for a long time.

C: (*nodding*)

T: And, Michelle, if you did begin to feel differently for the first time in a long time, if that cloud lifted, what would be different? How could you tell?

C: (*long pause*) Maybe it wouldn't be so hard to get up in the morning.

T: Yeah.

C: To tell you the truth, I didn't get out of the bed at all yesterday morning. I've got a 15-year-old, and I told her that she was going to stay home because I just didn't feel, the cloud was so bad, I just didn't feel like getting out of bed.

T: Mmm huh. And, if the cloud began to lift, the black fog started to clear, what would be different?

C: I would have a reason for getting out of bed.

T: You would have a reason?

C: I would give myself a reason. Up until now, when I wake up in the morning, I usually lie in bed and give myself reasons to *stay* in bed.

T: Ahh hah. You would be giving yourself reasons to get out of bed.

C: (*nods head*) Mmm huh.

T: What kinds of reasons would you be giving yourself?

In the dialogue that followed, the client identified several reasons she thought would motivate her get out of bed. The conversation then shifted to other changes that Michelle would notice once the "black cloud" lifted. As suggested in Chapter 4, care was then taken to ensure that the changes she described were stated in small, specific, concrete, behavioral, achievable, and proactive terms. For example, she was asked:

- What else would be different if the black cloud lifted?
- What would be the *smallest* sign that the black cloud was lifting?
- What would be the *first* sign?
- When you no longer had to spend so much time struggling with the black cloud, what would you be doing more of *instead*?
- *Who* would be the first person to notice that you had won the battle with the black cloud? What would *that person* notice different about you that would tell him or her that the battle was finally won?
- *Where* do suppose you would be when you first noticed the changes? What will have happened just before that would have contributed to the change? What will happen after that would help maintain it?

When engaging in future-oriented work, helping clients describe the future they desire in these terms tends to make that future more salient to the present (de Shazer et al., 1986). The detail, in other words, lends an aura of reality, implying that the future the client is describing is possible to achieve in the present. In many instances, possibility even becomes connected with reality when the increasingly detailed description elicits recollections of having experienced all or at least part of what is being described (Miller & Berg, 1995).

By the end of the first visit, Michelle's affect had brightened considerably. She had even recalled a few examples of having experienced some of what she was describing. The therapist concluded the session by noting the improvement in her affect and giving Michelle a future-oriented assignment to "Look for evidence of the changes you have been describing occurring during the coming week." With regard to this particular assignment, several recent studies suggest that clients who are given assignments that encourage them to assume or act "as if" changes will be occurring are more optimistic and more likely to report improvement in subsequent sessions than clients who are given tasks that are structured around their problem (e.g., monitoring the occurrence or pattern of the problem [McKeel, 1996]). Subsequent sessions with Michelle confirmed these results.

Before moving on, it should be mentioned that therapists need not be as directive as in the case of Michelle in order to bring a future orientation to treatment. Clients frequently provide opportunities for the therapist to join them in a discussion of their hopes and dreams for the future. When such opportunities arise, the therapist can simply follow the client's lead and amplify the discussion.

Case Example: I Thought I'd Be President

As an example of simply listening for and then amplifying the client's introduction of a future time frame, consider dialogue taken from a case with a man who came to treatment because of depression. The client had been recounting his history of failed relationships, drug abuse, and legal difficulties when the following exchange took place:

Client: My life has not turned out the way I thought it would when I was coming up.

Therapist: (*sympathetically*) It hasn't?

C: Nah.

T: You had lots of dreams, hopes, then?

C: Yeah, I did (*pausing and then with laughter*). I thought I'd be President.

T: Of the United States?

C: Uh huh (*laughs*).

T: (*laughs*) Sounds like you'd like things to be more like you thought they'd be when you were coming up?

C: (*looks away, nodding affirmatively*)

T: If things started to be a little more like that, what would be different?

As the excerpt illustrates, the therapist chooses to hear the client's assessment of his childhood as evidence of hope for something better in the future rather than despair over lost opportunities in the past. The dialogue that followed was increasingly future-oriented, as the therapist and client worked together to create (or recreate) a vision of how the client wanted his life to be different. Changes in the client's affect over the course of the session indicated that some of the hope he had experienced in the past was being recaptured in the present.

⊁ *Treatment should enhance or highlight the client's feeling of personal control.*

Another robust finding from the positive illusions research is that people who believe they can influence or modify the course of life events—in other words, who have a sense of personal control—tend to cope better and adjust more successfully when those events are negative or stressful. Importantly, this is true whether the belief in personal control is veridical or not! As researchers Taylor, Wayment, and Collins (1993) point out, simply *believing* one "has the means to influence, terminate, or modify a noxious event [helps people] cope better with those events" (p. 329).

At the same time, as reviewed in Chapter 3, research on psychotherapy has established a link between successful treatment outcome, on the one hand, and clients' general belief in their ability to influence the course of life events, on the other. You may recall that this research showed that clients who believe that the outcome of specific events is dependent on their own behavior are more likely to have positive treatment outcomes. As one final example of such findings, consider a study conducted by Beyebach, Morejon, Palenzuela, and Rodriguez-Arias (1996), which investigated the relationship between psychotherapy outcome and three different cognitive variables: (1) self-efficacy, or a person's estimation of his or her ability to put a given operation into action; (2) locus of control, the belief a person has about his or her ability to influence the outcome of life events; and (3) success expectancies, or a person's estimation of the probability that a particular outcome will occur. Using well-established measures and a panel of independent judges blind to the hypotheses of the study, the researchers found that only one of the three variables was significantly related to treatment outcome—locus of control. Specifically, clients who *believed* that the outcome of life events was contingent on their behavior were three times more likely to experience a successful outcome in therapy than clients who typically viewed events as being outside of their personal control.

Such research highlights the importance of therapists' working to enhance clients' feelings of personal control. This can be accomplished in any number of ways. For example, the therapist can simply listen for and then amplify any references clients make to their actions having an impact on the outcome of daily events. Depending on the style of the therapist and presentation of the client, the therapist can also be more direct, for example, asking questions or making direct statements that presuppose client influence over events occurring in his/her life. Finally, and perhaps most important, the therapist can be mindful of the inherent hierarchy or power imbalance that exists in the therapeutic encounter and work to flatten that heirarchy and empower the client. This latter suggestion is especially important, as the following two examples illustrate, in cases where external circumstances (e.g., mandated treatment, life-threatening situations) have in reality curtailed clients' personal control or power.

Case Example: Meeting the Prophet

Client: I am the Prophet.

Therapist: Good morning.

C: (*looking away*)

T: This is quite an honor for me. I've never met a prophet before.

C: (*continues to look away*)

T: (*tentatively*) What should I call you?

The preceding dialogue, taken from the opening moments of a first session with a man in an inpatient psychiatric setting, is a nice illustration of attempting to enhance the personal control of a client whose real power has been curtailed by external circumstances. In this case, the 36-year-old man had been admitted to the hospital for evaluation and treatment after being arrested by the police for threatening people in a local shopping area. While seemingly small and insignificant, the therapist's greeting, comment, and question all cast the client in a position of power and control. Specifically, the comment places the client in a position of respect relative to the therapist, while the question shifts control over the direction of the interview to the client. In the dialogue that follows, the therapist continues to work to empower the client.

C: (*angrily*) I have been called to warn the wicked people of God's coming judgment.

T: From the looks of it, it seems like you're being treated like every other prophet in history.

C: (*turns toward the therapist, nods affirmatively*)

T: (*continuing*) Disbelieved, locked up, perse . . .

C: (*nodding affirmatively*) They will be punished! (*turns away*)

T: (*pause*) That's what you're trying to prevent, right?

C: (*turning toward the therapist*) Yes, but if they don't heed the warning, they *will* be punished.

T: You . . .

C: (*interrupting*) Not by me (*pointing toward the ceiling*). By *God*!

T: You have a difficult job, uh, calling. A lot of responsibility rests on your shoulders.

C: *God* called me.

T: (*nodding*) There must be some good reason for that?

C: (*nodding affirmatively*) God has His reasons.

T: What do suppose God sees in you that gave Him reason to call you?

Nearly everything the therapist does in this excerpt presupposes client control and influence — from the statement about the client's tremendous responsibility to the question about the reasons God chose the client to "warn the people." In the dialogue that followed, the man went on to identify some of his strengths, including, among other things, his faithfulness, dedication, sincerity, and kindness. Care was taken to acknowledge each of his strengths and to elicit concrete and specific examples of how he displayed them on a regular basis. Over the course of the interview, the man became less agitated, established and maintained eye contact, and, by the end of the meeting, started talking about what he would need to *do* in order to get out of the hospital. This latter discussion, in particular, was taken as evidence of the client's beginning to believe in his own power and influence.

Case Example: Keeping Cool

Another example of helping clients whose sense of personal control has been curtailed by external circumstances can be found in the case of Michael. Briefly, Michael had just been promoted to the position of manager in a local fast food outlet when the store was held up at gunpoint by several masked men. While no one was hurt in the robbery, Michael questioned the way he had responded to the crisis. In particular, he said he felt bad about "freezing up" and not doing more to protect his employees and help the police identify the robbers. Even though fellow employees and an employee assistance counselor had reassured Michael about the appropriateness of his response to the life-threatening situation, he continued to experience nagging doubts about his performance. For this reason, several weeks after the event he was referred for therapy. The following excerpt, occurring several minutes into the first visit, is a typical example of how the therapist worked with Michael to help him regain a sense of personal control.

Client: I froze, I just froze.

Therapist: Uh huh. And then?

C: They [the robbers] were, they were screaming. They were telling everybody, "Get down on the ground or we'll blow your f-ing heads off." Running around, waving their guns.

T: Gawd. What did you do?

C: I, I, I didn't say anything.

T: What *did* you do?

C: (*pausing*) I sort of, you know, I motioned . . .

T: For everyone to get down.

C: Yeah.

T: Wow, how did you, I mean, how were you able to do that?

C: (*shaking head*)

T: I mean, you know, you say you froze but, I don't know, it sounds more like you kept your cool.

C: (*looking back at the therapist*) Hmm.

T: How did you do that? How did you know that that was the right thing to do?

C: (*pauses, shakes head*) I don't know, I never thought of it like that. Maybe, maybe, um, just instinct.

T: You mean, maybe you're just naturally able to keep your cool? Not do things that might, I don't know, make things worse?

C: I did think about that.

T: About?

C: About not, about, I'm, well, there are all these people at the store and all the employees and I was scared about somebody getting hurt, killed.

T: So you kept your cool?

C: (*nodding*)

The therapist asks Michael questions that presuppose a sense of control and/or influence over his response to the robbery. The implication of this line of questioning is that Michael reacted to the situation with forethought as well as in the appropriate way. The therapist continued to use similar questions and responses throughout the session. By the end of the visit, Michael was already beginning to talk more confidently about his response to the robbery.

⌁ Treatment should "de-person-alize" the client's problems, difficulties, or shortcomings.

In 1985, the New York Mets battled for and eventually lost the Eastern Division pennant to the St. Louis Cardinals. The loss, according the team's players and manager, was "not our fault!" Indeed, if anything, the statements of the players and manager made over the course of the entire season evinced a pattern of blaming their errors and poor performance on everything but themselves: "The heat was too much," "It was one of those days," and "Some moisture must have gotten on the ball." In contrast, statements made by the players and manager of the Cardinals indicated that they held themselves responsible for their performance on the field—good and bad: "*I* am having a lot of trouble concentrating," "*I* was bummed out," and "*I* don't have the expertise." The result? Baseball fans will recall not only that the following year the Cardinals performed terribly—winning less that half of their games—but that the Mets went on to win the World Series! Adding insult to injury, some very interesting research has found that the Mets' style of blaming external circumstances for their shortcomings may have been the critical factor in their victory.

In 1990, Seligman summarized a series of studies he and his colleagues had conducted examining the relationship between various explanatory styles and performance in certain activities (i.e., sports, business, school, health, and psychological adjustment). In contrast to conventional wisdom, the researchers found that a style of attributing poor performance to external circumstances not only did not hinder but was actually was predictive of success above and beyond objective talent (e.g., test scores, batting averages). At the same time, the researchers found that a style of attributing failure to internal causes was predictive of failure regardless of innate ability.

In explaining these seemingly paradoxical results, Seligman pointed out that a style of attributing poor performance to external circumstances allows people to separate themselves from their difficulties—to "de-person-alize" their problems. The result? They maintain their self-esteem and are able to "try harder and come back from defeat" (1990, p. 166). On the other hand, a style of attributing poor performance to internal causes leads people to "person-alize" their difficulties—in other words, to think of themselves as untalented, incapable, or worthless, and, as one might expect, eventually to stop trying.

The results of the studies by Seligman and colleagues have direct implications for clinical work, specifically with helping clients believe there are possibilities. In this regard, the data indicate that therapists can enable their clients to "try hard and come back from defeat" by helping them depersonalize the problems or difficulties they bring to treatment. In other words, therapists should talk about problems in a way that separates those problems from the client, a way that says, in essence, "Yes, you *have* a problem, but *you* are not the problem."

Separating clients from their problems has been, albeit for a different reason, a fairly routine activity in psychotherapy practice (Miller, 1994a).[2] Consider, for example, the entire process of assigning a psychiatric diagnosis. Given that there is relatively little evidence that psychotherapy exerts diagnostic-specific benefits or, for that matter, that diagnosis affects the type of treatment a client will receive, the whole activity might be more parsimoniously viewed as a way of helping clients depersonalize their difficulties (see Cummings, 1986). Indoctrinating clients into clinical belief systems that situate the cause of mental or emotional suffering outside of their direct control or influence can also be viewed as a way of depersonalizing problems.[3] In essence, these belief systems

---

[2]As noted in the beginning of this chapter, the primary reason has been the assumption that understanding the origin and evolution of problems is a necessary precondition for their resolution.

[3]A very clear example of this is the disease model of addiction (cf. Alcoholics Anonymous, 1977). When treated with this model, clients are taught to believe that they are not personally responsible for *having* a drinking or drug use problem because they have a primary, progressive, and irreversible "disease" that *causes* them to use chemicals (cf. Johnson, 1973). A very similar idea stands at the core of the secular alternative to Alcoholics Anonymous, Rational Recovery. This model posits that problem drinkers and drug users have an "addictive voice" originating in a primitive part of the brain that expresses an

send the message, "*You*, client, are not the problem; rather, *your* (childhood, brain chemistry, unmonitored negative thoughts, rogue genes, experiences with aliens or trauma from previous lives, whatever) is the problem."

It is possible to help clients depersonalize their difficulties without assigning a diagnosis or schooling them in a particular clinical belief system. Most therapists do this when they structure the therapeutic conversation in a way that implies that the client's difficulties are either normal or expected given certain circumstances (e.g., phase of life, response to events [O'Hanlon & Weiner-Davis, 1989])—for example, when a therapist suggests to parents that the problematic behavior of their adolescent is typical for children of that age group or tells a grieving client that most people experience tearfulness and sadness following the death of a loved one. As an illustration of this, consider the following short excerpt taken from a session with a women who was grieving the death of her husband:

Client: I still think of him a lot [her late husband].

Therapist: Of course.

C: Sometimes I think I think about him more now than I did when he was alive.

T: Uh huh. (*sympathetically*) I've heard that before.

C: (*curious*) You have?

T: Yeah, I can't speak from my own experience, but when I've worked with people who've lost a loved one, I've heard them say that exact thing, "I think of them more now than ever."

C: (*thoughtful*) Hmm.

---

appetite for psychoactive substances and directs their behavior toward consumption. Here again, drinkers or drug users are not considered personally responsible for *having* the voice, since it stems from an unconscious, irrational, and primitive part of the brain over which they have no control.

T: I don't know if it's a blessing or a curse but they've said it.

C: (*thoughtfully*) Hmm. Maybe it is, it's, it's so hard when, I miss him so much but I wouldn't want to just go on and not think of him. That wouldn't be, we lived together for so many years. Maybe it is a blessing.

Finally, in keeping with the tone of this book, it should be noted that therapists can also help clients depersonalize the difficulties that bring them to treatment by simply listening for and then amplifying how clients describe themselves as separate from their difficulties. Clients frequently do talk about their difficulties as being separate from themselves, for example, as something they are at war with, in the grips of, struggling to defeat, battling against, or working to fend off. When such opportunities arise, the therapist need only adopt the client's description of the problem as a separate and distinct entity and then utilize it to enable the client to continue his/her problem-solving efforts. [4] The point of this particular suggestion—and, for that matter, all of the suggestions in this chapter—is *not* to help clients figure out what they actually need to do to solve the problem(s) that brought them into treatment; rather, the point is to help them recapture their belief in the possibility of change.

Case Example: It's Got Me

This dialogue is taken from a session with a female client who had presented for treatment because of depression.

Client: I can't do anything anymore. I just sit around, I don't do anything.

Therapist: Uh huh.

---

[4]Recent writers label this activity "externalizing," a process which "basically entails the linguistic separation of the problem from the personal identity of the client" (O'Hanlon, 1995, p. 21; cf. Johnson & Miller, 1994; White, 1986; White & Epston, 1990).

C: I don't work. Quit my job, actually quit a bunch of jobs. This thing, it's just got me.

T: This thing?

C: I don't know, these feelings, depression, it's like it's got me.

T: The depression, it's got you.

C: (*nodding, then looking toward the ground*) Yeah.

As the excerpt illustrates, the client separates herself from the problem she is having—in this case, depression—by first calling it a "thing" and then describing that "thing" as something that has hold of her. The dialogue continued for several more minutes, with the therapist first adopting and then later amplifying the description of the problem as an entity separate and distinct from the client. As the session continued, the client began to make references to what she was doing now, as well as what she had done in the past, to loosen herself from the grip of the depression-thing. Again, the therapist listened attentively and then amplified the client's statements.

C: Almost nothing I've done works. The therapy, the medication . . .

T: What has worked? I mean, you say, "almost nothing." What has worked to keep this depression-thing at bay?

C: It's more like it's holding me, tight, like a bear hug or something like that (*making a bear hug with her arms*).

T: Okay. When have you noticed that the depression, its hug is, that there's a little more breathing room? That you're not being held so tight?

A number of minutes were spent exploring what was different during those times when the client felt that the depression did not have as tight a hold on her. The session concluded with a discussion of potential ways for the client to escape or at least lessen the depression's grip. Over the course of the visit, the client's affect gradually brightened and she left feeling more hopeful about the possibility of change in the future.

SUMMARY AND CONCLUSION

Placebo factors make up as much as 15% of the variance in treatment outcome, about the same as model and technique factors. These factors include the hope and positive expectations for change that clients experience simply by being in treatment. All therapists have ways of interacting with clients and conducting treatment that facilitate hope and positive expectations for change. Based on research in social and clinical psychology, this chapter has offered some additional suggestions and recommendations for augmenting the contribution of placebo factors to psychotherapy outcome, namely having a healing ritual and bringing a possibility-focus to treatment.

6

"A GIFT FROM GOD"

A Case Example

> Client: The doctor said maybe I have a chemical imbalance. But I don't buy that . . .
> Therapist: Okay, any other ideas?

A UNIFYING language for psychotherapy, based on the four pantheoretical or common curative factors, has been presented in the preceding chapters. What follows in this chapter are case excerpts exemplifying a therapy informed by this language. The process of *empowering existing client strengths and molding treatment to fit the client's goals and expectations* is illustrated though clinical dialogue and commentary.

THE CLIENT

Bob is a 40-year-old male of European descent, married 10 years with no children. He is a college graduate and manages a large retirement community. Bob's presenting complaint is that he is depressed. According to him, the condition began after a series of deaths of friends and family. He complained of sleep disturbance, feelings of fear and foreboding, headaches and stomach distress, difficulty concentrating on tasks, troubling images of his own death, inability to get out of bed in the morning, and suicidal ideation.

Bob saw Dr. T., a well-regarded therapist, for 10 sessions and began taking antidepressant medication. Although a va-

riety of topics were explored and several different intervention strategies attempted, the client reported little improvement. Both client and therapist felt the therapy had reached
a standstill. Dr. T. referred the case for consultation, hoping
for a new direction. Dr. T. attended Bob's first meeting,
observing the session with a team behind a one-way mirror.

EXCERPT ONE: THE OPENING
MOMENTS OF THE FIRST VISIT

Therapist: Well, this is kind of a strange process, so it might
take a couple of minutes to get acclimated to a group
behind the mirror observing. It's kind of strange for me
when I start out, so we can both be anxious together here
for a few minutes.

Client: Okay.

T: What will happen is we'll talk for a while, about 45 minutes, and then we'll take a break. Then I'll go back behind
the mirror and talk with the team and see if they have any
suggestions or feedback they want to give you, and then
I'll come back and share that with you. The idea is for Dr.
T. to get ideas about ways to go to help the difficulties
that you came to see him about. I'm sure he told you that
was the purpose of all this.

C: Right.

T: I may get a phone call or two while we're in here so if the
phone rings, it is for me (*both laugh*), so I'll answer it and
I'll share what they say. Probably what they will say is,
"Will you ask about this or follow up on that?" Or maybe
they have a specific question that I haven't asked and I
need to ask you. So, what will be helpful for us is what
brought you to see Dr. T. and, if that problem still exists,
what is bringing you here to see me?

C: Okay, I guess basically it was depression as the result of three deaths of family members and a close working friend. I manage a retirement home and I've got a five-member board of trustees and one of them very suddenly died. He was 68 years old but he had not been sick to the point where someone expected him to suddenly have a heart attack. I guess just a combination of things, an aunt that was like a second mother to me died with cancer last fall. My grandmother who had been in a rest home for eight years also passed on. She went first, then my aunt, then the board member.

T: Okay. That's a lot.

C: And, it all just kind of hit at one time. I realized that I was unable to get up in the morning, and that I didn't want to get up. Suicidal tendencies were there, very definitely.

T: Sounds like things got really tough.

C: The suicidal thoughts have not been with me recently. I think the combination of the drug that I'm taking and talking this out and, I guess maybe, some of the things I'm trying to do for myself have helped a little bit.

T: Great. What else is helping, in addition to talking it out and the drug?

Commentary

The therapist begins the session by explaining the consultation process. He shares his own anxiety about meeting before the consulting team, hoping, as may be obvious, to make Bob as comfortable as possible. The client goes on to describe the depression, as well as attribute it to three recent deaths. Importantly, he also mentions some improvement that has occurred as a result of steps he has already taken. This was the first that Dr. T. had heard that Bob thought there was any improvement. As noted, Dr. T. believed that therapy was stalled and not working.

In the ensuing conversation, the client comments on his success to date in coping with the depression and his views about its nature. The therapist follows the client's lead, addressing his remarks and questions to the client's agenda. The therapist is also change-focused in his approach, listening, for example, for what else Bob does to help himself.

EXCERPT TWO: THE SESSION CONTINUES, MORE CHANGE, NEW GOALS FOR THERAPY

T: Great. What else is helping in addition to talking it out and the drug?

C: I manage a retirement home. I had two assistants. One was a new person on staff and the other one was a gentleman who has been there for many years, who retired, and the new gentleman took over doing some of the things that I was doing myself. The new person had considerably more supervisory abilities and quickly took over day-to-day operations. As a result, I became uninvolved in the things I always did before.

T: Uh huh.

C: So I'm trying to reinvolve myself. One of the things that Dr. T. and I decided was, in order to get the adrenaline flowing in the morning, is for me to get myself involved in a project, and that has been helping in the morning.

T: Okay.

C: It's still a drag to get up in the morning and rolling, and in the past, before this depression had come on, I was very much of a morning person. It's a difficult thing to deal with because basically I have been a very upbeat person all my life.

T: Okay, the point in time when you started to feel the difference was after these three deaths kind of pounded you in succession?

C: Yes. This all occurred last fall, so in January was when I started with Dr. T. But I guess what I'm still trying to look for is what caused this other than the three deaths.

T: You think there is something other than the three deaths? Frankly that's a lot, that's a heck of a lot at one time to be able to adjust to. Three deaths is a significant sequence of events to have to incorporate into the way you live life each day. "Well, she died, she died, and he died and I'm just going to get up and go to work just as if nothing has happened and my life hasn't changed at all and I had no feelings for these people." Death of loved ones also puts you in confrontation with your own mortality as well as the actual loss that those people represent to you. There certainly could be other reasons for your depression, but that certainly is a neon sign. One death is hard enough, but three important people in your life in that short a period of time is really beyond normal coping mechanisms.

C: Well, that's right, it is a lot, and if that's the case, then I guess I don't need to look much farther. But, I was also looking at the idea of having a family. My wife and I talked about having a family, but we have not been successful and so, you know, you look at your mortality and not having anyone to take care of you in, you know, down the line.

T: So the deaths were a trigger point and brought to the surface other things that also were a bother to you, like not having any children.

C: Right. And the struggle to have a baby has been tough. Lots of doctors and lots of disappointments.

T: Okay, you've been the physician route and . . .

C: We're still dealing with that now.

T: Okay, wow, I did that for four years and finally we were successful but what a pain that whole process was. Medications and surgery for both of us, and still year after year nothing happened and finally . . . That's really a very depressing sequence of events to go through as well. You want a child and you can't make it happen, with all the unwanted babies in the world and all the aborted babies in the world and here you'd like to have a baby and you can't have it. That's really a very difficult process to go through. It sounds like you have a whole lot going on in your life that would tend to make a person feel depressed. If that's what you're facing too and going through, no wonder you're depressed.

C: Really! It's been a real pain.

T: That's a lot for someone to contend with. But even given how many things are going on in your life, it also sounds like you are doing various things to help yourself. The antidepressant is one area that is helping, and seeing Dr. T. is another area that is helping, and you've noticed that if you get involved in something in the morning, it gets you going. Is there anything else that's helping?

Commentary

Exploring the client's resources and successes in helping his depression reveals a very important piece of information about the client's world view: that is, he is looking for the "cause" of the depression in something other than the three deaths. As pointed out in Chapter 5, knowing the client's world view may prove valuable when attempting to choose an orientation or treatment procedure that will be credible to the client. For this reason, the therapist follows the client and explores his views of what else besides the deaths may be contributing to his current difficulties. Along the way, the therapist is careful to validate Bob not only about the deaths but also about the difficulties he has experienced with starting a family. The client's struggles are highlighted as important and his feelings of depression legitimized given the difficult circumstances.

The therapist, mindful of the contribution of Bob's strengths to positive treatment outcome, affirms his efforts to alleviate the depression and works to enhance his feelings of personal control over that outcome. The therapist and the team monitor the client's responses. The validating comments are consistently met with head nods and verbal confirmations. The strongest came when the therapist disclosed having had similar difficulties having a child.

Overall, the therapeutic relationship is progressing; the topics of conversation are flowing from the client and the client's goals are about to be addressed. In the dialogue that follows, the therapist continues to focus on change and highlights what Bob has done to tackle his depression. He also listens to other ideas the client has regarding the cause of the depression.

EXCERPT THREE: MORE STRENGTHS, IDENTIFYING *THE* GOAL

T: Is there anything else that's helping?

C: I'm trying to lose some weight.

T: Wow.

C: Low self-esteem has been part of the problem.

T: From your weighing more than you think you should?

C: That has been part of the problem. Some board members have been needling me — and I know I'm overweight — and the doctor has told me I'm overweight. But I really didn't take it to heart until this all came to a head. I realized that part of the problem is low self-esteem as a result of being overweight.

T: And you are trying to do something about that, too?

C: Right.

T: Geez.

C: I lost about twenty pounds.

T: Wow, that's incredible! Losing weight is more difficult than stopping drinking, or smoking, or any other habits, because unlike those other things we can't live without food, so it's a lot more difficult. And given all the other things you are going through, losing weight is pretty impressive.

C: Well, I just cut down on all pop, and I cut down on all snacking, and I enjoyed both of those, and just said "use very limited amount or none," and that has taken a lot off. And I'm trying to do some exercise.

T: Um mmm.

C: I guess another, another problem, if you look at the job and everything else, I am very much of an outside person. I used to get out on the grounds a little bit and do some things. Now I'm more relegated to the office. I'm still trying to get out and yet my board of trustees would like to see me in the office managing the office and trying to increase sales.

T: Uh huh.

C: I have not told them that I am out doing things, but as long as the sales are really good, they don't really look at the other side of it.

T: They don't need to know everything you do.

C: That's right.

T: So you're also trying to be more active and be more out-doorsy in terms of affecting your weight and your mood as well. Sounds like you're doing a number of things to help yourself feel better and all of them are helping somewhat.

C: I would like it to move quicker.

T: I'm amazed at how much you've done given the events and kinds of issues that you are dealing with, how far you have actually moved with all the things that you are doing. You've put into action all these different ways of address-ing your depression from a really multidisciplinary way — mind and body, activity and self-esteem — a lot of different ways of approaching it. You put together a really effective plan, although it is not going quite as fast as you'd like it to go. From where I sit, although I realize that I'm not the one experiencing it, and it is never fast enough, but it sounds to me like you're really going high speed. So I'm pretty amazed that you're doing as well as you are given what you described to me.

C: Thanks, I'm trying, but I guess I can't put my finger on *why* it actually started.

T: Uh huh.

C: I think I was leading up to the depression prior to the deaths.

T: Oh, okay.

C: And the deaths kind of set me over.

T: Okay.

C: And I'd like to be able to answer that question in my own mind. I went through a complete physical in January thinking that it might be physical as opposed to mental. I had a stomachache, or I had a headache, or I had some other psychosomatic problem and didn't want to work.

T: Uh huh, your body was telling you something.

C: Another idea I have been kicking around is my whole work ethic. All I've ever done is work. Realizing that I'm still the general manager of the operation, but yet I could probably have more banking hours than the other people, but that's not ever been my upbringing.

T: Uh huh.

C: And uh, I thought that I always needed to be there and so I was. Now, I'm not so sure.

T: Uh huh. Sounds like you're doing a lot of reevaluation of your core assumptions about life.

C: I'm trying to. As I said, I've not ever had this problem before.

T: Okay. I want to make sure I'm following you. You've done a lot. You've made progress. You were kicked this depression ball and got it on the one-yard line and you have, by seeing Dr. T., taking the antidepressant, getting yourself involved in a project in the morning, exercising and losing weight, being outdoors more, and reevaluating your beliefs about life, family, and work, you've moved yourself down to . . . ?

C: The opponents' 40-yard line.

T: The 40-yard line. Okay. If you were to go to the opponents' 30-yard line with this depression, what would you see yourself doing different than you're doing now?

C: Getting off the antidepressants and I guess feeling better about myself and, uh . . .

T: Okay.

C: So I guess I'd like to be to the opponents' goal line, quicker than what I'm doing. And again reiterating, I'd like to know what initiated the depression.

T: Okay. So it sounds like finding out what initiated it is

pretty important to you in terms of making yourself feel better.

C: Yeah, very important.

Commentary

The therapist affirms, compliments, and validates Bob's efforts and struggles. Through the conversation Bob's goal becomes very clear: he wants to know *why* he became depressed. While he also wants to get off the antidepressant and feel better about himself, identifying the cause of the depression is his main interest. In order to facilitate a strong therapeutic alliance, this must be the focus of treatment. Focusing on his strengths and current successes would probably not be enough for Bob. As noted in Chapter 4, treatment is enhanced when clients' strengths are combined with the goals they have for treatment in the context of the therapeutic relationship. Similarly, making suggestions or offering other solutions for the depression would not conform to his hopes and wishes for treatment. Bob's view is that finding the cause of his depression is the way to "get to the goal line."

EXCERPT FOUR: EXPLORING CAUSES

T: Okay. So it sounds like finding out what initiated it is pretty important to you in terms of making yourself feel better.

C: Yeah, very important.

T: Okay.

C: Because the three deaths are definitely a major feature, and yet, the depression—on looking back, I feel with the stomach problems, and the headaches, and not being at work, was going on before the deaths occurred.

T: What's your hunch about that?

C: The doctor said maybe I have a chemical imbalance. But I don't buy that because why all of a sudden did things get bad? I never had this problem before.

T: Uh huh. Any other ideas?

C: Well, Mother's Day and the end of May, generally that is a very busy time at the Home preparing for summer visiting. We worked a lot of overtime in the past few years trying to get things in order and, uh, I think I was physically and even mentally drained at that point in time. From there until about September, I was having the so-called physical problems.

T: Okay.

C: And I guess I can't put my finger on it. Was it the result of the overtime that set me low?

T: Good question. Bob, how would you know that you had come onto the correct explanation of what initiated the depression?

C: I'm not sure I would. I'm trying to put my finger on it. Is it a result of working 150 hours of overtime beyond the six days a week that I work for summer preparation?

T: Oh, geez, that's a lot.

C: So realistically, if we look at that, is that the cause? Is that the initial cause? Is it the new supervisor who is capable of running things without me? Is it that? Is it a mid-life crisis at age 40, you know, is it?

T: Uh huh.

C: A number of things I have tried to itemize and put into some order, trying to figure out why this depression happened.

T: Uh huh.

C: And I've told myself in the back of my mind with the new

supervisor, he's got things better in order than we've had in the past. He has talked me into hiring some additional people to make this summer visiting work out.

T: Uh huh. Sounds like a smart guy.

C: Yeah. Because it was a drain on me last year. As I said I'm not getting any younger and there's other things I'd like to do with my life besides working all the time.

T: I'm glad to hear that. I had a crazy thought and I wanted to bounce it off of you. It sounds kind of weird, so bear with me a little bit.

Commentary

Once again, as in previous excerpts, the therapist is mindful of the client's resources. In addition, the therapist works to establish a strong therapeutic alliance with the client by responding empathically and accepting his view of therapeutic alliance and goal for the treatment—that is, discovering the cause of his depression, not just learning how to deal with it.

The dialogue shows how accommodating the client's view of the alliance results in the client's providing important information about both the goals and tasks of therapy. If therapy is going to be successful, it will have to provide Bob with an answer to his question. To discount his request or ignore his desire for "insight" in favor of a pure focus on solutions, exceptions, or problem interruption would have likely fallen short.

EXCERPT FIVE:
A NEW "CAUSE" EMERGES

T: I'm glad to hear that. I had a crazy thought and I wanted to bounce it off of you. It sounds kind of weird, so bear with me a little bit. Do you think it's possible that your physical problems and the depression are exactly what you needed to have you look at the way you were living your life? It's like, "Bob, I'm trying to get your attention here and if you don't start doing something different, your quality of life is starting to go down the toilet. It's time to start looking at it." People are inherently very wise, and at some level inside us, after a while, something is going to let us know that we need to look at life a little differently.

C: *I would totally agree.* Whether it be myself or the good Lord above—and I believe in Him—I believe there are reasons that we don't know why things occur. Maybe this is it. Yes.

T: Okay. I wanted to see if that made sense to you because, as you were talking, it certainly seemed like a fall-out, that your internal wisdom guided by Him let you know that it was time to start looking at the way you lived your life and to address that for yourself in a productive way. It certainly has turned out that way. The functional fall-out of the depression is that you have done several things to change your life. You have wound up looking very closely at your life, the way you're living it, the way you approach life, maybe the way you're going to approach your family and future.

C: Yes, I certainly have.

T: Problems can function in a lot of different ways for people, and as strange as it sounds, they're not all bad. Sometimes they open up totally new vistas for people to look at their lives and to change their lives, and sometimes it takes that kind of a message before a person will stop and say, "Wait a minute, there is something not right. I need to refocus. Life is going to pass me by. There are more important things in my life than going to work and doing the job. There's my family, my future, and what I'm going to give to the next generation, or whether or not I am going to be a part of making the next generation." And the thing that becomes more important is our own quality of life and how we experience it. Sometimes it takes something radical to get our attention, especially when it has been so ingrained in us that, you know, go get it, go to work every day, push and do your best, do the job right, no job is worth doing unless you do it well, and drive, drive, drive. And those are important values, but there's got to be some limit to those values in terms of how long and far you express them in your life. A lot of times, especially for men in our culture, it takes the rug being pulled out from under you to say, "Oh, okay, that's not going to work for me anymore and maybe there are some more important things in life." Does that make sense?

C: Yeah, sure, that makes a lot of sense, because the depression has definitely made me focus on my quality of life. Before it was, well, every day this is what I'm going to do, boom, boom, boom. Now it's, how can I accomplish this and then also get this accomplished, with regard to some of the personal things in my life and that type of thing. It's like a gift from God, a chance to focus my life differently.

Commentary

Together, the client and therapist explored several possible causes of his depression (i.e., the deaths, inability to have a child, the overtime, a mid-life crisis, the new supervisor, and low self-esteem). When these explanations fell short, the therapist offered a new "cause" for Bob's depression, suggesting that it was just what he needed in order to help him begin to reevaluate his life. As the dialogue illustrates, Bob responded with strong agreement, personalizing the "cause" by positing divine inspiration for the depression.

The "cause" suggested by the therapist emerged from the

conversation with Bob and was an attempt to pull together several important elements of his presentation — in particular, his successes, his contemplative style, his recent reevaluation of life, and his search for the "real" cause of his depression. In the final analysis, the procedure worked because it reflected these elements, *not* because it was clever reframe. Bob simply got what he was asking for from therapy — a good reason for having been depressed.

A break occurred at this point, during which the therapist consulted with the team behind the one-way mirror. After a few minutes, the therapist returned with the team's input. Basically, the feedback highlights the client's strengths as discovered in the interview and, given the client's verbal endorsement of the proposed cause, reiterates the conclusions that emerged from the interview.

EXCERPT SIX: TEAM FEEDBACK
AND CONCLUSIONS

T: One of the hardest things of my life is bringing therapists to a close when they're discussing things. They're a bunch of long-winded folks. There was a lot of consensus, which says a lot about your presentation, which was very clear. We did arrive at three things that we want to say to you as a team. One thing, the team was very impressed with your insightfulness about all of this.

C: Thank you. I appreciate that.

T: You obviously have given it a lot of deep and considered thought. And that really showed. You have a lot of insight into this whole experience. They were very impressed by that and they wanted me to tell you, that because, of course, a lot of people aren't that way. The team was also very impressed with all the things you have done to address this depression problem. There are at least half a dozen things that you have done and are doing—taking an antidepressant, seeing a therapist, losing weight, getting involved in an activity in the morning, thinking more toward taking time off, just to mention some. All these things that you are doing to address this problem are really impressive, so you've been not only insightful but also action-oriented in looking at your life and making changes. And that was also really impressive. I was also quite amazed, and that was shared by the team, that you've been able to do so much. Frankly, they really wanted me to tell you to *do all you're doing because it's working*. It's obviously working. You're not all the way where you want to be, but you're on the road there and that's really quite apparent. And the only thing along with "keep doing what you're doing" is they wanted to suggest that you consider slowing down a little bit, not stopping, or not cutting back on all those things, but slowing down. This is a long-term life change kind of an issue or set of issues that you are dealing with. They are not the kinds of things that you put a check mark on your appointment book about. They're wholesale life changes, addressing basic core assumptions about life that you're struggling with, and that's not an overnight process. That's something that's going to be done over time, with consideration, especially given the meaning of it all. If—and it makes a lot of sense to me, and it made a lot of sense to the team—what we talked about earlier in terms of it being a message to you or even a gift from God for you to reevaluate your life, allow it to unfold for yourself. If, indeed, it is such a gift or serving that function for you, contemplate that and give it consideration because it's an important thing that has happened to you. Maybe something to consider is to go slow and appreciate that aspect of it, if you're following me there.

C: I think so. In other words, don't be so depressed that it's not working as quickly as you want it to work because the depression is there for a good reason.

T: Yes, yes, exactly, and that reason is working. It's providing something for you that you indeed are taking great advantage. And of course, it *is* serving you well in a lot of ways, although that's an odd way of looking at something negative like depression, but it also is serving a very positive function. So those were the messages they wanted me to convey to you. You can pick up with Dr. T. from there and I appreciate your courage in subjecting yourself to this process.

C: I found it was a bit intriguing and very helpful.

T: Well, your willingness to try different things is certainly to your credit and I think speaks well to your ability to handle it all. You're on the right road. I certainly enjoyed talking to you.

C: I appreciate it very much. Thank you.

Commentary

Dr. T., Bob's therapist, was surprised by the many strengths and successes that Bob reported in the visit. He was particularly struck by the fact that Bob believed progress had been made given that both he and Bob had talked about feeling stuck. In this regard, the critical factor was being change-focused—that is, actively listening for and then amplifying the client's report of differences, change, or improvement. Dr. T. reported that many of the same issues had been discussed in the sessions he had with Bob and noted how the style of conversation in the consultation helped Bob acknowledge the ability he had to influence his feelings.

The follow-up session to the consultation interview turned out to be the last meeting. Bob had taken charge of his life and the depression. In the session, he discussed at length what the depression had been teaching him about his life. He intimated that the depression allowed him to reexamine what he wanted to do with his vocational and personal life. He attributed most of the refocusing to God, saying that the more he thought about it the more the whole thing felt like God's will. Another session was scheduled but later canceled by Bob because he felt that further treatment was not necessary. A follow-up call six months later found the client feeling much improved—not perfect—but off antidepressant medication and continuing to work on aspects of his life that his "gift from God" had helped him identify.

Discussion

Client factors

The case of Bob illustrates the differential impact of the four factors comprising the unifying language for change. Client factors speak to clients' inherent resources and abilities to exploit chance events as opportunities for change. The consultation with Bob, while carefully attending to his distress and goals for therapy, focused on his progress and was directed toward his accomplishments. Bob's resources were central to success.

Relationship/alliance factors

Relationship factors provide the interpersonal context for successful therapy, as well as the foundation for any intervention. Bob felt understood and his struggles were considered important. The topics that Bob indicated as relevant were respected and explored, and Bob's goals were addressed both in the course of the interview and in the intervention itself.

Intervention is effective to the extent that it is based in a strong alliance and validates the client. The "gift" aspects of

Bob's depression flowed from an interview that accommodated Bob's expectations. The explanation that was offered relied on Bob's accomplishments, validated his struggles, and answered his question about the depression.

Placebo factors

Last place in terms of significance to outcome is shared by placebo and specific technique factors. Placebo effects include improvement that results from the client's awareness of participating in a healing ritual as well as the hope that is inspired when the therapist engages in activities that increase the client's expectation of a favorable outcome. The consulting therapist believed in Bob's abilities, repeatedly commented upon his accomplishments, and suggested the inevitability of change given Bob's multifaceted plan of attack. The consultant's and team's stated admiration encouraged hope for additional changes.

While the client's condition fit the diagnostic criteria for depression, the diagnosis had been of little help in selecting a remedy for Bob or predicting his success in treatment. The diagnosis gave a flat and colorless picture of the client; it simply did not capture the important features of his life. Knowledge of Bob's unique circumstance and goals for therapy were far more helpful in the treatment process.

Technique and treatment of choice

Because techniques account for only approximately 15% of change, they are only possibilities that may or may not prove useful in the unique circumstance of the client. The selection of technique, therefore, must go beyond the mere prescriptive matching of client problems with so-called treatments of choice. Viewing "treatments of choice" as possibilities allows the selection of a particular technique on the basis of its fit with the client—that is, fit with the client's resources, the therapist's style, the relationship with the client, and the client's belief in the helpfulness of the technique.

Bob had already been given the so-called treatments of choice for depression (i.e., antidepressant medication and cognitive-behavioral treatment). Although the drug had helped, Bob did not believe he had a biochemical imbalance and actually wanted to be off of antidepressants. In addition, the cognitive-behavioral therapy he had received had not addressed his primary concern. The techniques employed in this case primarily highlighted his strengths and successes and addressed his major concern. The role of techniques and models in a unifying language is considered in detail in the next chapter.

CONCLUSIONS

This case illustrates the unifying language for psychotherapy: client, relationship, placebo, and technique factors. The success here came about through a proactive dependence on client strengths, respect for the client's perceptions of the alliance, and an abiding faith in both the client and his direction.

7 STRUCTURE AND NOVELTY

The Role of Models and Techniques in Psychotherapy Outcome

>Each therapist eventually evolves his own therapeutic method, which is a composite of the methods he has learned, the experiences he has had, and his specific personality traits.
>
>*Lewis Wolberg, 1977, p. 973*

>Schools of care constitute cultures. . . . Each culture of healing provides its practitioners with ideas that relieve our anxious recognition of our ignorance and helplessness in the face of the sufferings of patients.
>
>*Robert Fancher, 1995, pp. 30–31*

B Y NOW, it is probably clear that the importance of models and techniques has been inflated in psychotherapy. The loud and historically incessant fanfare about their virtues obviously is ill-deserved or, pending new research establishing their peremptory worth, at least premature. Even so, their contribution to therapeutic outcome cannot be denied. Recall that the outcome literature suggests that as much as 15% of the variance is attributable to these two elements (Lambert, 1992). For this reason, every therapist should be familiar with and have the ability to use a number of treatment models and techniques.

Given that the research has so consistently demonstrated that the various therapeutic approaches achieve roughly equivalent outcomes, however, one might ask what role models and techniques should play in a therapy informed by a unifying language. How exactly should they be viewed when so much of the variance is controlled by other factors — 85% to be exact (40% extratherapeutic factors, 30% relationship factors, and 15% placebo factors)? The present chapter seeks to answer these questions.

MODELS AND
TECHNIQUES AS PRACTICE

When finger point at moon, don't look at finger or you'll miss the moon.

Bruce Lee, Enter the Dragon

On one of his many trips abroad, anthropologist/philosopher Gregory Bateson observed the members of a Japanese family displaying respect toward the father (Simon, 1996). Bateson noticed that the daughters, in particular, seemed to go to great lengths to demonstrate their high regard for him by bowing and generally showing excitement on his return home from work. Ever the anthropologist, Bateson sought out one of the daughters in order to find out why she and her sister had so much respect for their father. Contrary to what he expected to hear, however, the daughter informed him that she and her sister did *not* respect their father. Rather, she said, "We *practice* showing him respect so that if we ever meet anyone we really respect we will know how to show it" (Simon, 1996, p. 53).

This story hints at an answer to the question about the role of models and techniques. When guided by a unifying language, therapeutic technique ceases being a reflection of a particular theoretical doctrine or school (e.g., dynamic, cognitive-behavioral, solution-focused) and becomes, as Simon (1996) has suggested, "a practice which teaches *the therapist*, through naming, enactment, and talking to colleagues, the attitudes and values from which [therapeutic] work is generated" (p. 53, emphasis added; see also Fancher, 1995). In other words, just as bowing provided the two daughters in Bateson's story with a method for learning respect, models and techniques provide therapists with learnable, replicable, and structured ways for developing/practicing the values, attitudes, and behaviors consistent with the core ingredients of effective psychotherapy — that is, the common factors.

Therapeutic technique provides clinicians with something akin to a magnifying glass that brings together, focuses, and concentrates the forces of change, narrows them to a point in place and time, and causes them to ignite into action. The research literature indicates that focus and structure are essential elements of effective psychotherapy. In fact, studies conducted to date suggest that one of the best predictors of negative outcome in psychotherapy is a *lack* of focus and structure (Mohl, 1995). In what some (cf. Lambert & Bergin, 1994) have described as one of the "most careful empirical investigations" ever conducted on the subject, researcher Sachs (1983) found that failure to provide a structure or focus in therapeutic sessions — an error that occurred with a surprising degree of frequency in those studied — had a greater impact on treatment outcome than the personal qualities of either the therapist or the client (Mohl, 1995).

The challenging question, given the large number of choices available, is which structure or focus the therapist should adopt when working with a particular client. To paraphrase Paul (1967) and others (Kiesler, 1966; Krumboltz, 1966), "What treatment, conducted by whom, is most effective for this individual with that specific problem and under which set of circumstances?" In this regard, at the present time the data indicate that the particular orientation or technique is actually of less importance than the degree to which that orientation or technique helps the therapist develop/practice attitudes and behaviors that are consistent with the common factors and fit with the client's world view and expectations for treatment. For example, it would obviously not be in the best interest of the client or the therapy if the model or technique that was utilized engendered a pessimistic view of people or required a protracted dependence on the therapist. Neither would it be helpful if the approach somehow managed to erode the esteem or self-efficacy of the client or conflicted with the client's personal values or religious beliefs. Surprisingly, a number of treatment models and techniques exist that may unwittingly produce these very effects.

Interpreting transference interpretations

As one example of a technique that may vitiate the contribution of the common factors, consider transference interpretations. According to Henry, Strupp, Schacht, and Gaston (1994), the "transference interpretation represents the central defining technique of psychodynamic psychotherapy" (p. 469). In spite of the rising popularity of other approaches — including eclecticism — psychodynamic models continue to enjoy widespread popularity and influence (Jensen, Bergin, & Greaves, 1990). Within the various psychodynamic approaches, transference interpretations have a long and rich tradition. Historically, much trust was placed in their mutative power. Research to substantiate the special effects of this sort of intervention has been long in coming and now that data are amassing — particularly in the last decade — a different picture emerges.

In the most recent edition of the *Handbook of Psychotherapy and Behavior Change*, Henry et al. (1994) review the extant empirical literature on the actual performance of transference interpretations in psychodynamic therapy. Contrary to the often favorable and celebrated reports appearing in case descriptions and clinical summaries, research results show that the use of transference interpretations may actually damage the therapeutic alliance and do not, as has traditionally been assumed, repair already poor alliances. Transference interpretations, even when followed by an emotional response by the client, do not possess any unique therapeutic effect. Moreover, this sort of interpretation is apt to arouse more defensive responding from the client than other types of interventions. Although a defensive response is accommodated, even predicted, by psychodynamic theory, whatever benefit is achieved by the interpretation must be balanced against other research findings demonstrating that defensive responding is linked to poorer therapeutic outcomes (Henry et al., 1994, pp. 475–477).

Regardless of the motivation or intent of the therapist, the problem with transference interpretations is that their root content is predicated on certain critical assumptions about clients' psychology and the human condition that run counter to the common factors. As Wile (1984) describes it:

> Clients are seen as gratifying infantile impulses, being defensive, having developmental defects, and resisting the therapy. Therapists who conceptualize people in these ways may have a hard time making interpretations that do not communicate at least some element of this pejorative view. (p. 353)

It is not difficult to see how clients would object to reductionistic remarks that attack and undermine a self already enfeebled and probably, in part, prompted the original request for therapy.

This is not to say that for some clients at some time transference interpretations may not prove useful. Indeed, existing research suggests that the ideal conditions for productive transference interpretation "appear to be accurate interpretations (however defined) delivered with relatively low frequency to more highly functioning patients" (Henry et al.,

1994, p. 476). It should also be added here that the highly functioning patients would also need to agree with the world view promoted by the particular psychodynamic theory presupposed in the interpretation's content. That is, if the client subscribes to the belief that people are motivated by infantile or instinctual impulses, interpretations or explanations with that thesis would then be plausible and potentially therapeutic.

Confronting confrontation

Another popular and widely used therapeutic technique is confrontation. Indeed, according to Matuschka (1985), this technique is "part of *every* psychotherapeutic relationship" (p. 195, emphasis added). Confrontation is usually defined as pointing out double messages, discrepancies, or incongruities between or among the client's thoughts, attitudes, behaviors, and even "body language" (see Egan, 1975; Evans, Hearn, Uhlemann, & Ivey, 1979; Ivey & Simek-Downing, 1980). As Ivey and Gluckstern (1976) write, "In a confrontation individuals are faced directly with the fact that they may be saying other than that which they mean, or doing other than that which they say" (p. 46).

Most of the major schools of therapy pay special attention to inconsistencies and discrepancies because those inconsistencies and discrepancies are thought to reflect the very traits, defense mechanisms, or intentional misrepresentations that stand in the way of therapeutic change (Ivey & Gluckstern, 1976). This is particularly evident, for example, in the field of drug and alcohol treatment, where for the last several decades treatment has been virtually synonymous with confrontation. Based on a view of clients as "resistant," "unmotivated," and "in denial," well-known and popular advocates of this approach have taught that "Victims of the disease do not submit to treatment. . . . They [must be] forced to seek help" (Johnson, 1973, p. 1).

Here again, however, research to substantiate the special effects of this sort of intervention—in the treatment of clients with drug and alcohol problems, as well as clients in general—has been long in coming. And, once again, now that the data are amassing, a different picture emerges. Consider one representative study conducted by Miller, Benefield, and Tonigan (1993) on the treatment of clients with drug and alcohol problems. In this study, the researchers found that a directive-confrontational style resulted in significantly more resistance from clients, poorer treatment outcomes, and more client drinking (when measured at one-year follow-up) than a supportive-reflective therapeutic style. Other researchers have found that confrontive approaches may actually harm those who are in the greatest need of help. Consider, for instance, a study by Annis (1979) that found that participation in confrontational group therapy caused clients with a negative self-image to be worse at the conclusion of the treatment than subjects who received no treatment at all! While clients high in self-esteem did slightly better than the control subjects in this study, one is left to wonder how much better they might have done had they *not* been subjected to the treatment procedure in the first place.

Such findings are not limited to therapeutic work with clients who have drug and alcohol problems. For example, using cluster analysis, Elliot (1985) created a taxonomy of helpful and nonhelpful events occurring in psychotherapy. Not surprisingly, the most common helpful interpersonal event was the clients' feeling that the therapist either understood or was sympathetic to their situation or difficulty. The most nonhelpful events identified in the study were those in which the client felt misunderstood, inaccurately perceived, criticized, or pressured by the therapist. Depending on the particular study, anywhere from 25% to 40% of total outcome variance is accounted for by factors that make up a supportive-reflective, client-directed approach to treatment (Duncan & Moynihan, 1994; Patterson, 1984). And yet, each time a new approach enters the therapy model market-place—especially when applied to a controversial or politically charged client population—confrontation is often considered the treatment of choice. Witness the recent rise of highly confrontational treatment approaches aimed at perpetrators of domestic violence or sexual abuse.

Confrontation suffers from the same problem as transference interpretations; that is, the technique is based on assumptions inconsistent with the common factors. It is hard to imagine, for example, how a therapist who views clients as "victims of a disease [who must be] forced to seek help" could foster a strong therapeutic alliance, work collaboratively with clients, or facilitate hope and a positive expectation for change. Less dramatic, but equally difficult to imagine, is how a therapist who believes that clients contain personality traits and underlying defense mechanisms that cause them to conceal important information or communicate in incongruent ways would not communicate at least some of those pejorative beliefs to clients.

Arguing that confrontation, transference interpretations—or any model or technique for that matter—could be executed in a manner consistent with a supportive-reflective style misses the point. Techniques do *not* cause change. As Kiesler (1995) points out, "techniques . . . do not specify the essential components among the relatively complex treatment packages *nor the psychological mechanisms responsible for their respective successes*" (p. 98). Rather, models and techniques are the proverbial "finger pointing at the moon." The more a model or technique helps the therapist look in the direction of the common factors, the more helpful that model or technique will be. Focus on the finger, however, and the therapy misses the moon.

Therapists can evaluate the degree to which a particular model or technique points in a therapeutic direction by asking the following questions:

- Does the orientation or strategy fit with, support, or complement the client's world view? If so, how?
- Does the theory or intervention fit with or complement the client's expectations for treatment? How so? Can it be tailored to fit?
- Does the particular strategy capitalize on client strengths, resources, abilities? How?
- To what extent does the orientation/intervention take into account and use the client's environment and existing support network?
- Does the method identify or build on the spontaneous changes that clients experience while in therapy? How?
- To what degree does the orientation/technique identify, fit with, or build on the client's goals for therapy?
- Would the client describe the therapeutic interaction resulting from the adoption of the particular strategy or orientation as empathic, respectful, and genuine?
- How does the orientation or intervention increase the client's sense of hope, expectancy, or personal control?
- How does the method or orientation contribute to the client's sense of self-esteem, self-efficacy, and self-mastery?

Structuring the common factors is not, however, the only way that models and techniques can be useful to clinicians. In the next section, one additional use is explored.

MODELS AND
TECHNIQUES AS NOVELTY

Do not become the slave of your model.

Vincent van Gogh

> This deceptively simple formula, *more of the same*, is one
> of the most effective recipes for disaster that has gradually
> evolved on our planet. In the course of hundreds of mil-
> lions of years, it has led to the extinction of entire species.
>
> *Paul Watzlawick, 1983, p. 31*

Within the first year of his presidency, Jimmy Carter invited Anwar Sadat, the president of Egypt, and Menachem
Begin, the prime minister of Israel, to come to the United
States for a series of high-level talks aimed at fashioning a
peace agreement between the two countries (Carter, 1993).[1]
Buoyed by his recent election to the presidency and motivated
by a strong desire to prevent the bloodletting that had occurred in the last Israeli-Egyptian conflict, Carter had come
to believe that he could succeed where several previous ad-
ministrations had failed. After nearly two weeks of extraordinary diplomacy and meticulous negotiation, however, the
meetings at the secluded presidential retreat in Maryland
seemed destined to suffer the same fate as previous efforts.
Indeed, shortly after arriving at Camp David, the two Middle
Eastern leaders stopped speaking to each other and would
not even agree to meet in the same room! Discouraged, Carter began packing his bags to return to the White House. As
he was preparing to leave, however, something quite unexpected and totally unplanned occurred, which broke the
stalemate.

President Carter went to the cabin of Prime Minister Begin
to deliver some photographs of the three men that had been
taken earlier. Begin had wanted Presidents Carter and Sadat
to sign a picture for each of his eight grandchildren. According to Carter, Begin became emotional as he looked at the
pictures and read each of the personalized inscriptions. Obviously, the photographs caused him to think about the fate
of his grandchildren — and Israeli children in general — in the

---

[1]Thanks to Joe Eron for relating this story and pointing out the connection
with psychotherapy.

event of another confrontation with Egypt. He promised to look at the latest peace proposal once again. Shortly thereafter, he called and accepted the agreement.

In a quite different arena, psychiatrist Michael Balint (1968) described his treatment of a woman in her late twenties who originally sought therapy because of "an inability to do anything." After two years of regular, on the couch, object-relations-informed psychoanalytic treatment, the woman had made little progress. The real breakthrough in the treatment came only when Dr. Balint encouraged the woman to do a somersault in his office. This recommendation came on the heels of the woman's recollection that she could not do somersaults when she was a child. The woman, Dr. Balint reports, immediately "got up from the couch and, to her great amazement, did a perfect somersault without any difficulty" (p. 129). Thereafter, Balint noted marked improvements in the woman's emotional, social, and professional life.

As unrelated and different as these two stories seem, they do, in fact, illustrate an additional way that models and techniques can be useful to clinicians; that is, models and techniques provide clinicians with alternative ways of conceptualizing and conducting treatment when progress is not forthcoming. Though unplanned, it was the *change* in Carter's approach that led to resolution of the impasse between Prime Minister Begin and President Sadat. In short, he stopped doing what wasn't working—negotiating with the two leaders—and did something different. Interestingly enough, that something different—bringing the personalized photographs—capitalized on the common factor of hope and expectancy, since it caused Prime Minister Begin to begin thinking about how he wanted things to be different in the future. Doing something different was likewise at the heart of the story related by Balint—that is, he shifted from a passive-analytic style to an active-directive mode.

In years past, treatment failures were most often interpreted within the frame of reference of a particular model or theoretical school (Watzlawick, 1986).[2] The result, as has previously been pointed out, is that theoretical doctrine was preserved at the expense of the client or therapist. Clients were labeled either resistant to change or inappropriate for psychotherapy while therapists were considered inadequately trained or countertransferentially impaired. Nowadays, however, with over 400 therapy models and techniques to choose from, there is little reason for continued allegiance to a particular theoretical orientation when that way of thinking about or conducting treatment is not producing results. Instead, another model or technique can be considered. No blame need be assigned; therapists and clients can simply change their minds, go back to the smorgasbord, so to speak, and make another selection. In other words, it would seem that the different schools of therapy may be at their most helpful when they provide therapists with novel ways of looking at old situations, when they empower therapists to *change* rather than *make up* their minds about clients.

Research confirms that clients are more likely to benefit from and be satisfied with treatment when their therapists are flexible in orientation and do not try to convince them of the utility or rightness of any single approach (Kuehl, Newfield, & Joanning, 1990). This is not to say that therapists should switch orientations willy-nilly every time progress is not immediately evident; rather, we would suggest that theoretical or technical orthodoxy always be considered secondary to whether or not progress is being made. Studies indicate that this is not the case. For example, Kendall (1992) found that the majority of therapists who were treating—and

[2]In this regard, it is interesting to note that Balint seemed to have a hard time letting go of his model following the success of his client. In the pages that follow the story, he goes to great lengths to explain the improvements *within* the object-relations perspective.

who were expected to continue treating—clients who were *not* making progress had not developed any alternative plans for treatment. Lack of progress—and by implication, lack of eventual success—was, instead, attributed solely to the clients, with therapists seeing themselves and the therapy they offered as the least likely cause of treatment failure.

One way for therapists to determine that a change of mind is called for is to be, as was described in Chapter 3, more change-focused in their clinical work; that is, to be mindful of—to listen for or inquire about—any changes that the client experiences before, during, or between treatment sessions. All large-scale, meta-analytic studies of client change indicate that the most frequent improvement occurs early in treatment. Specifically, between 50 and 60% of clients experience significant symptomatic relief within one to seven visits—figures which increase to 75% after six months and 85% at one year (Howard, Kopta, Krause, & Orlinsky, 1986; Smith, Glass, & Miller, 1980; Steenbarger, 1992, 1994; Talmon, 1990; Talmon, Hoyt, & Rosenbaum, 1988). Moreover, these same data, as Orlinsky and Howard (1986) point out, "suggest a course of diminishing returns with more and more effort required to achieve just noticeable differences in patient improvement" (p. 361). In other words, as far as timing is concerned, the data indicate that therapists should consider doing something different when they fail to hear or elicit reports of progress from clients within several hours rather than months of therapy. As an example of this, consider the following brief case example.

Case Example: Some Reflections on Stuckness

Denise was a client in her mid-thirties who had been coming to regular weekly sessions for one month. Her therapist conceptualized treatment in brief therapy terms and, consistent with that approach, attempted to help Denise set small, realistic goals and identify the strengths and competencies she possessed that could be used to achieve them. In spite of the best efforts of the therapist, however, Denise was not able to specify with any degree of clarity exactly what she hoped to accomplish by being in therapy. Moreover, exploring her strengths and resources only seemed to exacerbate the depressing feelings that had originally motivated her to seek treatment. By the end of the fourth visit, both Denise and the therapist agreed that treatment was stalled and that something different needed to happen. The therapist suggested that the next session include a reflecting team — a format in which a group of therapists watch the session from behind a one-way mirror and then, after switching places with the client and therapist near the end of the hour, openly discuss their ideas, questions, and thoughts about what they have seen and heard (Andersen, 1987, 1991; Freedman & Combs, 1996). Denise agreed.

As planned, Denise and the therapist ended the next session by sitting behind the one-way mirror and listening to the team's reflections about the visit. Many questions and ideas were brought up and discussed by the team. For example, several team members brought up the possibility and/or need to augment the talk therapy with some form of biological intervention (i.e., medication). Other team members disagreed, however, suggesting instead that the strict goal orientation of the current approach might be preventing Denise from feeling heard and understood. These latter members wondered, in particular, if the treatment might be more successful if the therapist simply slowed down and listened a bit more. Still others believed that the present approach had simply not been given enough time to work and expressed concern about proceeding without clear objectives for fear of the treatment becoming interminable.

In all, the discussion lasted several minutes. Following this, Denise and the therapist resumed their positions in front of the one-way mirror to process the team's discussion. As the following dialogue illustrates, Denise's own reflections helped the therapist change his mind about the best way to approach the treatment:

T: Well, what do you think?

C: (*firmly*) I know I don't want to take medication.

T: (*nodding*) You do.

C: Yeah, I don't want to take pills.

T: Okay, so . . .

C: I just, I just want to *talk*.

T: I was wondering about that, if, you know, because we've mostly focused, talked about *goals* and I was wondering, after listening to the team, if maybe I haven't been listening and if I should set that aside and just talk.

C: (*nodding*)

T: That would be more helpful.

C: (*nodding*) Yeah, and I mean, there's nothing specific, no secret, you know, that I like *have* to say.

T: Okay, more like just talking.

C: Mmm huh, and I don't agree that it will take forever either.

T: Okay, you don't.

C: No.

T: (*laughing*) Okay, I guess I agree, 'cause, um, what will take forever is continuing to do more of this same stuff that isn't helping. That will take forever.

Denise and the therapist continued to talk for a few more minutes about both the team discussion and the direction of future treatment. In the sessions that followed, the therapist utilized a client-centered approach to guide him in adopting the attitude and behaviors that Denise (and the several members of the team) thought would be helpful (Rogers, 1951).

CONCLUSION

Whether switching from passive to active, intrapsychic to interpersonal, individual to interactional, therapists can still utilize the unifying language as a guide to choosing alternative treatment approaches. In this regard, orientations that help the therapist adopt a different way of identifying or approaching the client's goals, establishing a better match with the client's motivational level or stage of change, capitalizing on chance events, or utilizing or becoming aware of external factors or environmental supports are likely to prove the most beneficial in resolving a treatment impasse. In the next chapter, a detailed example of using the unifying language as a guide to changing treatment approaches is offered.

8 GETTING A LIFE

A Case Example

> Therapist: So, how are you doing?
>
> Client: I feel pretty good today because I knew I was going to come down and see you.

IN CHAPTER 6, a case was presented that fell together rather quickly when guided by a unifying language. As a way of illustrating some of points made in the last chapter regarding models and techniques, the present chapter discusses a case from the other end of the continuum—a case that is not resolved quickly, smoothly, or completely. Instead, the client's goals evolve throughout the process and differing technical orientations are adopted in order to provide new directions to prevent the treatment from floundering. This case illustrates how a unifying language holds the therapy together through the ebb and flow of therapeutic process and, at times, tragic circumstances of the client.

THE CLIENT

Dottie is a 46-year-old woman of European descent referred to treatment by a psychologist on the rehabilitation unit where Dottie's mother received treatment following a stroke. The psychologist made the referral because Dottie engages in a number of highly repetitive rituals. A treatment team observes from behind a one-way mirror while the therapist and Dottie explore the rituals that Dottie feels compelled to engage in — rituals that consist, for the most part, of repetitively washing her hands between household chores and checking and rechecking nearly everything she does until she is exhausted.

SESSION ONE: THE BROKEN RECORD

Client: I'm obsessive-compulsive. It's awful, it's overwhelming, it makes the smallest little thing that anybody else does without thinking about it, like washing dishes, or mailing a letter, or writing out a check, or washing their hair, or taking a bath, or cleaning their shoes, an ordeal. Everything's stupid, but I can't help it. I take it out on myself, and I say, "Dottie, you stupid blankity, blankity, blank, blank, blank." I drive myself nuts!

Therapist: Sounds incredibly frustrating, just terrible agony for you. Everything becomes a major production.

C: I describe it as a broken record. My brain will go so far, and then it hits the crack, and the needle comes all the way back to here, and I go so far, and I hit the crack. It takes me half the day to do anything, like even getting ready to come here. I see a psychiatrist, Dr. R. He's a doll. But he never takes me seriously. I think that he thinks I make all this up. Yeah, he kind of laughs at me, and says, "Dottie, I don't know what we're going to do with you." I don't think he ever took me seriously. Now he just gives me medication.

In the opening moments of the first session, Dottie reveals her feeling that the previous therapist did not take her or her problem seriously. Whether her assessment matches the previous therapist's or not matters little at this point in time. Rather, as indicated in Chapter 4, what is critical is accommodating the current treatment to the client's view of a helpful therapeutic relationship. In this regard, the therapist accepts Dottie's statement at face value and makes a concerted effort to communicate concern about the rituals and the pain they cause. To do otherwise would, as it had in the previous treatment, prevent the formation of a therapeutic alliance.

The therapist becomes more and more change-focused as the session continues to unfold. Several periods of time are uncovered during which no compulsive behavior occurred. For example, the therapist learns that Dottie did not engage in any hand-washing or other ritualized behaviors when her mother first had the stroke. Neither does she experience the compulsions when she is engaged in doing something for the first time. When pushed for details about these periods of success, however, Dottie has difficulty explaining the difference between the times when the rituals do and do not occur.

By the end of the hour, Dottie and the therapist have agreed on the goal for treatment: to be completely rid of the rituals. The therapist gives a future-oriented homework assignment to Dottie—specifically, to think about how her life will be different once the rituals have stopped—and schedules an appointment for the following week.

T: One thing that really strikes us is that you have been in a very frustrating and depressing situation, because of the compulsive behavior, for a long, long time, and frankly we're amazed that you're doing as well as you are. You made it clear the agonizing process you have to go through to get ready to leave the house, so you're quite a trooper to be able to pull it together to even come here.

C: Well, thank you, I take that as a compliment. (*laughs*) Thank you.

T: We were wondering if, for next time, you might give some thought to what will be different in your life once these rituals *are* gone?

C: That's an interesting thought, because I have never once thought how it would be different. I thought I wish I could just clean this room the way other people do, I, but I never thought about what it would actually be like if I did it.

SESSION TWO: A QUESTION OF HOPE

When Dottie returned the following week, she began the session by reporting that she had been able, on two separate occasions, to accomplish some activities without performing her rituals. Thereafter, most of the session was spent investigating how these changes had occurred and, as discussed in Chapter 3, helping potentiate their recurrence by "blaming" them on Dottie's hard work. She explained her role in the following way:

C: Every morning I have asked myself, "Now, what is today going to be like if I don't go through all my rituals?" And, a couple of times, I can't tell you why, I've been pretty good. I've been better than I can remember being for years. I can't explain why, but there were a couple of times when I just went and did something like anybody else would've. That question must have hit a button somewhere, because it helped. I felt hopeful. It helped a couple of times, and there hasn't even been help a couple of times in the past. And thinking about that in the mornings, gives me a sense of weight lifted off. There were a couple of times when I didn't do the washing of my hands in between the jobs. So, for me, just not washing my hands was entirely different. All those times I talked to Dr. R., he never helped me as much as you guys. Because never, in my life, had it occurred to me to wonder how my day would be if I wasn't like that. You made me turn it into the present. And I appreciate this, very much.

According to Dottie, the future-oriented homework assignment helped orient her away from both the past and the burden of the rituals and toward life she wanted to lead in the present and future. Given the success of the assignment, Dottie was asked to continue thinking about how her life would be different if she didn't engage in any rituals.

SESSIONS THREE AND FOUR

Session three continued in much the same vein. The focus of the treatment remained on the rituals and Dottie continued to make slow but consistent progress. In the fourth session, however, things began to change. Dottie returned expressing a strong desire to talk about her mother.

C: I want to talk about something different today, if we may.

T: Okay.

C: I'm not doing well at all. I had one of those days when, my stomach is just churning. It's about my Mom — I can hardly stand being around her.

T: Okay.

C: I'm an only child, and she has always controlled me with her guilt and demands. She did Dad the same way. And I have always let her control me. I can never get her approval, no matter what I do. I know I'm as much at fault for letting her get away with it. I do what she wants because it's just easier, because if you don't it's just constant nagging. She controls and criticizes me constantly. She always has. She especially criticizes me about the rituals. I'm really bitter, and I'm really angry, and I'm really resentful. And this is the worst that I have felt about her and my relationship and situation. I feel trapped. I just feel like some poor little raccoon in a leg-hold trap, that I want to chew my own leg off to get away. This last two weeks, I wasn't able to do anything, I made no improvement. My mother just drives me nuts. But if you ever see her, you're gonna say, "How could Dottie say that?" Because here's this tiny little 83-year-old lady, with silvery white hair, and little, rosy cheeks, and these little hands with arthritis in them.

T: It makes her all the more powerful, a master manipulator.

C: I think you hit the nail on the head.

As the dialogue illustrates, Dottie broadened the therapeutic conversation to include her relationship with her mother. She shared her frustration and resentment about never being able to please her mother as well as the control her mother seemed to have over her. These feelings were validated by the therapist and Dottie was encouraged to elaborate further. Years of bitterness then flooded into the session. In the process, the client voiced the idea that her mother's perpetual dissatisfaction and demands for perfection might be at the core of her compulsive behavior. Dottie had, in fact, introduced the idea about her mother in the first session. However, for whatever reason, it was not heard and the result was a narrow view of her goals and a sole focus on changing the compulsive behaviors. In a way, Dottie rescued the team from a stilted approach when she brought up her mother again.

Here is what Dottie said about her mother in the first session:

C: I don't know if it goes back to my mother always wanting me to win, always pushing me, always demanding perfection. She wanted me to be the valedictorian, but there were two of us, we were co-valedictorians. I was the happiest girl in the world because we both ended up with a 4.0, and I was so happy that there were two of us, that I was not

the valedictorian and somebody else was salutatorian. My
mother made my life miserable because I wasn't first and
the only first. And I can still to this day remember how
happy I was, actually disappointing her.

SESSION FIVE AND SIX

In the next session, time was taken to address Dottie's
feelings of being controlled by her mother. A variety of strategies was explored for dealing with her mother. In each case,
the suggestions that were offered depended on the client's
resources and previous successes, addressed her goal of feeling less controlled by her mother, and were formulated
jointly with Dottie. Despite this, Dottie returned for her sixth
session having not followed through with any of the ideas.

C: I couldn't do it. That's how ingrained I am. I tried but my
   stomach turned. I absolutely didn't have it in me to do
   anything. I had such high hopes when I left here but when
   it came down to it. . . . It seemed like I could and even
   seemed like it would be fun, but yet I couldn't do it.

T: Do you have any ideas why?

C: I think that it is so ingrained in me to please her. I felt I
   had no choice but to do what I was told. It's just like being
   five instead of forty-six. You know, it's dumb.

T: I don't think it is dumb. It is the way things have been in
   your house for the last forty-six years; it's a hard pattern
   to break out of. Perhaps the ideas considered were too big,
   too much defying your mother and risking her disap-
   proval.

Dottie conveys her disappointment at not being able to
follow through with the ideas that were generated in the
previous session. The therapist normalizes her view of it as

dumb and validates the hardship in changing such a long-standing pattern. At the break, noting her disappointment and feeling disappointed themselves, the team and therapist discuss the possibility of adopting a different theory to think about and offer alternative directions for the case. So far, the biologically-oriented intervention of her previous therapy had not proven useful. Neither had pursuing times when the rituals did not occur or developing strategies for dealing with her mother's control in the current treatment.

The therapist and team explore a number of different theories in an attempt to change *their* minds about the case. Still staying with Dottie's presented direction regarding the relationship with her mother, the team adopts a different view of Dottie's compulsive behavior, tentatively suggesting that it may keep her from leaving her "needy" mother in the lurch.

T: You're the one who always takes the brunt for the whole thing. The team and I were thinking — and of course, we don't know for sure — these rituals may actually have served a positive purpose.

C: Hmm.

T: Yeah, in thinking about how your life would be different if you didn't have the rituals, we immediately recognized that you would probably leave your mother.

C: Huh.

T: In a way, by bearing the brunt, the pain and exhaustion of your rituals, you don't feel good about yourself and the result is, you stay. If you didn't have them, we can only guess that you would have left her a long time ago. You would be out enjoying other people your own age, socializing with other people, maybe dating. You often say how stupid this all is. We wonder if the rituals — or at least beating yourself up about them constantly — keep you sacrificing your own life to take care of your mom. That's perhaps why it was so difficult to do some of the things we talked about last week. If you start breaking the mold in any way, your needy mother would probably be threatened and maybe even turn up the heat.

C: That makes a lot of sense, but I don't want to be in that role. Gawd, that is a lot. I need to think about it.

The introduction of this different view of Dottie's situation was an attempt to help the therapist and team get unstuck, and simultaneously another way of validating the difficulty Dottie had in standing up to her mother.

SESSION SEVEN

Shortly before session seven, Dottie's mother took a turn for the worse and required emergency surgery. The result was an increase in the level of care and responsibility that Dottie had to assume for her mother. For most of the session, the therapist basically listened and provided support while the client recounted the events of the previous few days. Eventually, however, the client returned to the content of the last session.

C: She looked me straight in the eye and she said in this feeble little voice, "Well, it looks like you might finally get what you've been talking about." And, I said, "What's that, Mama?" knowing full well what was coming, and she said, "Maybe you won't have to put up with me anymore."

T: Oh, geez.

C: This could have been her last words—to leave the guilt on me. Sometimes I just feel like, oosh.

T: No wonder. With all that's happened. She is an expert at this, isn't she?

C: You are absolutely one million percent right. Nothing is easy. This woman has not gone to the bathroom for nine days so I have to give her the enema. I don't like this stuff. This mineral oil enema would not even go in. I'm squeezing that little bottle as hard as I can. You know an enema isn't even easy.

T: Oh, wow. What an ordeal.

C: Oh, it's been awful.

T: It's been a hellish time. I'm surprised you look as good as you do. Her near death, your having total care for her, plus her still being her demanding and guilt-manipulating self.

C: I'm to the point now where I can't even say when I get up in the morning how is today going to be different because at this point my rituals are practically inconsequential.

T: They are just overshadowed right now. I don't want to paint a gloomy picture, but it doesn't sound like you have much of a life right now. You're providing total nursing care for your mother and it's very frustrating. She's a handful emotionally and so demanding and then you add all the physical problems on to that and, my gosh, what an impossible situation. How can you have any life at all?

C: I don't know. What you said the last time really made me think. I guess the only conclusion that I came to was that I hate to think I'll keep sacrificing my life to make her happy. I need to let it go, let go of this baggage between my mom and me. I need to get a life! How can I do that?

T: It'll be real hard, Dottie. Until you pursue other things, every time you see your mother you'll think of your 150 thousand interactions with her. No one could put up with that day after day, week after week, month after month. No one else in the world could deal with that situation. If it continues you'll get more and more and more depressed and frustrated, and that concerns me. How much of your life do you think revolves around your mother?

C: About 98%.

T: How much do you think you need to let go of to feel better?

C: Well, I think I'm at the point where I'm hanging on by my fingernails now. I'd like to be about 85% of my life taking care of her. At this point 85% sounds good. I'll definitely work on it because I'm exhausted. But I feel better having talked with you and gotten it all off my chest because you can't, you can't go on like this. I can't go on feeling like I could just kill her all the time.

T: No. That just reflects how frustrated you are because of this situation and that you need to get some relief.

C: And quite honestly, I feel cheated.

T: Well, you *are* cheated, as the team and I said last week, you are cheated out of your life right now, and that's just not fair.

C: I think I'm finally to the point where I realize that I've got to do something. I've got to make some changes.

Dottie shares her frustrations and the therapist commiserates. As a result of the previous week's work, a different goal for therapy begins to emerge — one of "letting go" of the "baggage" with her mother and getting a life. The goal is articulated as 13% less involvement with her mother. The session reaches a crescendo when Dottie takes responsibility for needing to do something different. An assignment is given to consider what that 13% change might look like in practical terms.

SESSION EIGHT: NOT SUCH A
TERRIBLE SCOUNDREL

T: So, how are you doing?

C: Well, I don't know why exactly, but the rituals have not been as bad. They have not been as bad since the last time I was here. The last time when I was here I really felt so much better afterwards. I always feel better afterwards. But last time I really felt better after we had talked.

T: Good.

C: And we are not yelling and fighting all the time like we were the three or four weeks before I came the last time.

T: How come?

C: I think that the key was, when I said, which I had not verbalized to anybody because I was ashamed to, when I said that I really feel like I am being cheated and you said, "Well, you are." That really made me feel like, well, you know, maybe I'm not such a terrible scoundrel. I thought it was not normal to feel like I'm being cheated. But now, maybe I'm not so awful to think that I'm being cheated. That's the one thing that I just thought so much about. I just felt good after last time. I mean I felt better about *me*.

T: Great.

C: So I think maybe getting that off my mind and actually telling somebody about how frustrated I was. Getting that out and then you saying, "Well, you really are being cheated." Those are the things that stick in my mind.

T: Okay. You have been cheated out of a large part of life. There's not a lot in your life or in your world that contributes to having good self-esteem. Ninety-eight percent is with your mother and there aren't a lot of self-esteem boosters there.

C: Well, I'm gonna start doing some things to let go and get
a life. I'm going to investigate nursing homes.

Dottie reports substantial improvement since the previous
visit. She feels better about herself and accepts a far more
benign view of herself in her situation with her mother. As a
result, she is not engaging in the rituals and she is fighting
less with her mother. Her resolve "to do something different"
has carried over from the previous session and she makes it
concrete by committing to check out nursing homes.

SESSION NINE

The client returns for session nine having followed
through with the assignment she gave herself at the end of
the last visit. In the process of recounting her efforts, she
notes the occurrence of a chance event that has added fuel to
the fires of change.

C: Anyway, I've talked to social services about if Mom
would have to go into a nursing home, and all of that, so
now I just need to do some waiting.
T: Okay, so waiting for now.
C: Yeah. I also had a real high and a real low since last time.
We got an offer on some land we own in the country. I
really got a lot done. I was rushing around. I was going to
the county offices — I was even standing up straight and
walking, instead of going along with my usual hound dog
slump — and got maps and photographs. I was doing
things.
T: Wow, how did you get yourself going when you accomplished all those things?

C: 'Cause I thought something good was going to happen.

T: That the land was going to sell?

C: Yeah, and I don't want to sell that land but maybe there comes a time when you have to let go of things that you can't keep care of.

T: That's right. The land *and* your mother.

C: While that was going on, I just felt good for a change. I felt like something was going to happen. I felt there was light at the end of the tunnel. And I was doing things that I hate to do. I was doing figure work—I mean it was incredible what I did. And I cleaned the house. I don't do stuff like that. You know I have to make a big production out of everything. And for that one week, I had hopes for something new and different.

T: Okay.

C: And maybe getting out from under this rock that I feel is hanging over my head. But then, the roof fell in, the couple backed out of the deal, and I got so disappointed. But then I must have regrouped.

T: No wonder you felt so bad, you had a lot of hope riding there. But I'm also not surprised you have regrouped.

C: At the time, I realized that I felt good. I was just zipping around and acting kind of normal for a couple of weeks. You know, doing stuff. And feeling decent about things. And I did things that normally I have trouble doing. I just felt better.

T: You didn't have as much problem with the rituals.

C: Uh uh, I didn't.

T: Great! What were you hoping for had it sold? Are we talking money relief? Or what else did that mean to you?

C: Maybe the bigger picture—of not just the money—but of actually letting go, instead of trying to hang on by my fingernails. That's the bigger picture. That had not really dawned on me. I was thinking that we can pay this bill, and have a little bit of money, and we could pay this off. But, there is a bigger picture. And I had not consciously realized the bigger thing behind it until now. So that'll give me a lot to think about—about how different I felt because I'm letting go.

T: You are on the right track!

The chance circumstance of the offer on the land resulted in Dottie jumping into immediate action. She experienced what her life could be like and recognized how much better she felt. Dottie connected her improvements to the "letting go" process. The fortuitous event not only offered the opportunity for Dottie to act and feel "normal" but also fit into a framework for understanding and continuing the changes. Dottie also, once again, demonstrated her amazing resilience after the deal fell through. The session also included a discussion about muscle tension, which Dottie initiated, and the team offered relaxation possibilities. Dottie was given a progressive muscle relaxation tape to try.

SESSION TEN:
CONTINUING TO LET GO

T: So how's it going?

C: I felt better this morning when I got up than I have in a long, long time and I think that it might be for a couple of reasons. You know you gave me the tape four weeks ago today, and I started playing it. And now, I've gotten it so I can relax everything. Last night it really felt good. And I just thought so much about how good I felt about thinking I was going to let go of something. I've tried to do that in little ways because apparently I can't do anything in a big way. I have to do it in a little way. To me it's a big way, but to somebody else, it is nothing, and then I'm starting to say, "But I'm not so and so and who cares what so and so would do!"

T: Great!

C: One example of me starting to get a life was that my cousin Shelley and I went out last Tuesday night a week ago. We went out for dinner and we got yogurt and we had such a pleasant evening, just talking. I've also been throwing stuff away, a kind of letting go. When I let go my rituals are better.

T: Great. We really encourage you to keep on your current path. Keep doing the relaxation. Also it seems that letting go is very important, especially given how great you felt when you were involved with selling the land, so continue to pay attention to small ways of letting go and getting a life.

C: Okay, you guys will never know how many times in the course of a day your names are in my head. Every little thing is a little victory for me — not comparing to anybody else — and I think you would be proud of me for this.

DISCUSSION

No further sessions took place with Dottie. The distance to the clinic combined with the increasing care for her mother ultimately prevented further treatment. Long-term telephone follow-up revealed, however, that Dottie was continuing to care for her mother and struggle to "let go." She did report having times that were very good in which she did positive things away from her mother. During these times, she noted that the rituals diminished. Dottie also reported that she experienced low points in which she felt overwhelmed and the rituals were "especially bad."

The unifying language can be used to make sense of the treatment that occurred with Dottie. First, the extratherapeutic factors: throughout treatment, Dottie was viewed as capable and resourceful. The team and therapist depended on her resourcefulness and made every effort to encourage her active participation in treatment. The chance event of the potential sale of the land helped Dottie to experience that she could have a life outside of her mother; although it did not turn out well, it gave her hope about her life. This event was incorporated into the treatment and Dottie utilized it to accomplish things she previously perceived as impossible.

Relationship factors played a significant role throughout the sessions with Dottie. In particular, a concerted effort was made to ensure Dottie's positive evaluation of the relationship. The flexibility in this regard seemed to enhance the strength of the relationship with Dottie. The relationship was also strengthened by the continuous accommodation of the treatment to the evolving goals of the client (e.g., from reducing rituals to dealing with her mother's control, to letting go and getting a life).

Technical factors also played a role in the treatment. Elements of solution-focused, strategic, behavioral, and family systems were utilized in an attempt to fit the client's abilities, goals, and views, as well as to offer different possibilities when treatment stalled.

Epilogue

> Then they said, "Come let us build ourselves a city, and a tower with its top in the heavens, *and let us make a name for ourselves.*" The Lord came down to see the city and the tower . . . and said, " . . . Come let us go down, and confuse their language there, so that they will not understand one another's speech." So the Lord scattered them abroad. . . . Therefore it was called *Babel, because there the Lord confused the language of all the earth.*"
>
> *Genesis 11:1, 4–5, 7–9*

> When the day of Pentecost had come, they were all together in one place. All of them were filled with the Holy Spirit and began speaking in other languages, as the Spirit gave them ability. And at this sound the crowd gathered and was bewildered, *because each one heard them speaking in the native language of each.* All were amazed and perplexed. . . . But others sneered and said, "They are filled with new wine."
>
> *Acts of the Apostles 2:1,4, 6, 12–13*

IN THE preceding chapters, we have attempted to spell out a basic vocabulary for a unifying language of psychotherapy practice. We do not believe that the particular vocabulary we have offered in this volume is the only way to view or unify the various schools of practice; rather, it is one way to suggest that the time for some unifying dialogue has come. For this reason, we invite and look forward to other attempts at building bridges between the various traditions and disciplines that make up psychotherapy. The particular language that is eventually adopted or used to describe our various commonalities matters much less to us than the development of a more ecumenical spirit and direction.

Writing this book has been both a personal and professional journey—as much an attempt to force us to evolve beyond the traditions in which we were steeped as it was an effort to warn the field about the consequences of continuing with business as usual. We must confess, however, that a sense of loss has accompanied our evolution in the direction of the common factors. While writing, there were many times that we caught ourselves looking back longingly to the promise of the models that first captured our personal and professional interest. Moreover, we are still tempted by ads promising to teach us a new and improved psychotherapy that will do what forty years of outcome research virtually guarantees it cannot (e.g., vanquish the unknown and provide faster, more enduring therapeutic results). At present, we have chosen to understand the temptation to respond to such promises as evidence of hope: that is, hope in the possibility of helping others solve their problems and relieve their suffering—the very hope that leads most therapists to enter the profession in the first place but that somewhere along the way is displaced onto models and techniques.

Bibliography

Acierno, R., & Hersen, M. (1994). Review of the validation and dissemination of eye-movement desensitation and reprocessing: A scientific and ethical dilemma. *Clinical Psychology Review, 14*, 287–299.

Adler, A. (1963). *The practice and theory of individual psychology.* Paterson, NJ: Littlefield, Adams.

Adler, A. (1964). *Problems of neurosis.* New York: Harper & Row.

Alcoholics Anonymous World Wide Services, Inc. (1977). *Alcoholics Anonymous* (3rd ed.). New York: Author.

Allport, G. (1964). Mental health: A generic attitude. *Journal of Religion and Health, 4*, 7–21.

American Psychiatric Association (1994). *Diagnostic and statistical manual of mental disorders.* Washington, DC: American Psychiatric Association.

Andersen, T. (1987). The reflecting team: Dialogue and meta-dialogue in clinical work. *Family Process, 26*, 415–428.

Andersen, T. (Ed.) (1991). *The reflecting team: Dialogue and dialogues about dialogues.* New York: Norton.

Andreas, C. R., & Andreas, S. (1990). Briefer than brief. *Family Therapy Networker, 14*(2), 36–42.

Annis, H. M. (1979). Group treatment of incarcerated offenders with alcohol and drug problems. *Canadian Journal of Criminology, 21*, 3–15.

Ansbacher, H., & Ansbacher, R. (1956). *The individual psychology of Alfred Adler.* New York: Basic.

Bachelor, A. (1988). How clients perceive therapist empathy. *Psychotherapy, 25*, 227–240.

Bachelor, A. (1991). Comparison and relationship to outcome of diverse dimensions of the helping alliance as seen by client and therapist. *Psychotherapy, 28*, 534–549.

Balint, M. (1968). *The basic fault.* London: Tavistock.

Bandura, A. (1977). Self-efficacy: Toward a unifying theory of behavior change. *Psychological Review, 84*, 191–215.

Bandura, A. (1986). *Social foundations of thought and action.* Englewood Cliffs, NJ: Prentice-Hall.

Bandura, A., & Schunk, D. H. (1981). Cultivating competence, self-efficacy, and intrinsic interest through proximal self-motivation. *Journal of Personality and Social Psychology, 41*, 586–598.

Barlow, D. (1988). *Anxiety and its disorders.* New York: Guilford.

Barlow, D., & Wolfe, B. (1981). Behavioral approaches to anxiety disorders. *Journal of Consulting and Clinical Psychology, 49*, 448–454.

Berg, I. K., & Miller, S. D. (1992). *Working with the problem drinker: A solution-focused approach.* New York: Norton.

Bergin, A. E. (1971). The evaluation of therapeutic outcomes. In A. E. Bergin & S. L. Garfield (Eds.), *Handbook of psychotherapy and behavior change: An empirical analysis.* New York: Wiley.

Berkman, A. S., Bassos, C. A., & Post, L. (1988). Managed mental health care and independent practice: A challenge to psychology. *Psychotherapy, 25*, 434–440.

Berman, J. S., & Norton, N. C. (1985). Does professional training make a therapist more effective? *Psychological Bulletin, 98*, 401–406.

Beutler, L. E. (1989). The misplaced role of theory in psychotherapy integration. *Journal of Integrative and Eclectic Psychotherapy, 8*, 17–22.

Beutler, L. E., Machado, P. P., & Neufeldt, S. A. (1994). Therapist variables. In A. E. Bergin & S. L. Garfield (Eds.), *Handbook of Psychotherapy and Behavior Change* (4th ed.). New York: Wiley.

Beyebach, M., Morejon, A. R., Palenzuela, D. L., & Rodriguez-Aris, J. L. (1996). Reserach on the process of solution-focused therapy. In S. D. Miller, M. A. Hubble, & B. L. Duncan, (Eds.), *Handbook of solution-focused brief therapy.* San Francisco: Jossey-Bass.

Boedecker, A. L. (1994). We have allowed therapy to grow unchecked, unregulated. *The National Psychologist, 3*(3), 14.

Bohart, A. & Tallman, K. (1996). The active client: Therapy as self-help. *Journal of Humanistic Psychology, 36*, 7–30.

Booth (1948). Psychodynamics in parkinsonism. *Psychosomatic Medicine, 10*, 1–14.

Bower, B. (1995). EMDR: Promise and dissent. *Science News, 148*(17), 270, 272.

Brandon, D. (1976). *Zen in the art of helping.* London, England: Arkana.

Butler, S. F., & Strupp, H. H. (1986). Specific and nonspecific factors in psychotherapy: A problematic paradigm for psychotherapy research. *Psychotherapy, 23*, 30–40.

Butler, W., & Powers, K. (1996). Solution-focused grief therapy. In S. D. Miller, M. A. Hubble, & B. L. Duncan (Eds.), *Handbook of solution-focused brief therapy*. San Francisco: Jossey-Bass.

Cannon, W. B. (1942). "Voodoo" death. *American Anthropologist, 44*(2), 169–181.

Carlinsky, J. (1994). Epigones of orgonomy. *Skeptic, 2*(3), 90–92.

Carter, J. (1993). *Talking peace: A vision for the next generation*. New York: Dutton Children's Books.

Chambless, D. L. (June, 1996). Identification of empirically supported psychological interventions. *Clinician's Research Digest (Supplemental Bulletin), 14*(6), 1–2.

Chang, J., & Phillips, M. (1993). Michael White and Steve de Shazer: New directions in family therapy. In S. Gilligan & R. Price (Eds.), *Therapeutic conversations*. New York: Norton.

Christensen, A., & Jacobson, N. (1994). Who (or what) can do psychotherapy: The status and challenge of nonprofessional therapies. *Psychological Science, 5*(1), 8–14.

Clement, P. W. (1994). Quantitative evaluation of 26 years of private practice. *Professional Psychology: Research and Practice, 25*(2), 173–176.

Clinicians Research Digest (July, 1994). How effective are marital and family therapies? *12*(7), 1.

Cohen, P., & Cohen, J. (1984). The clinician's illusion. *Archives of General Psychiatry, 41*, 1178–1182.

Coyne, J. (1982). Undressing the fashionable mind. *Family Process, 21*, 391–396.

Covey, S. R. (1989). *The 7 habits of highly effective people*. New York: Simon and Schuster.

Coyne, J. (1994). The rush to be brief [Letter to the editor]. *Family Therapy Networker, 18*(5), 8.

Cross, D. G., Sheehan, P. W., & Kahn, J. A. (1980). Alternative advice and counseling psychotherapy. *Journal of Consulting and Clinical Psychology, 48*, 615–625.

Cummings, N. A. (1986). The dismantling of our health system: Strategies for the survival of psychological practice. *American Psychologist, 41*(4), 426–431.

Dawes, R. M. (1994). *House of cards: Psychology and psychotherapy built on myth*. New York: Free Press.

de Shazer, S. (1988). *Clues: Investigating solutions in brief therapy*. New York: Norton.

de Shazer, S. (1991). *Putting difference to work*. New York: Norton.

de Shazer, S. (1993). Commentary: de Shazer & White: Vive la difference. In S. Gilligan & R. Price (Eds.), *Therapeutic conversations*. New York: Norton.

de Shazer, S. (July 15, 1994). Presentation at Therapeutic Conversations Conference II. Washington, DC.

de Shazer, S., Berg, I., Lipchik, E., Nunnally, E., Molnar, A., & Gingerich, W. (1986). Brief therapy: Focused solution development. *Family Process, 25*(2), 207–222.

Doherty, W. J., & Simmons, D. S. (January, 1995). Clinical practice patterns of marriage and family therapy: A national survey of therapists and their clients. *Journal of Marital and Family Therapy, 21*(1), 3–16.

Doherty, W. J., & Simmons, D. S. (January, 1996). Clinical practice patterns of marriage and family therapy: A national survey of therapists and their clients. *Journal of Marital and Family Therapy, 22*(1), 9–26.

Duncan, B. L. (1989). Paradoxical procedures in family therapy. In M. Ascher (Ed.), *Therapeutic paradox*. New York: Guilford.

Duncan, B. L., Hubble, M. A., & Miller, S. D. (1997). *Psychotherapy with impossible cases: Efficient treatment of therapy veterans*. New York: Norton.

Duncan, B. L., & Moynihan, D. W. (1994). Applying outcome research: Intentional utilization of the client's frame of reference. *Psychotherapy, 31*(2), 294–302.

Duncan, B. L., Solovey, A. D., & Rusk, G. S. (1992). *Changing the rules: A client-directed approach to therapy*. New York: Guilford.

Durrant, M., & Kowalski, K. (1993). Enhancing views of competence. In S. Friedman (Ed.), *The new language of change*. New York: Guilford.

Efran, J. S., & Green, M. A. (1994). Overpromised, underresearched: Where's the science in psychotherapy? *Family Therapy Networker, 18*(5), 97–102.

Egan, G. (1975). *The skilled helper*. Monterey, CA: Brooks/Cole.

Ekeland, I. (1993). *The broken dice*. Chicago: University of Chicago Press.

Elliot, R. (1985). Helpful and nonhelpful events in brief counseling: An empirical taxonomy. *Journal of Counseling Psychology, 32*(3), 307–322.

Elkin, I. (1994). The NIMH treatment of depression collaborative research program: Where we began and where we are. In A. E. Bergin & S. Garfield (Eds.), *Handbook of psychotherapy and behavior change* (4th ed.). New York: Wiley.

Evans, D. R., Hearn, M. T., Uhleman, M. R., & Ivey, A. E. (1979). *Essential interviewing: A programmed approach to effective communication*. Monterey, CA: Brooks/Cole.

Fancher, R. (1995). *Cultures of healing*. New York: Freeman.

Ferenczi, S. (1985). In Judith Dupont (Ed.), *The clinical diary of Sandor Ferenczi*. Cambridge, MA: Harvard University Press.

Fisch, R., Weakland, J., & Segal, L. (1982). *The tactics of change*. San Francisco: Jossey-Bass.

Follette, W. (1991). Taking up the cudgel: Activism and science. (Interview with Neil S. Jacobson). *The Scientist Practitioner, 1*(4), 8–18.

Frances, A., Clarkin, J., & Perry, S. (1984). *Differential therapeutics in psychiatry: The art and science of treatment selection*. New York: Brunner/Mazel.

Frank, G. H. (1964). The effect of directive and nondirective statements by therapists on the content of patient verbalization. *Journal of General Psychology, 71*, 323–328.

Frank, J. D. (1973). *Persuasion and healing: A comparative study of psychotherapy*. Baltimore, MD: Johns Hopkins University Press.

Frank, J. D. (1976). Psychotherapy and the sense of mastery. In R. L. Spitzer & D. F. Klein (Eds.), *Evaluation of psychotherapies: Behavioral therapies, drug therapies and their interaction* (pp. 47–56). Baltimore, MD: Johns Hopkins University Press.

Frank, J. D. (1990). Foreword. In M. Talmon, *Single session therapy*. San Francisco, CA: Jossey-Bass.

Frank, J. D., & Frank, J. B. (1991). *Persuasion and healing: A comparative study of psychotherapy* (3rd ed.). Baltimore, MD: John Hopkins University Press.

Frazer, Sir James George (1920). *The golden bough*. New York: Collier.

Frederick, C., & Phillips, M. (1992). The use of hypnotic age progressions as interventions with acute psychosomatic conditions. *American Journal of Clinical Hypnosis, 35*(2), 89–98.

Freedman, J., & Combs, G. (1996). *Narrative therapy: The social construction of preferred realities*. New York: Norton.

Freud, S. (1990). In W. Boehlich (Ed.), *Letters of Sigmund Freud to Edward Silberstein*. Boston: Harvard University Press, p. 56.

Garb, H. (1989). Clinical judgement, clinical training, and professional experience. *Psychological Bulletin, 105*, 387–392.

Garduk, E. L., & Haggard, E. A. (1972). Immediate effects on patients of psychoanlytic interpretations. *Psychological Issues, 7*(4).

Garfield, S. L. (1971). Research on client variable in psychotherapy. In S. L. Garfield & A. E. Bergin (Eds.), *Handbook of psychotherapy and behavior change: An empirical analysis*. New York: Wiley.

Garfield, S. L. (1982). Eclecticism and integration in psychotherapy. *Behavior Therapy, 13*, 610–623.

Garfield, S. L. (1987). Towards a scientifically oriented eclecticism. *Scandinavian Journal of Behaviour Therapy, 16*, 95–109.

Garfield, S. L. (1989). *The practice of brief psychotherapy.* New York: Pergamon.

Garfield, S. L. (1994). Research on client variables in psychotherapy. In A. E. Bergin & S. L. Garfield (Eds.), *Handbook of psychotherapy and behavior change* (4th ed.). New York: Wiley.

Garfield, S. L., & Bergin, A. E. (Eds.) (1971). *Handbook of psychotherapy and behavior change: An empirical analysis.* New York: John Wiley.

Garfield, S. L., & Bergin, A. E. (1994). Introduction and historical overview. In A. E. Bergin & S. L. Garfield (Eds.), *Handbook of psychotherapy and behavior change* (4th ed.). New York: Wiley.

Garfield, S. L., & Wolpin, M. (1963). Expectations regarding psychotherapy. *Journal of Nervous and Mental Disease, 137*, 353–362.

Gediman, H. K., & Lieberman, J. S. (March 14, 1996). An interview with Dr. Helen K. Gediman and Dr. Janice S. Lieberman. *Psychotherapy Books News, 30*, 7.

Gilovich, (1991). *How we know what isn't so.* New York: Free Press.

Goldfried, M. R., & Newman, C. F. (1992). A history of psychotherapy integration. In J. C. Norcross & M. R. Goldfried (Eds.), *Handbook of psychotherapy integration.* New York: Basic.

Goleman, D. (December 24, 1991). In new research optimism is the key to a successful life. *New York Times,* B5–6.

Gordon, D., & Meyers-Anderson, M. (1981). *Phoenix: Therapeutic patterns of Milton H. Erickson.* Cupertino, CA: Meta.

Gould, R. A., & Clum, G. A. (1993). A meta-analysis of self-help treatment approaches. *Clinical Psychology Review, 13*(2), 169–186.

Gravitz, H., & Bowden, J. (1987). *Recovery: A guide for adult children of alcoholics.* New York: Simon & Schuster.

Grosskurth, P. (1991). *The secret ring: Freud's inner circle and the politics of psychoanalysis.* Reading, MA: Addison-Wesley.

Grunebaum, H. (1988). What if family therapy were a kind of psychotherapy? A reading of the *Handbook of Psychotherapy and Behavior Change. Journal of Marital and Family Therapy, 14*, 195–199.

Haley, J. (1985). *Conversations with Milton H. Erickson: Changing individuals* (vol. 1). New York: Triangle.

Haley, J. (1986). *Uncommon therapy: The psychiatric techniques of Milton H. Erickson, M.D.* New York: Norton.

Haley, J. (1993). How to be a therapy supervisor without knowing how to change anyone. *Journal of Systemic Therapy, 12*(4), 41–52.

Haley, J. (1994). Zen and the art of therapy. *The Family Therapy Networker, 18*(1), 54–60.

Hammond, D. C., Hepworth, D. H., & Smith, V. G. (1977). *Improving therapeutic communication.* San Francisco, CA: Jossey-Bass.

Hattie, J. A., Sharpley, C. F., & Rogers, H. F. (1984). Comparative effectiveness of professional and paraprofessional helpers. *Psychological Bulletin, 95,* 534–541.

Held, B. (1991). The process/content distinction in psychotherapy revisited. *Psychotherapy, 28*(2), 207–217.

Held, B. (1995). *Back to the future.* New York: Norton.

Henry, W. P., Strupp, H. H., Schacht, T. E., & Gaston, L. (1994). Psychodynmaic approaches. In A. E. Bergin & S. L. Garfield, (Eds.), *Handbook of psychotherapy and behavior change* (4th ed.). New York: Wiley.

Herink, R. (Ed.) (1980). *The psychotherapy handbook: The A to Z guide to more than 250 different therapies in use today.* New York: New American Library.

Hester, R. K., Miller, W. R., Delaney, H. D., & Meyers, R. J. (November, 1990). *Effectiveness of the community reinforcement approach.* Paper presented at the 24th Annual Meeting of the Association for the Advancement of Behavior Therapy. San Francisco, CA.

Hoffman, E. (1994). *The drive for self: Alfred Adler and the founding of individual psychology.* Reading, MA: Addison-Wesley.

Hollon, S. D., & Beck, A. T. (1994). Cognitive and cognitive-behavioral therapies. In A. E. Bergin & S. L. Garfield (Eds.), *Handbook of psychotherapy and behavior change* (4th ed.). New York: Wiley.

Horvath, A. O., & Luborsky, L. (1993). The role of the alliance in psychotherapy. *Journal of Consulting and Clinical Psychology, 61,* 561–573.

Howard, K. I., Kopte, S. M., Krause, M. S., & Orlinsky, D. E. (1986). The dose-effect relationship in psychotherapy. *American Psychologist, 41*(2), 159–164.

Hubble, J. P., & Koller, W. C. (1995). The parkinsonian personality. In W. J. Weiner & A. E. Lang (Eds.), *Advances in neurology: Behavioral neurology of movement disorders* (vol. 65). New York: Raven.

Hubble, M. A. (1993). Therapy research: The bonfire of the uncertainties. *The Family Psychologist: Bulletin of the Division of Family Psychology, 9*(2), 14–16.

Hubble, M. A., & O'Hanlon, W. H. (1992). Theory countertransference. *Dulwich Centre Newsletter, 1,* 25–30.

Hubble, M. A., & Solovey, A. D. (1994). Ambassadorship in medical rehabilitation: A remedy for noncompliance. *Journal of Systemic Therapies, 13*(3), 67–76.

Hunsley, J., & Glueckauf, R. L. (1988). The utilization of chance occur-

rences in strategic therapy. *Journal of Strategic and Systemic Therapies,*
    7(4), 73–81.

Imber, S. D., Pilkonis, P. A., Harway, N. I., Klein, R. H., & Rubinsky,
    P. A. (1982). Maintenance of change in the psychotherapies. *Journal
    of Psychiatric Treatment and Evaluation, 4,* 1–5.

Ivey, A. E., & Gluckstern, N. (1976). *Basic influencing skills participant
    manual.* North Amherst, MA: Microtraining.

Ivey, A. E., & Simek-Downing, L. (1980). *Counseling and psychother-
    apy.* Englewood Cliffs, NJ: Prentice-Hall.

Jacobson, N. (1995). The overselling of psychotherapy. *Family Therapy
    Networker, 19*(2), 40–52.

Jensen, V. H. (1977). *Helping relationships: Skills development manual
    for training professional, paraprofessional, and lay counselors.* Provo,
    UT: Brigham Young University Press.

Jensen, J. B., Bergin, A. E., & Greaves, D. W. (1990). The meaning
    of eclecticism: New survey and analysis of components. *Professional
    Psychology, 21,* 124–130.

Johnson, B. (1973). *I'll quit tomorrow.* New York: Harper & Row.

Jordan, J. S., Harvey, J. H., & Weary, G. (1988). Attributional biases in
    clinical decision making. In D. C. Turk & P. Salovey (Eds.). *Reasoning,
    inference, and judgement in clinical psychology.* New York: Free Press.

Johnson, L., & Miller, S. D. (1994). Modification of depression risk
    factors: A solution-focused approach. *Psychotherapy, 31*(2), 244–353.

Joseph, L. E. (1994). *Common sense: Why it's no longer so common.*
    New York: Addison-Wesley.

Kaminer, W. (1992). *I'm dysfunctional, you're dysfunctional.* Reading,
    MA: Addison-Wesley.

Katagiri, D. (1988). *Return to silence.* Boston, MA: Shambhala.

Kazdin, A. E. (1980). Acceptability of time-out from reinforcement proce-
    dures for disruptive child behavior. *Behavior Therapy, 11,* 329–344.

Kazdin, A. E. (1986). Comparative outcome studies of psychotherapy:
    Methodological issues and strategies. *Journal of Consulting and Clini-
    cal Psychology, 54,* 95–105.

Kendall, P. C. (1992). When clients don't progress: Influences on and
    explanations for lack of therapeutic progress. *Cognitive Therapy and
    Research, 16,* 269–281.

Kessler, R. S., & Miller, S. D. (1995). The use of a future time frame in
    psychotherapy with and without hypnosis. *American Journal of Clini-
    cal Hypnosis, 38*(1), 39–46.

Kiesler, D. J. (1966). Some myths of psychotherapy research and the
    search for a paradigm. *Psychological Bulletin, 65,* 110–136.

Kiesler, D. J. (1995). Some myths of psychotherapy research and the search for a paradigm: Revisited. *Psychotherapy Research, 5*(2), 91–101.

Kirk, S., & Kutchins, H. (1993). *The selling of DSM: The rhetoric of science in psychiatry.* New York: Aldine de Gruyter.

Kiser, D., Piercy, F., & Lipchi. E. The integration of emotion in solution-focused therapy. *Journal of Marriage and Family Therapy, 19*(3), 233–242.

Kissin, B., Platz, A., & Su, W. H. (1971). Selective factors in treatment choice and outcome in alcoholics. In N. K. Mello & J. H. Mandelson (Eds.), *Recent advances in studies of alcoholism* (pp. 781–802). Washington, DC: U. S. Government Printing Office.

Kivlighan, D. M. (1989). Changes in counselor intentions and response modes and in client reactions and session evaluation after training. *Journal of Counseling Psychology, 36,* 471–476.

Knesper, D. J., Pagnucco, D. J., & Wheeler, J. R. C. (1985). Similarities and differences across mental health service providers and practice settings in the United States. *American Psychologist, 40,* 1352–1369.

Koss, M. P., & Butcher, J. N. (1986). Research on brief psychotherapy. In S. L. Garfield & A. E. Bergin (Eds.), *Handbook of psychotherapy and behavior change* (3rd ed.). New York: Wiley.

Koss, M. P., & Shiang, J. (1994). Research on brief psychotherapy. In A. E. Bergin & S. L. Garfield (Eds.), *Handbook of psychotherapy and behavior change* (4th ed.). New York: Wiley.

Kottler, J. (1991). *The compleate therapist.* San Francisco: Jossey-Bass.

Kowalski, K., & Durrant, M. (1990). Overcoming the effects of sexual abuse: Developing a self-perception of competence. In M. Durrant & C. White (Eds.), *Ideas for therapy with sexual abuse.* Adelaide, Australia: Dulwich Centre.

Kral, R. (1986). Indirect therapy in the schools. In S. de Shazer & R. Kral (Eds.), *The family therapy collections: Indirect approaches in family therapy.* Rockville, MD: Aspen.

Kral, R., & Kowalski, K. (1989). After the miracle: The second stage in solution-focused brief therapy. *Journal of Strategic and Systemic Therapies, 8*(2–3), 73–76.

Kraft, K. (1988). *Zen: Tradition and transition.* New York: Grove.

Kristol, E. (June, 1990). Declarations of codependence. *American Spectator.*

Krumboltz, J. D. (1966). *Resolution in counseling: Impacts of behavioral science.* Boston, MA: Houghton-Mifflin.

Kuehl, B. P., Newfield, N. A., & Joanning, H. (1990). A client-based description of family therapy. *Journal of Family Psychology, 3,* 310–321.

Kupst, M. J., & Shulman, J. L. (1979). Comparing professional and lay expectations of psychotherapy. *Psychotherapy, 16,* 237–243.

Lakoff, R. (1990). *Talking power*. New York: Basic.

Lambert, M. J. (1992). Implications of outcome research for psychotherapy integration. In J. C. Norcross & M. R. Goldfried (Eds.), *Handbook of psychotherapy integration*. New York: Basic.

Lambert, M. J., & Bergin, A. E. (1994). The effectiveness of psychotherapy. In A. E. Bergin & S. L. Garfield (Eds.), *Handbook of psychotherapy and behavior change* (4th ed.). New York: Wiley.

Lamberti, D. (1994). At bat. *Northwest Traveller, 27*(9), 65.

Lawson, D. (1994). Identifying pretreatment change. *Journal of Counseling and Development, 72*, 244–248.

Lerner, M. (1995). The assault on psychotherapy. *Family Therapy Networker, 19*(5), 44–52.

Levitt, E. E. (1966). Psychotherapy research and the expectation-reality discrepancy. *Psychotherapy, 3*, 163–166.

Liberman, B. L. (1978). The maintenance and persistence of change: Long-term follow-up investigations of psychotherapy. In J. D. Frank, R. Hoehn-Sarix, S. D. Imber, B. L. Liberman, & A. R. Stone (Eds.), *Effective ingredients of effective psychotherapy*. New York: Brunner/Mazel.

Lipchik, E. (1988). Purposeful sequence for beginning the solution-focused interview. In E. Lipchik (Ed.), *Family therapy collections: Interviewing*. Newbury Park, CA: Sage.

Lipchik, E. (March/April, 1994). The rush to be brief. *Family Therapy Networker, 18*(2), 34–39.

Lisson, R. C. (1995). [Letter to the editor]. *Family Therapy Networker, 19*(2), 11.

Locke, E. A., Shaw, K. N., Saari, L. M., & Latham, G. P. (1981). Goal setting and task performance: 1969–1980. *Psychological Bulletin, 90*, 125–152.

Lytle, R. A. (1993). An investigation of the efficacy of eye-movement desensitization in the treatment of cognitive intrusions related to memories of a past stressful event. *Dissertations Abstracts International, 54-09*(B), 4926.

Mahoney, M. (1991). *Human change processes: The scientific foundations of psychotherapy*. New York: Basic.

Markus, H., & Nurius, P. (1986). Possible selves. *American Psychologist, 41*, 954–969.

Marmar, C., Horowitz, M.J., Weiss, D., & Marzialie, E. A. (1986). The development of the therapeutic alliance rating system. In L. Greenberg & W. Pinsof (Eds.), *Psychotherapeutic process: A research handbook* (pp. 367–390). New York: Guilford.

Martin, C. (1989). *University of Utah Review, 22*(5), 2.

Martin, G., & Pear, J. (1983). *Behavior modification: What it is and how to do it.* Englewood Cliffs, NJ: Prentice-Hall.

Matuschka, E. (1985). Treatment, outcome, and clinical evaluation. In T. E. Bratter & G. G. Forrest (Eds.), *Alcoholism and substance abuse: Strategies for clinical intervention.* New York: Free Press.

Matheson, D., Bruce, R., & Beauchamp, K. (1978). *Experimental psychology: Research design and analysis.* New York: Holt, Rhinehart, and Winston.

McCall, R. B. (1980). *Fundamental statistics for psychology* (3rd ed.). New York: Harcourt, Brace, Jovanovich.

McKeel, A. J. (1996). A clincian's guide to research on solution-focused brief therapy. In S. D. Miller, M. A. Hubble, & B. L. Duncan (Eds.), *Handbook of solution-focused brief therapy.* San Francisco, CA: Jossey-Bass.

Meador, B., & Rogers, C. (1979). Person-centered therapy. In R. J. Corsini (Ed.), *Current psychotherapies* (2nd ed.). Itasca, IL: Peacock.

Metcalf, L., Thomas, F., Duncan, B. L., Miller, S. D., & Hubble, M. A. (1996). What works in solution-focused brief therapy: A qualitative analysis of client and therapist perceptions. In S. D. Miller, M. A. Hubble, & B. L. Duncan (Eds.), *Handbook of solution-focused brief therapy.* San Francisco, CA: Jossey-Bass.

Miller, S. D. (1992). The symptoms of solution. *Journal of Strategic and Systemic Therapies, 11,* 1–11.

Miller, S. D. (1994a). The solution conspiracy: A mystery in three installments. *Journal of Systemic Therapies, 13*(1), 18–37.

Miller, S. D. (1994b). Some questions (not answers) for the brief treatment of people with drug and alcohol problems. In M. Hoyt (Ed.), *Constructive therapies.* New York: Guilford.

Miller, S. D. (1995). Solution-focused brief therapy: Focusing on "what works" in clinical practice [Workshop handouts]. Chicago, IL: Author.

Miller, S. D. (1996). Working with Michael: Giving up models, methods, and techniques. *L'Effet Spirale, 4*(1), 7–8.

Miller, S. D., & Berg, I. K. (1991). Working with the problem drinker: A solution-focused approach. *Arizona Counseling Journal, 16*(1), 3–12.

Miller, S. D., & Berg, I. K. (1995). *The miracle method: A radically new approach to problem drinking.* New York: Norton.

Miller, W. R. (1986). Increasing motivation for change. In W. R. Miller & N. H. Heather (Eds.), *Addictive behaviors: Processes of change.* New York: Plenum.

Miller, W. R. (1987). Motivation and treatment goals. *Drugs and Society, 1,* 131–151.

Miller, W. R., Benefield, R. G., & Tonigan, J. S. (1993). Enhancing motivation for change in problem drinking: A controlled comparison of two therapist styles. *Journal of Consulting and Clinical Psychology, 61*(3), 455–461.

Miller, W. R., & Hester, R. K. (1989). Treating alcohol problems: Toward an informed eclecticism. In R. K. Hester & W. R. Miller (Eds.), *Handbook of alcoholism treatment approaches.* New York: Pergamon.

Mohl, D. C. (1995). Negative outcome in psychotherapy: A critical review. *Clinical Psychology, 2,* 1–27.

Morrock, R. (1994). Pseudo-psychotherapy: UFOs, cloudbusters, conspiracy, and paranoia in Wilhelm Reich's psychotherapy. *Skeptic, 2*(3), 93–95.

Mosak, H. H. (1978). Adlerian psychotherapy. In R. J. Corsini (Ed.), *Current psychotherapies* (2nd ed.). Itasca, IL: Peacock.

Murphy, J. J. (1996). Solution-focused brief therapy in the school. In S. D. Miller, M. A. Hubble, & B. L. Duncan (Eds.), *Handbook of solution-focused brief therapy.* San Francisco, CA: Jossey-Bass.

Murray, E. J., & Jacobsen L. I. (1971). The nature of learning in traditional and behavioral therapy. In A. E. Bergin & S. L. Garfield (Eds.), *Handbook of psychotherapy and behavior change: An empirical analysis.* New York: Wiley.

Murphy, P. M., Cramer, D., & Lillie, F. J. (1984). The relationship between curative factors perceived by patients in psychotherapy of depression: An exploratory study. *British Journal of Medical Psychology, 57,* 187–192.

Nisbett, R., & Ross, L. (1980). *Human inference: Strategies and shortcomings of social judgement.* Englewood Cliffs, NJ: Prentice-Hall.

Nunnally, E., de Shazer, S., Lipchik, E., & Berg, I. (1986). A study of change: Therapeutic theory in process. In D. Efron (Ed.), *Journeys: Expansion of the strategic-systemic therapies.* New York: Brunner/Mazel.

Nylund, D., & Corsiglia, V. (1994). Becoming solution-focused forced in brief therapy: Remembering something important that we already knew. *Journal of Systemic Therapies, 13*(1), 5–12.

O'Hanlon, B. (1987). *Taproots: Underlying principles of Milton Erickson's therapy hypnosis.* New York: Norton.

O'Hanlon, B. (March/April, 1990a). Debriefing myself: When a brief therapist does long-term work. *Family Therapy Networker, 14*(2), 48–49.

O'Hanlon, B. (1990b). A grand unified thoery for brief therapy: Putting problems in context. In J. Zeig & S. Gilligan (Eds.), *Brief therapy: Myths, methods, and metaphors.* New York: Brunner/Mazel.

O'Hanlon, B. (1991). Not systemic, not strategic: Still clueless after all these years. *Journal of Strategic and Systemic Therapies, 10*(3–4), 105–109.

O'Hanlon, B. (1995). The third wave. *Family Therapy Networker, 18*(6), 18–25, 28–29.

O'Hanlon, B., & Hexum, A. L. (1990). *An uncommon casebook: The complete clinical work of Milton H. Erickson, M.D.* New York: Norton.

O'Hanlon, B., & Weiner-Davis, M. (1989). *In search of solutions.* New York: Norton.

O'Hanlon, B., & Wilk, J. (1987). *Shifting contexts: The generation of effective psychotherapy.* New York: Guilford.

O'Regan, B. (1985). Placebo: The hidden asset in healing. *Investigations: A Research Bulletin, 2*(1), 1–3.

Orlinsky, D. E., Grawe, K., & Parks, B. K. (1994). Process and outcome in psychotherapy—noch einmal. In A. E. Bergin & S. L. Garfield (Eds.), *Handbook of psychotherapy and behavior change* (4th ed.). New York: Wiley.

Orlinsky, D. E., & Howard, K. I. (1986). Process and outcome in psychotherapy. In S. L. Garfield & A. E. Bergin (Eds.), *Handbook of psychotherapy and behavior change* (3rd ed.). New York: Wiley.

Patterson, C. H. (1984). Empathy, warmth, and genuineness in psychotherapy: A review of reviews. *Psychotherapy, 21*, 431–438.

Patton, M., & Meara, N. M. (1982). The analysis of language in psychological treatment. In R. L. Russell (Ed.), *Spoken interaction in psychotherapy.* New York: Irvington.

Paul, G. (1967). Strategy in outcome research in psychotherapy. *Journal of Consulting Psychology, 31*, 109–118.

Penn, P. (1995). Feed forward: Future questions, future maps. *Family Process, 23*(3), 299–310.

Perloff, L. S. (1983). Perceptions of vulnerability to vicitimization. *Journal of Social Issues, 39*, 41–61.

Phillips, M., & Frederick, C. (1992). The use of hypnotic age progressions as prognostic, ego strengthening and integrating techniques. *American Journal of Clinical Hypnosis, 35*(2), 99–108.

Prochaska, J. O. (1991). Prescribing to the stage and level of phobia patients. *Psychotherapy, 28*, 463–468.

Prochaska, J. O. (1993). Working in harmony with how people change naturally. *The Weight Control Digest, 3*, 249, 252–255.

Prochaska, J. O. (1995). Common problems: Common solutions. *Clinical Psychology: Science and Practice, 2*, 101–105.

Prochaska, J. O., & DiClemente, C. C. (1982). Transtheoretical therapy:

Toward a more integrative model of change. *Psychotherapy, 19,* 276–288.

Prochaska, J. O., & DiClemente, C. C. (1984). *The transtheoretical approach: Crossing traditional boundaries of therapy.* Homewood, IL: Dow Jones-Irwin.

Prochaska, J. O., & DiClemente, C. C. (1992). The transtheoretical approach. In J. C. Norcorss & M. R. Goldfried (Eds.), *Handbook of psychotherapy integration.* New York: Basic.

Prochaska, J. O., DiClemente, C. C., & Norcross, J. C. (1992). In search of how people change. *American Psychologist, 47,* 1102–1114.

Putnam, F. W., Guroff, J. J., Silberman, E. K., Barban, L., & Post, R. M. (1986). The clinical phenomenology of multiple personality disorder. *Journal of Clinical Psychiatry, 47,* 285–293.

Rabkin, R. (1983). *Strategic psychotherapy: Brief and symptomatic treatment.* New York: Meridian.

Reimers, T. M., Wacker, D. P., Cooper, L. J., & De Raad, A. O. (1992). Acceptability of behavioral treatments for children: Analog and naturalistic evaluations by parents. *School Psychology Review, 21,* 628–643.

Report of the Research Task Force of the National Institute of Mental Health (1975). Research in the service of mental health (DHEW Publication No. ADM 75–236). Rockville, MD: DHEW.

Reuterlov, H., Lofgren, T., Nordstrom, K., & Ternstrom, A. (in press). "What's better?": Clients' reports of change in second and subsequent sessions. *Brief Therapy.*

Roper Organization (1992). *Unusual personal experiences: An analysis of data from three national surveys.* Las Vegas, NV: Bigelow Holding Company.

Rogers, C. (1951). *Client centered therapy: Its current practice, theory, and implications.* Chicago, IL: Houghton Mifflin.

Rosen, S. (1982). *My voice will go with you.* New York: Norton.

Rosenzweig, S. (1936). Some implicit common factors in diverse methods in psychotherapy. *American Journal of Orthopsychiatry, 6,* 412–415.

Rossi, E. (1980). *The Collected Papers of Milton Erickson on Hypnosis* (vol. I–IV). New York: Irvington.

Sachs, J. S. (1983). Negative factors in brief psychotherapy: An empirical assessment. *Journal of Consulting and Clinical Psychology, 51,* 557–564.

Sagan, C. (1980). *Cosmos.* New York: Random House.

Sanchez-Craig, M. (1980). Random assignment to abstinence or contolled drinking in a cognitive-behavioral program: Effects on drinking behavior. *Addictive Behavior, 5,* 35–39.

Schauble, P. G., & Pierce, R. M. (1974). Client in-therapy behavior: A therapist guide to progress. *Psychotherapy, 11*, 229–234.

Selekman, M. D. (1989). Taming chemical monsters: Cybernetic-systemic therapy with adolescent substance abusers. *Journal of Strategic and Systemic Therapies, 8*(2), 5–10.

Selekman, M. D. (1991). The solution-oriented parenting group: A treatment alternative that works. *Journal of Strategic and Systemic Therapies, 10*(1), 37–50.

Seligman, M. E. P. (1975). *Helplessness: On depression, development, and death*. San Francisco, CA: Freeman.

Seligman, M. E. P. (1990). *Learned optimism*. New York: Knopf.

Shadish, W. R., Montgomery, L. M., Wilson, P., Wilson, M. R., Bright, I., & Okwumabua, T. (1993). Effects of family and marital psychotherapies: A meta-analysis. *Journal of Consulting and Clinical Psychology, 61*, 992–1002.

Shapiro, F. (1989a). Efficacy of the eye movement desensitization procedure in the treatment of traumatic memories. *Journal of Traumatic Stress Studies, 2*, 199–223.

Shapiro, F. (1989b). Eye movement desensitization: A new treatment for post-traumatic stress disorder. *Journal of Behavior Therapy and Experimental Psychiatry, 20*, 211–217.

Shostrom (1966). *Three approaches to therapy*. Santa Ana, CA: Psychological Films.

Simon, D. (1996). Crafting consciousness through form: Solution-focused therapy as a spiritual path. In S. D. Miller, M. A. Hubble, & B. L. Duncan (Eds.), *Handbook of solution-focused brief therapy*. San Francisco, CA: Jossey-Bass.

Smith, D. (1982). Trends in counseling and psychotherapy. *American Psychologist, 37*, 802–809.

Smith, M. L., & Glass, G. V. (1987). *Research and evaluation in education and the social sciences*. Englewood Cliffs, NJ: Prentice-Hall.

Smith, M. L., Glass, G. V., & Miller, T. I. (1980). *The benefits of psychotherapy*. Baltimore, MD: Johns Hopkins University Press.

Snyder, C. R., Irving, L. M., & Anderson, J. R. (1991). Hope and health. In C. R. Snyder & D. R. Forsyth (Eds.), *Handbook of social and clinical psychology*. New York: Pergamon.

Speisman, J. C. (1959). Depth of interpretation and verbal resistance in psychotherapy. *Journal of Counseling Psychology, 23*, 93–99.

Steenbarger, B. N. (1992). Toward science-practice integration in brief counseling and therapy. *The Counseling Psychologist, 20*, 403–450.

Steenbarger, B. N. (1994). Duration and outcome in psychotherapy: An integrative review. *Professional Psychology, 25*(2), 111–119.

Stein, D. M., & Lambert, M. J. (1984). On the relationship between therapist experience and psychotherapy outcome. *Clinical Psychology Review, 4*, 1–16.

Strupp, H. (1971). *Psychotherapy and the modification of abnormal behavior.* New York: McGraw-Hill.

Strupp, H. H. (1995). The psychotherapist's skills revisted. *Clinical Psychology, 2*, 70–74.

Strupp, H., Hadley, S. W., & Gomez-Schwartz, B. (1974). Specific versus nonspecific factors in psychotherapy: A controlled study of outcome. *Archives of General Psychiatry, 36*, 1125–1136.

Szasz, T. (1994). Diagnoses are not diseases. *Skeptic, 2*(3), 86.

Talmon, M. (1990). *Single session therapy.* San Francisco: Jossey-Bass.

Talmon, M., Hoyt, M. F., & Rosenbaum, R. (December, 1988). *When the first session is the last: A map for rapid therapeutic change.* Paper presented at the Fourth International Congress on Ericksonian Approaches to Hypnosis and Psychotherapy. San Francisco, CA.

Task force report on promotion and dissemination of psychological procedures (1993). Washington, DC: American Psychological Association.

Taylor, S. E. (1989). *Health psychology* (2nd ed.). New York: McGraw-Hill.

Taylor, S. E., & Brown, J. D. (1988). Illusion and well-being: A social psychological perspective on mental health. *Psychological Bulletin, 103*, 193–210.

Taylor, S. E., Wayment, H. A., & Collins, M. A. (1993). Positive illusions and affect regulation. In D. M. Wegner & J. W. Pennebaker (Eds.), *Handbook of mental control.* Englewood Cliffs, NJ: Prentice-Hall.

Thompson, A. P. (1986). Changes in counseling skills during graduate and undergraduate study. *Journal of Counseling Psychology, 33*, 65–72.

Thorton, C. C., Gottheil, E., Gellens, H. K., & Alterman, A. I. (1977). Voluntary versus involuntary abstinence in the treatment of alcoholics. *Journal of Studies on Alcohol, 38*, 1740–1748.

Todes, C. J., & Lees, A. J. (1985). The pre-morbid personality of patients with Parkinsons disease. *Journal of Neurology, Neurosurgery, and Psychiatry, 48*, 97–100.

Torem, M. (1992). Back from the future: A powerful age progression technique. *American Journal of Clinical Hypnosis, 35*(2), 81–88.

Truax, C. B., & Carkhuff, R. R. (1967). *Toward effective counseling and psychotherapy.* Chicago, IL: Aldine.

Uchiyama, K. (1993). *Opening the hand of thought: Approach to Zen.* New York: Penguin.

Vaihinger, H. (1925). *The philosophy of "as if": A system of the theoretical, practical and religious fictions of mankind.* New York: Harcourt, Brace and Company.

Van Gennep, A. (1960). *The rites of passage.* Chicago, IL: University of Chicago Press.

Veroff, J., Kulka, R. A., & Douvan, E. (1981). *Mental health in America.* New York: Basic.

Viscott, D. (1972). *The making of a psychiatrist.* New York: Arbor House.

Walter, J., & Peller, J. (1992). *Becoming solution-focused in brief therapy.* New York: Brunner/Mazel.

Waters, D., & Lawrence, E. (1993). Creating a therapeutic vision. *Family Therapy Networker, 17*(6), 53–58.

Watkins, C. E., Jr., Lopez, F. G., Campbell, V. L., & Himmell, C. D. (1986). Contemporary counseling psychology: Results of a national survey. *Journal of Counseling Psychology, 33,* 301–309.

Watzlawick, P. (1983). *The situation is hopeless, but not serious.* New York: Norton.

Watzlawick, P. (1986). If you desire to see, learn how to act. In J. Zeig (Ed.), *The evolution of psychotherapy.* New York: Brunner/Mazel.

Weakland, J. (1993). Conversation—but what kind? In S. Gilligan & R. Price (Eds.), *Therapeutic Conversations.* New York: Norton.

Weakland, J. (1995). [Letter to the editor]. *Family Therapy Networker, 19*(5), 16.

Weinberg, J. (1995). Common factors aren't so common: The common factors dilemma. *Clinical Psychology, 2,* 45–69.

Weiner-Davis, M., de Shazer, S., & Gingerich, W. (1987). Building on pretreatment change to construct the therapeutic solution: An exploratory study. *Journal of Marital and Family Therapy, 13*(4), 359–364.

Weinstein, N. D. (1980). Unrealistic optimism about future life events. *Journal of Personality and Social Psychology, 39,* 806–820.

Weinstein, N. D. (1982). Unrealistic optimism about susceptibility to health problems. *Journal of Behavioral Medicine, 5,* 441–460.

Weinstein, N. D. (1984). Why it won't happen to me: Perceptions of risk factors and susceptibility. *Health Psychology, 3,* 431–457.

Weiss, B. L. (1988). *Many lives, many masters.* New York: Fireside.

White, M. (1993). Commentary: The histories of the present. In S. Gilligan & R. Price (Eds.), *Therapeutic conversations.* New York: Norton.

White, M. (1986). Negative explanation, restraint, and double description: A template for family therapy. *Family Process, 25*(2), 169–183.

White, M., & Epston, D. (1990). *Narrative means to therapeutic ends.* New York: Norton.

Wile, D. B. (1984). Kohut, Kernberg, and accusatory interpretations. *Psychotherapy, 21*, 353–364.

Wilson, S. A., Becker, L. A., & Tinker, R. H. (1995). Eye movement desensitization and reprocessing (EMDR): Treatment for psychologically traumatized individuals. *Journal of Consulting and Clinical Psychology, 63*(6), 928–937.

Witt, J. C., Elliot, S. N., & Martens, B. K. (1984). Acceptability of behavioral interventions used in the classroom. *Behavioral Disorders, 9*, 95–104.

Wolberg, L. (1954). *The technique of psychotherapy.* New York: Grune and Stratton.

Wolberg, L. (1977). *The technique of psychotherapy* (3rd ed.). New York: Grune and Stratton.

Zilbergeld, B. (1983). *The shrinking of America.* Boston: Little, Brown.

Zimet, C. N. (1989). The mental health care revolution: Can psychology survive? *American Psychologist, 44*(4), 703–708.

Index

accountability
    language for providing, ix
    of therapists, to third-party payers,
        11–12
Acierno, R., 129
action stage, of change, 102
Adler, A., 68, 122, 144
affect, in Parkinson's disease, 19–20
affirmation, by the therapist, 118
alcoholism
    client's competence in managing, case
        example, 66–68
    comparison of traditional approach
        with learning-based counseling,
        135–36
    treatment emphasizing a cause out-
        side the client, 156
    see also drug and alcohol treat-
        ment
alliance, see therapeutic alliance / rela-
    tionship
Allport, G., 123
ambassadorship, as a metaphor for re-
    spect, 115
analysis, of outcomes of models of ther-
    apy, 3–4
Andersen, T., 195
Anderson, J. R., 31
Andreas, C. R., 4
Andreas, S., 4
Annis, H. M., 188
Ansbacher, H., 68
Ansbacher, R., 68
anticipation, as defense, 103

attention, and empathy, 112
attitude, underlying empathy, 112

Bachelor, A., 28, 111
Balint, M., 192
Bandura, A., 56, 106
Barban, L., 126
Barlow, D., 3
Barrett, W., 22
Bassos, C. A., 11
Bateson, G., 183
Beauchamp, K., 132
Beck, A. T., 144
Becker, L. A., 130
behavior therapy, comparison with psy-
    choanalytically oriented therapy,
    16–17
belief
    in a healing ritual, 131–32
    in personal control, and coping,
        149–50
Benefield, R. G., 188
Berg, I. K., 4–5, 11, 45, 53, 59, 61,
    88, 106, 127, 144, 147
Bergin, A. E., 2, 4, 7, 13, 15, 16, 42,
    56, 60, 77, 84, 124, 184, 185
Berkman, A. S., 11
Berman, J. S., 13
*Better, Deeper, and More Enduring
    Brief Therapy* (Ellis), 21
between-session change
    case examples, 51–54, 54–56,
        78–80
    extratherapeutic factors in, 49–51
Beutler, L. E., 127, 135, 136

Beyebach, M., 43, 106–7, 150
bias in evaluation
    of client responses to therapies, 14,
        102
    of failure in therapy, 193
biological psychiatry versus talk ther-
    apy, 2–3
Boedecker, A. L., 12
Bohart, A., 36
bone pointing, in psychotherapy, 125–
    28
Booth
    on Parkinson's disease, 20
Bowden, J., 61
Bower, B., 129
Brandon, D., 112
brief strategic therapy, "go slow" in-
    junction from, 96–98
brief therapy
    case example, 194–97
    claims about, 21–22
    evaluation of outcomes, 4–5, 6
Bright, I., 2
Brown, J. D., 142
Bruce, R., 132
Butcher, J. N., 5
Butler, S. F., 106
Butler, W., 145

Campbell, V. L., 15
Cannon, W. B., 125
caring, by the therapist, and outcome
    of therapy, 83
Carkhuff, R. R., 110
Carlinsky, J., 126
Carter, J., 191
causes
    and effects, optimism and being well-
        adjusted, 143
    exploring
        case example, 171–73
        therapist's speculations, 173–76
    identification of, and change, 127
    and treatment, 125–26
Chambless, D. L., 3
chance, role in pretreatment change,
    42–44
Chang, J., 8
change
    between-session, 49–56
    and cause identification, 127
    confrontation to encourage, 187–88

expectation for
    facilitating in therapy, 128–60
    and success of therapy, 31
    focus on, by therapists, 40–44
    future orientation to encourage, case
        example, 57–59
    hoping for, 122–60
    readiness for, 87–104
        case example, 176
    stage of, and motivational readiness,
        88–90
    in treatment approach, 205
    unifying language as a guide for,
        197
    unconventional forms of, 192
character analysis, for explaining Par-
    kinson's disease, 20
Christensen, A., 13, 36
Clarkin, J., 5
Clement, P. W., 11–12, 13
client-centered therapy, 86–120
clients
    acceptability of a procedure to, and
        success in therapy, 135–39
    attributing the success of therapy to,
        56–62
    competence of, 214
    focus on, 62–70
    contribution of
        to change, 60–62
        to the success of therapy, 32–33,
            34–80, 176–78
        to the therapist-client relationship,
            27
    enlightened state of, analogy with
        Soto Zen Buddhism, 38–39
    goals for therapy, and outcomes,
        107–8
    literature on the incompetence of,
        24–26
    participation in the preparation stage
        of change, 101–2
    rating by
        of the therapeutic alliance, 28, 85
        of the therapist, 70–76
    treatment failures attributed to, 193
    validation experienced by, 117–20
    view of therapeutic models, 29–30
    view of therapy and therapists, 23,
        111
        study of alcoholism treatments,
            135–36

view of the therapeutic relationship, 110–20
"clinician's illusion," about duration of therapy, 5
Clum, G. A., 36
cluster analysis, for identifying helpful events in psychotherapy, 188–89
cognitive-behavioral therapies
for anxiety, 3
causes assigned to problems in, 126
cognitive variables, study of effect on therapy outcome, 150
Cohen, J., 5
Cohen, P., 5
collaboration, in drug and alcohol treatment, 105–6
Collins, M. A., 142, 143, 149
Combs, G., 195
common factors
leading to a unifying language, 24–31
in successful therapy models, 15–18
techniques for pointing in the direction of, 189–90
communication, therapist's use of language, 71–72
competence, client's, 62–65
case examples, 66–68, 79–80
confrontation, confronting, 187–90
contemplation stage of change, 94–100
context, of motivation, 88
Cooper, L. J., 135
core conditions
for effecting change in clients, 86–87
for effective psychotherapy, 27–28, 111
Corsiglia, V., 85
courtesy, to reluctant clients, 91
Coyne, J., 11, 85
Cramer, D., 124
credibility of a procedure, 135–36
case example, 136–39
and knowing the client's world view, 167
Cross, D. G., 77
Cummings, N. A., 11, 126, 156

Dawes, R. M., 14, 125
De Raad, A. O., 135
de Shazer, S., 8, 9, 11, 42, 88, 126, 127, 144, 147
deception, by a client in therapy, 141

defensive responding, and transference interpretations, 186
Delaney, H. D., 135, 136
de-person-alization, 154–60
depression
case examples, 109–10, 113–14, 148–49, 158–60, 163
team feedback, 176–81
and client competence, 62–65
extratherapeutic factors in success of therapy, 34–35, 51–54
outcomes of pharmacologic and psychotherapeutic interventions, 3
therapeutic relationship example, 81–82
diagnosis, categories for, increase in, 60–61
Diagnostic and Statistical Manual of Mental Disorders (APA), 25, 60
DiClemente, C. C., 88, 89, 91, 95, 101, 102, 104, 127
differences among models of therapy
importance to the therapist, 7, 9–10
documentation, of therapy outcomes, 12–13
Doherty, W. J., 2, 5
dopamine, and motor disorder in Parkinson's disease, 20
Douvan, E., 77
Drinker's Check-up, 91–92
drop-out rates, in therapy, and outcome measures, 4
drug and alcohol treatment
clients' goals in, versus assigning clients to programs, 105
outcomes of action-oriented programs, 102
outcomes of confrontational approaches, 188–89
see also alcoholism
drug treatment, evaluation of, compared with state of change, 89–90
Duncan, B. L., 4, 18, 28, 39, 85, 88, 95, 96, 120, 189
Durrant, M., 8

eclecticism, in therapeutic practice, 15–16
Efran, J. S., 43
Egan, G., 187
Ekeland, I., 40
Elkin, I., 3

Elliot, R., 188
Elliot, S. N., 135
Ellis, A., 21, 70
empathy
   case example, 113–14
   clients' experience of, 111
   as a core condition for effecting
      change, 87, 112–14
   in siding with a client on slow
      change, 97–98
empowerment, of factors the therapist
   has in use, 39–40
environment
   social network, 77–78
   supportive, in the contemplative
      stage of therapy, 95
Epston, D., 8, 145, 158
Erickson, M., 35, 72
ethics
   of teaching clients the belief systems
      of therapists, 127
   of using effective therapeutic ap-
      proaches, 14
Evans, D. R., 187
"exceptions" versus "unique outcomes,"
   8–9
expectations
   for change
      facilitating in therapy, 128–60
      and success of therapy, 31
   clients' versus therapists', 51
   negative effects of, 125
   role of, in successful psychotherapy,
      124
   see also hope, creation of
externalizing the problem, 158
extratherapeutic factors
   becoming mindful of, 39–80
   and outcomes of therapy, 24–26,
      34–37, 214
   supportive environment, in the con-
      templative stage of therapy,
      95
Eye Movement Desensitization and Reprocessing (EMDR), 129–31

faith, in a therapeutic procedure, 132
falsification, of a therapeutic hypothe-
   sis, 14
Family Therapy Networker, 12
Fancher, R., 182, 184
Ferenczi, S., 34, 116

Fisch, R., 88, 96, 98, 102
flexibility, 214
focus on possibility, 141–43
frame of reference, client's, using in
   therapy, 136–39
Frances, A., 5
Frank, G. H., 111
Frank, J. B., 30, 42, 126, 130, 143
Frank, J. D., 6, 10, 17, 30, 42, 56,
   126, 130, 143
Frazer, James George, 130
Frederick, C., 144
Freedman, J., 195
Freud, S., 2, 9, 60
future
   change in, case example, 57–59
   orientation toward, 143–49
      case examples, 145–148, 148–49
   potentiating change for, 56–62

Garb, H., 13
Gardner, J., 114
Garduk, E. L., 111
Garfield, S. L., 1, 5, 7, 11, 43, 51, 60,
   81, 125, 143
Gaston, L., 27, 185, 186–87
Gediman, H. K., 141, 142
Geenen, H., 26
genuineness
   as a core condition for effecting
      change, 87, 115–17
   humility and, 117
Gilovich, 14
Gingerich, W., 42, 127, 147
Glass, G. V., 13, 15, 132, 194
Gluckstern, N., 187
Glueckauf, R. L., 37
goals
   client's, 104–10, 214
      case examples, 164–67, 200–201,
         208
      selecting in the preparation stage,
         101
Goldfried, M. R., 16
Goleman, D., 31
Gomez-Schwartz, B., 17
Gordon, D., 72
"go slow" injunction, 96–97, 177
Gould, R. A., 36
Gravitz, H., 61
Grawe, K., 7, 27, 28, 87, 118, 136
Greaves, D. W., 185

Green, M. A., 43
Grosskurth, P., 9
guest, therapist as, precontemplative
    stage of therapy, 93–94
Guroff, J. J., 126

Hadley, S. W., 17
Haggard, E. A., 111
Hahn, R., 122
Haley, J., 37, 72
Hammond, D. C., 110
*Handbook of Psychotherapy and Be-
    havior Change*, 185
Harvey, J. H., 14
Harway, N. I., 59
Hattie, J. A., 13
healing ritual, to provide positive expec-
    tations, 129–31
Hearn, M. T., 187
Held, B., 127
Henry, W. P., 27, 185, 186–87
Hepworth, D. H., 110
Herink, R., 1
Hersen, M., 129
Hester, R. K., 105, 135, 136
Hexum, A. L., 72
Himmell, C. D., 15
Hollon, S. D., 144
homelessness
    attribution of factors leading to
        change, 57–59
    extratherapeutic factors, case exam-
        ple, 54–56
    and social network, case example,
        78–80
homeostasis, systemic, 41
homework
    conveying hope and expectation in,
        132–33
    future-oriented, 144, 200, 202
hope, creation of, 30–31
    case example, 201–2
    with homework assignments, 132–
        33
    see also expectations
Horowitz, M. J., 87
Horvath, A. O., 27, 28
Howard, K. I., 41, 50, 51, 194
Hoyt, M. F., 194
Hubble, J. P., 20
Hubble, M. A., 11, 15, 85, 88, 115,
    120

humility, and genuineness, 117
Hunsley, J., 37

iatrogenic resistance, 90
illusions, positive, of healthy people,
    142
Imber, S. D., 59
in-session change, reported by clients, 50
interest
    in results of a technique, 132–35
    of the therapist in results, case exam-
        ple, 133–35
Irving, L. M., 31
Ivey, A. E., 187

Jacobsen, L. I., 111
Jacobson, N., 13, 36
Jensen, J. B., 185
Jensen, V. H., 110
Joanning, H., 23, 193
Johnson, B., 156, 188
Johnson, L., 8, 106, 144, 158
joining the client, alternative to, 64–65
Jordan, J. S., 14
Joseph, L. E., 11

Kahn, J. A., 77
Kaminer, W., 25
Katagiri, D., 1
Kazdin, A. E., 2, 9, 135
Kendall, P. C., 193
Kessler, R. S., 144
Kiesler, D. J., 9, 184, 189
Kirk, S., 19
Kiser, D., 85
Kivilighan, 10
Klein, R. H., 59
Knesper, D. J., 5
Koller, W. C., 20
Kopte, S. M., 41, 50, 51, 194
Koss, M. P., 5, 22
Kottler, J., 129, 131
Kowalski, K., 8, 59, 132
Kraft, K., 38
Kral, R., 59, 132
Krause, M. S., 41, 50, 51, 194
Kristol, E., 61
Krumboltz, J. D., 184
Kuehl, B. P., 23, 193
Kulka, R. A., 77
Kupst, M. J., 50
Kutchins, H., 19

La Rochefoucauld, 34
Lakoff, R., 11
Lambert, M. J., ix, 2, 4, 7, 13, 15, 16,
    23, 24, 26, 27, 29–30, 36, 42,
    56, 77, 84, 124, 182, 184
Lamberti, D., 24
language
    of clinicians, x, 70–76
    emphasis on, to create a difference,
        11
    in psychotherapy, 70–76
lapses, in change, planning for, 103
Latham, G. P., 106
Lawson, D., 42
learning, from a setback, 67–68
Lee, B., 183
Lees, A. J., 19–20
legislation, proposed, requiring demon-
    strated efficacy of therapies,
    12
Lerner, M., 13
Levitt, E. E., 5
Liberman, B. L., 56
Lieberman, J. S., 141, 142
Lillie, F. J., 124
Lincoln, Abraham, 11
linguistic style
    case example, 73–76
    matching the therapist's with the cli-
        ent's, 70–76
Lipchik, E., 8, 11, 85, 127, 147
Lisson, R. C., 18
listening
    for change reported by clients, 194
    for a client's introduction of ideas,
        203–4
    as a condition for change, 45–46,
        46–49
    for evidence of client competence,
        62–70
    for evidence of improvement, 51
    relationship implied in, 81–82
    and respect, 115
    for separation of problems from the
        client, 158
Locke, E. A., 106
Lofgren, T., 50
Lopez, F. G., 15
Luborsky, L., 27, 28
lupus erythematosus, in a blind client,
    62–65
Lytle, R. A., 130

McCall, R. B., 42
Machado, P. P., 135, 136
McKeel, A. J., 148
Mahoney, M., 28, 50
maintenance stage, of change, 103
Making of a Psychiatrist, The (Viscott),
    116
managed care, effect on therapist-client
    relationships, 27
Many Faces of Deceit, The (Gediman
    and Lieberman), 141
marketplace, considerations in promo-
    tion of therapy models, 10
Markus, H., 143
Marmar, C., 87
marriage counseling, hope in, 122–
    23
Martens, B. K., 135
Martin, C., 141
Martin, G., 141
Marzialie, E. A., 87
Matheson, D., 132
Matuschka, E., 187
Meador, B., 87
Meara, N. M., 70, 71
Mencken, H. L., 17–18
Menninger, K., 103
Metcalf, L., 85
Meyers, R. J., 135, 136
Meyers-Anderson, M., 72
Miller, S. D., 4–5, 8, 11, 15, 41, 45,
    53, 59, 61, 85, 88, 106, 120,
    141, 144, 145, 147, 156, 158
Miller, T. I., 13, 15, 194
Miller, W. R., 89, 91, 94, 101, 102,
    105, 106, 135, 136, 188
modeling, of a successful therapeutic re-
    lationship, 110–11
models for therapy
    language use implied by, 74–75
    studies of effectiveness, 1–3
    as temptations, and as evidence of
        hope, 216
    view of human change as difficult,
        50–51
Mohl, D. C., 184
Molnar, A., 127, 147
Montgomery, L. M., 2
Morejon, A. R., 43, 106–7, 150
Morrock, R., 126
Mosak, H. H., 144, 145
motivation, of clients, 87–88

Moynihan, D. W., 18, 39, 189
Murphy, J. J., 135
Murphy, P. M., 124
Murray, E. J., 111

narrative therapy, claims about, and
  evaluation of, 21–22
Neufeldt, S. A., 135, 136
neurosis, extratherapeutic factors in
  therapy success, 35–36
Newfield, N. A., 23, 193
Newman, C. F., 16
Nisbett, R., 14
NLP Eye Movement Integration, ad
  for, 21
Norcross, J. C., 88, 89, 91, 101, 102,
  104
Nordstrom, K., 50
Norton, N. C., 13
novelty, in models and techniques,
  190–97
Nunnally, E., 11, 127, 147
Nurius, P., 143
Nylund, D., 85

obsessive-compulsive behavior, case example, 199–214
O'Hanlon, B., 4, 6, 8, 21, 41, 72, 126,
  157, 158
Okwumabua, T., 2
O'Regan, B., 128, 132, 140
"original sin" psychotherapy theory,
  61
Orlinsky, D. E., 7, 27, 28, 41, 50, 51,
  87, 118, 136, 194
outcome questions, 106
outcome research
  on client perceptions and success, 28
  on the contribution of the therapeutic
    relationship, 84–85
  on duration of therapy, and success
    of therapy, 51
  on pretreatment improvement and ul-
    timate success, 43
  about techniques, 2
outcomes
  and client's goals, for therapy, 107–8
  roles of models and techniques in,
    182–97

Pagnucco, D. J., 5
Palenzuela, D. L., 43, 106–7, 150

panic-related disorders, therapy of
  choice for, 3
paralysis agitans, in Parkinsonism, 19–20
Parkinsonism, 19–20
Parks, B. K., 7, 27, 28, 87, 118, 136
participation, by the client, in therapy,
  25–26
Patterson, C. H., 39, 84, 189
Patton, M., 70, 71
Paul, G., 184
Pear, J., 141
Peller, J., 59
Penn, P., 145
perception, client's
  of effort related to change, 57
  of respect, 115
Perloff, L. S., 143
Perls, F., 70
Perry, S., 5
personal control, enhancing the client's,
  149–54
  case examples, 151–52, 152–54
personalization, of a cause of a problem, 175–76
perspective, traditional therapist's,
  homeless alcoholic example, 59
Persuasion and Healing (Frank), 17
Phillips, M., 8, 144
phobic disorders, cognitive-behavioral
  therapies for, 3
physical illness
  lupus erythematosus, 62–65
  relationship to hope, 123–24
  rheumatoid arthritis, response of pa-
    tients to medication, 140
Pierce, R. M., 56
Piercy, F., 85
Pilkonis, P. A., 59
placebo factors, 124
  case example, 180
  comparison with client effort, 56–57
positive blame, 59
Post, L., 11
Post, R. M., 126
Powers, K., 145
practice, using models and techniques
  for, 183–84
precontemplation, stage of therapy,
  90–94
prediction
  of failure of therapy, 184
  of success of therapy, factors in, 43

predictive power, of the stages of
    change, 89
preparation stage, of change, 100–102
pretreatment change, 44–46
    case example, 46–49
    extratherapeutic factors in, 41–49
    prevalence, of dysfunction, profession-
        als' views of, 60–61
Prochaska, J. O., 4, 88, 89, 90, 91, 95,
    100, 101, 102, 103, 104, 127
psychiatric diagnosis, depersonalization
    through, 156
psychoanalytically oriented therapy,
    comparison with behavior ther-
    apy, 16–17
psychodynamic theory
    causes identified in, 126
    interpretation of transference in,
        185–87
Putnam, F. W., 126

Question, The, Adlerian technique of
    asking, 144
questions
    about between-session change, 53–
        54, 54–56
    about outcomes desired of therapy,
        106
    for potentiating change, 59
    about pretreatment change, 44–
        46

Rabkin, R., 143
Rational-Emotive Therapy, causes as-
    signed to problems in, 126
reality, in imagining a positive future,
    147–48
recovery-oriented therapists, causes as-
    signed to problems by, 126
reflecting team, using in stuck therapy,
    195–97
regression toward the mean, and pre-
    treatment change in the client,
    42–43
Reimers, T. M., 135
relationship, factors in, see therapeutic
    alliance/relationship
resistance, iatrogenic, 90
resources, community, for helping cli-
    ents, 76–78
respect, as a core condition for effecting
    change, 87, 114–15

Reuterlov, H., 50
rheumatoid arthritis, response of pa-
    tients to a placebo, 140
rituals, traditional, 130–31
Robert, R. H., 130
Rodriguez-Aris, J. L., 43, 106–7,
    150
Rogers, C., 27, 70, 86, 87, 197
Rogers, H. F., 13
Rosen, S., 35
Rosenbaum, R., 194
Rosenzweig, S., 17
Ross, L., 14
Rossi, E., 72
Rubinsky, P. A., 59
Rusk, G. S., 4, 28

Saari, L. M., 106
Sachs, J. S., 184
Sagan, C., 6
Sanchez-Craig, M., 105
Schacht, T. E., 27, 185, 186–87
Schauble, P. G., 56
Schunk, D. H., 106
Segal, L., 88, 96, 98, 102
Selekman, M. D., 8
self-efficacy
    and enduring change, 56–62,
        104
    see also personal control
self-esteem
    maintaining by depersonalizing poor
        performance, 155–56
    protecting with distortion, 142
Seligman, M. E. P., 144, 155
sexual relationship, pretreatment
    change, case example, 46–49
Shadish, W. R., 2
Shapiro, D. A., 2, 13, 15, 42, 84,
    124
Shapiro, F., 129
Sharpley, C. F., 13
Shaw, K. N., 106
Sheehan, P. W., 77
Shiang, J., 22
Shostrom, 70
Shrinking of America, The (Zilbergeld),
    61
Shulman, J. L., 50
Silberman, E. K., 126
Simek-Downing, L., 187
Simmons, D. S., 2, 5

Simon, D., 183
simplicity, in clinical presentation, 32–33
Singer, Isaac Bashevis, 128
Smith, D., 15
Smith, M. L., 13, 15, 132, 194
Smith, V. G., 110
smoking
  duration of precontemplative stage in therapy for, 91
  stages of change for clients in programs for cessation of, 102
Snyder, C. R., 31
social network
  case example, 78–80
  inquiry about, in therapy, 77–78
Solovey, A. D., 4, 28, 115
solution-focused brief therapy (SFBT), 85
  comparison with narrative therapy, 8–9
solutions, to problems in the helping professions, x
Speisman, J. C., 111
stability, traditional focus on, in clinical work, 41
Steenbarger, B. N., 194
Stein, D. M., 13
strategic school, 37–39
  "dangers of change" approach of, 98–100
strengths, case example, 167–71
structure
  for mobilizing placebo factors, 131
  models and technique, 182–97
Strupp, H. H., 17, 27, 86, 106, 185, 186–87
stuckness
  case example: Denise, 194–97
  case example: Dottie, 206
success
  client's, relating a therapeutic procedure to, 139–43
  factors contributing to
    expectancy, hope and placebo, 30–31
    extratherapeutic, 26, 36
    therapeutic technique, 28–30
    therapist-client relationship, 27
  suicidal ideation, case example: "A Gift from God", 163
Suzuki, D. T., 38
Szasz, T., 8

talk therapy versus biological psychiatry, 2–3
Tallman, K., 36
Talmon, M., 6, 42, 194
Taylor, S. E., 142, 143, 149
technique, therapeutic
  as a common factor in success, 28–30, 214
  case example, 180–81
  emphasis on, solution-focused brief therapy, 85
termination, after change, 103–4
Ternstrom, A., 50
theory, clinical, 1–18
therapeutic alliance / relationship
  case examples, 179–80, 214
  with clients in the preparation stage of change, 101–2
  common factor in the success of therapy, 26–28
  contribution of, to treatment outcome, 81–121
  facilitating, with a focus provided by the client, 171
  research on, 87
    acceptance of client goals, 105
therapist
  attitude of
    case example, 68–70
    and hope in therapy, 30–31, 68
  belief of
    about content of therapy, and outcomes, 85
    in procedures or rituals, 131–32
  changing a therapeutic approach, 205
  choice of, and etiology of a client's problems, 126
  contribution to the therapist-client relationship, 27
  factors contributing to effectiveness of, 13, 136
    strategic school, 37–39
  flexibility of, and progress in therapy, 193–94
  healing rituals of, 131–32
  as hero, 61–62
  importance of, in professional reviews, 25–26
  importance to, of differences among models, 9–10
  interest of, in results of a procedure, 132–35

therapist (*continued*)
  listening for successes, 178
  potentiating change by extrathera-
    peutic factors, 59
  relationship with the client, and clini-
    cal success, 26–28
  teaching of, by practice of a tech-
    nique, 183–84
  tentative attitude on the part of,
    116–17
  unifying language as a guide for, in
    changing a therapeutic ap-
    proach, 197
therapy
  advantage over no therapy, 14–15
  duration of
    clients' expectations, 51
    and degree of improvement, 194
    effect of setting time limits, 7
    and evaluation of success, 42
    and therapeutic model, 5
    and therapist-client relationships, 27
  modal number of sessions, 6
  technique for, and structure of
    change, 88–89
  treatment of choice, as a factor in suc-
    cess, case example, 180–81
Thomas, F., 85
Thompson, A. P., 10
Thought Energy Synchronization Therapy, 85
Three Approaches to Psychotherapy
  (film), approach to language in,
  70
Tinker, R. H., 130
Todes, C. J., 19–20
Tonigan, J. S., 188
Torem, M., 145
transference, interpreting interpretations of, 185–87
Truax, C. B., 110
trust, of the therapist in probability of
  change, 40–41

Uchiyama, K., 38
Uhleman, M. R., 187
unifying language
  building, for psychotherapy, 19–33

common factors comprising, 15–16
  case example, 214
  vocabulary for, 215–16

validation
  example: Shooting the Breeze, 119–
    20
  client's experience of, 117–20
  of a therapeutic method, bias in, 14
Van Gennep, A., 130
Veroff, J., 77
Veterans' Administration, study of the
  length of treatment, 5
Viscott, D., 116
vocabulary, of a unifying language, 22–
  23

Wacker, D. P., 135
Walter, J., 59
Watkins, C. E., Jr., 15
Watts, Alan, 38
Watzlawick, P., 14, 68, 125–26, 191,
  193
Wayment, H. A., 142, 143, 149
Weakland, J., ix, 88, 96, 97, 98,
  102
Weary, G., 14
Weinberg, J., 19
Weiner-Davis, M., 42, 127, 157
Weinstein, N. D., 143
Weiss, B. L., 126
Weiss, D., 87
Wheeler, J. R. C., 5
White, M., 8, 9, 145, 158
Wile, D. B., 186
Wilk, J., 4, 41
Wilson, M. R., 2
Wilson, P., 2
Wilson, S. A., 130
Witt, J. C., 135
Wolberg, L., 61, 115, 131, 182
Wolfe, B., 3
Wolpin, M., 51

Zen Buddhism, analogy with strategic
  therapy, 37–39
Zilbergeld, B., 61
Zimet, C. M., 11